ALSO BY LAURENCE STEINBERG

Adolescence

You and Your Adolescent: A Parent's Guide for Ages 10 to 20 (with Ann Levine)

When Teenagers Work: The Psychological and Social Costs of Adolescent Employment (with Ellen Greenberger)

SIMON & SCHUSTER

NEW YORK   LONDON   TORONTO

SYDNEY   TOKYO   SINGAPORE

CROSSING PATHS

HOW YOUR CHILD'S ADOLESCENCE TRIGGERS YOUR OWN CRISIS

LAURENCE STEINBERG

WITH WENDY STEINBERG

SIMON & SCHUSTER
Rockefeller Center
1230 Avenue of the Americas
New York, New York 10020

Copyright © 1994 by Dr. Laurence Steinberg

SIMON & SCHUSTER and colophon are registered trademarks of Simon & Schuster Inc.

Designed by Karolina Harris
Manufactured in the United States of America

10   9   8   7   6   5   4   3   2   1

Library of Congress Cataloging-in-Publication Data
Steinberg, Laurence D., date.
Crossing paths : how your child's adolescence triggers your own crisis /
Laurence Steinberg with Wendy Steinberg
p.   cm.
Includes bibliographical references and index.
1. Adolescence. 2. Middle age. 3. Parent and teenager.
I. Steinberg, Wendy. II. Title.
HQ796.S8262 1994
305.23'5—dc20   94-8910 CIP
ISBN 0-671-79758-1

ACKNOWLEDGMENTS

Many talented individuals contributed to this volume, and I acknowledge their help with gratitude and pleasure.

The research on which this book is based could not have been completed without the able assistance of our project team, which over the years involved several dozen undergraduate and graduate assistants. I am indebted, in particular, to Susan Silverberg, Ron Saletsky, Brenda Atkinson, Julie Elmen, Frances Sessa, Kelly Koski, and Sandy Sykora.

The research was supported by generous grants from the William T. Grant Foundation and the Graduate School of the University of Wisconsin—Madison. Special thanks are due as well to participants in a seminar entitled The Family at Adolescence, which was given in the Department of Child and Family Studies at the University of Wisconsin. Many of the ideas discussed here had their beginnings in that class.

Susan Silverberg's contribution to this work over the years has been especially significant. It was Susan who first convinced our research team that the transition of the firstborn child into adolescence was likely to be a significant event in the lives of parents. I am grateful to her for permitting us to draw freely on many of the findings initially reported in her doctoral dissertation.

Numerous colleagues have been helpful commentators over the years on many of the themes developed in this book. My thinking has been greatly influenced by Andy Collins, Catherine Cooper, Shirley Feldman, Hal Grotevant, Stuart Hauser, John Hill, Grayson Holmbeck, Sally Powers, Judi Smetana, and Jim Youniss.

I am indebted to John Kelly and to our agent, Barbara Lowenstein, for their advice and guidance during the early stages of developing the book, and to our editor, Bob Bender, for his thoughtful suggestions on the manuscript.

I am eternally grateful to the several hundred parents and teenagers who opened their homes and lives to us. I hope I have told their stories not only with accuracy, but with compassion and understanding.

My deepest words of gratitude go to my wife and coauthor, Wendy. This book would not have come to fruition had it not been for her belief in the value of this project, her willingness to collaborate with me on the manuscript, and her remarkable talent as a writer. Wendy's insightful ideas about the emotional interior of family life influenced the entire work, and her elegant and lyrical writing ensured that our families' stories were told with grace and passion.

To Benjamin,

at the threshold of adolescence

CONTENTS

PART I

PARENTS AT MIDLIFE

1. CROSSING PATHS

Our children, more than anyone or anything else, act as yardsticks for our assessment of ourselves. More than a mirror, and more than the gentle reminders from our spouses, they reveal to us that we are growing older, heavier, more wrinkled, less agile. As they grow and change, maturing into young adults, their natural, normal development highlights the crossing paths they and we are on.

The physical blossoming inherent in adolescence provides a cruel contrast to our midlife journey. It takes nothing more than a sideways glance with narrowed, critical eyes from your son or daughter to let you know that something is not right: The new pair of jogging shorts the young salesman at the sporting goods store insisted everyone was wearing look ridiculous on you; the black strapless dress that your good friend told you would be perfect for the black-tie affair you're attending is wrong. No one but your own child would shake his or her head in that blatantly honest way . . . and convey the absolute truth.

When I organized the Families at Adolescence Project, my goal was to follow a large group of families as their firstborn child made the transition from childhood into adolescence. I knew from my experience as a psychologist and expert on family relationships during adolescence that this was a particularly tumultuous period in the life cycle of the family. I had conducted several major research projects on parents and teenagers and found that this period was one of great flux in family relationships, a time during which parents had many questions but few solutions. And over the years, whether I was in my office or at a cocktail party, I was barraged by parents of teenagers desperate for advice and answers.

Knowing that this was a vulnerable and emotionally loaded time for parents and children, I wanted to examine the conflicts and tensions that typically arose in families as teenagers struggled for and established their sense of autonomy. I was also aware that most of the psychological literature about families with teenagers has focused on the impact parents have on their children, not the other way around. Our bookstores are filled with advice and testimony on the ways particular parenting styles affect a youngster's personality development, how discipline influences teenagers' behavior, why various approaches to parenting succeed or fail, and so on. Everything a parent does, we are told, in some way touches the child.

But what about the reverse? What impact do children have on their parents?

It was not until recently that social scientists began to explore the ways in which children's development affects their parents. Virtually all of this research, however, has focused on just two very specific passages in the family's life: the "transition to parenthood," when the first newborn arrives; and the transition into the "empty nest," when the last child, now a young adult, leaves home. So, in essence, our knowledge about how parents are affected by their children is limited to research on their arrival and departure.

But what about the intervening eighteen years that parents and children spend together? Don't the milestones children pass through influence their parents during this time as well? Although common sense tells us that they must, very little actually has been written about how the subtle—and not-so-subtle—changes that occur in the child reverberate through the parents' life. This seems an odd omission indeed, because a great deal takes place between the birth and the launching of a child that has a profound effect on parents' mental health and well-being.

The book you are about to read is about the crisis that many parents experience when their child becomes a teenager.

ABOUT THE STUDY

In designing research on what happens to "normal" families as they grow and change, it is important to begin with a sample of average people. Nothing can be more misleading than social science research based on atypical samples, such as families visiting a clinic for therapy or readers of some esoteric magazine. Ours was a random, community sample, drawn without the participants' knowledge of the purpose of our research. This is unlike studies that advertise for participants, thus drawing from a select population with specific characteristics or symptoms that the researcher knows beforehand will fit with the focus of the study. In this research, we focused on typical parents and teenagers.

I began the study by surveying all the fifth, sixth, eighth, and ninth graders at eight different schools in and around a medium-sized midwestern city. In order to ensure a balanced socioeconomic cross section, we drew from different parts of town. Our participants ranged from solid working-class and blue-collar parents to upper middle-class professionals and high-level executives. Single parent and stepparent families were well represented (more than one third of our families had been through a divorce), as well as intact families.

From our school surveys we identified 270 firstborn children between the ages of ten and fourteen. After contacting all of their parents to explain that we were conducting a study of family life, 204 families, or 75 percent, agreed to participate—a much higher rate of participation than that usually observed in social science research of this kind. (Many studies have participation rates around 30 percent.) We were astounded by the enthusiastic response and soon found out the reason why: Parents of this age group are extremely perplexed by the changes they see in their families and are interested in why this period of their lives is so disturbing. They were eager, almost desperate, to discuss their feelings and concerns with me and my expert staff.

Previous studies of adolescence generally have ignored parents' feelings during this time. The prevailing belief has been that adolescence involves change only for the child. Because I wanted to get a fuller picture of the whole family unit and what each member was going through, the feelings they were experiencing, and the different ways each was coping with the changes, I decided to explore the parents' states of mind as well. I wanted to see the process of a child's crossing into adolescence from both perspectives.

In order to ensure a complete and accurate measurement of this period in the family cycle, we used multiple methods of data collection in our study. My staff and I administered in-depth questionnaires, standardized tests, and conducted one-on-one interviews, all in the participants' homes over the three-year period. Of the parents, we asked hundreds of questions designed to measure their marital and job satisfaction, self-esteem, parenting roles and practices, attitudes and values, and physical and mental health. In the children, we measured different signs of adolescent development, including physical, mental, and emotional growth, as well as their attitudes toward parents and peers, school performance, self-esteem, social relationships, and psychological functioning. Because we spent endless hours with each family, compiling multiple viewpoints of the same picture, we were able to draw a total portrait of each household during this time.

I was surprised at how open and responsive the parents were to our very personal probings. Initially, I took the fact that so many parents were so eager to join our study as an indication of their desire for information about how to better understand their teenagers. What I did not realize was that many parents participated in our project not because they did not understand their child, but because they were confused about what was happening to themselves.

Parents' accounts were frequently disquieting. I'll never forget the look on one father's face when he told me a story about his teenage son. Jim, a litigation lawyer, was devastated when his teenage son sneered in his face that the last thing on earth he wanted to be was a lawyer. "Boy, did that tear me apart," Jim said. "I was stunned that he could hurt me so much. Especially when I realized it wasn't that long ago that he'd tell me he was going to be a lawyer when he grew up, 'just like Daddy.' That was when he was in a phase where I could do no wrong. That time has sure vanished."

Some adolescents don't verbalize their disapproval of their parents as bluntly as Jim's son had, but almost all of them go through a period of challenging, questioning, and criticizing their parents in every possible area of a parent's life. Adolescence, the transition from childhood to adulthood, is one of the most significant events that occurs within the family system, and the change it involves is not limited to just the child. The child's passage into adolescence reverberates throughout the entire household.

In the chapters that follow you will see through firsthand accounts of families from our project why this period is one of such unrest for so many parents. The families you will meet are real, not fictional. We have changed their names and disguised many of the details of their lives in order to protect their privacy, but the stories you will read are true.

After my interview with Jim, I went back to my office and stared at a picture on my desk of my son, Benjamin. I tried to imagine Benjamin, who was four then, turning on me, as Jim's son had turned on him. When I fast-forwarded the clock, the feeling hit me—what it would feel like when suddenly, for the first time, I wouldn't be idolized by Ben, that he wouldn't look to me for answers anymore, as he did constantly as a four-year-old. I empathized with Jim and wondered how parents coped with a child's pulling away, with his or her rejection of them, and how parents let that natural separation occur without pain. I recalled my own adolescence and replayed scenes with my own parents in my mind. I winced at the things I had said, at the hurt I must have inflicted, and realized how unaware I had been of my impact on them.

2. THE MERRICKS

BARBARA MERRICK

It was a perfect summer day, warm and breezy, in 1985 when I first met Barbara Merrick at her home. A striking-looking woman with long, dark wavy hair and intense sky-blue eyes, she looked like she had stepped right out of a picture book on Ireland. Her pale, freckled skin reminded me of those young rosy-cheeked women clad in thick cable-knit sweaters. Dressed in a sleeveless blouse and Bermudas that showed off her trim figure, Barbara seemed like an energetic woman, and young for her forty-one years. As she led me through a formally furnished living room, I recalled the story I'd heard from her husband, Stan, whom I'd interviewed the week before, about how they'd met. It was on a college trip to an island in Lake Michigan. On the ferry ride over, Stan had been standing on the upper deck, looking down, and that was when he first saw Barbara. She was smiling up at him, her hair blowing about her face, her arms hugging her bundled body, and he said he'd fallen in love with her the moment he saw her blue eyes.

I followed Barbara through French doors and out onto a spacious deck that was lined with pots of flowers. As I admired the view of the lake in the distance and the carefully tended garden beneath us, she poured us each a glass of iced tea. Friendly and talkative, Barbara described how the deck had been a family project. Stan, an architect, had drawn the plans while each family member made specific requests and suggestions. Barbara's wish was to have enough room for flowers and a big table for family dinners. Since it had been built, they'd "practically lived" out there, according to Barbara, eating most of their meals together at the large round table. As we sat amidst this perfect setting, beneath towering maple trees, I expected I was going to hear a lot about the Merricks' perfect lives.

Barbara Merrick worked in public relations for one of the hospitals in the area. She spoke enthusiastically about her job and the people she worked with. Having been there for over ten years, she said she was fortunate to be able to arrange her schedule so that she was home most afternoons with her two boys, Brian and Jason, aged eleven and eight. Stan worked for a small architectural firm downtown and had flexible hours, so he was available to help out with child care when necessary.

When I asked about her marriage, Barbara replied cheerfully that Stan was a wonderful husband, very caring and considerate. "We've always enjoyed each other's company," she said, "which is very important, I think—though I know Stan would like us to spend more time together without the boys. But I feel it's important to do things as a family. That's how mine was. And besides," she added dismissively, "there'll be plenty of time for us alone when the boys are grown."

Midway through our conversation, Barbara called Brian and Jason up from the yard where they had been playing and introduced them to me. I was impressed as each one came forward, shook my hand and looked me in the eye, each extremely well mannered. I noticed Brian had his mother's intense eyes and a serious air about him. The following week when I would interview him, I was to see just how serious and self-controlled he was. Jason, on the other hand, was spunky and lighthearted, the opposite of his older brother.

As Barbara and I talked for a while, I could see that the Merricks were a close family whose daily routines were carefully orchestrated by Barbara. I could imagine her picture-perfect dinners out on the beautiful deck, followed by a game of Monopoly or Parcheesi as the sun set behind the lake. Barbara appeared to me that afternoon as a woman who was very much in charge of herself and her life, and who was happy with it that way. I listened as she told me stories typical of dual-career couples—the occasional dilemmas of child-care scheduling and the juggling of household chores amidst dealings with aging relatives or occasional times of financial strain. But, all in all, the Merricks seemed to be a stable, content family who were open and communicative with one another. Shortly before I left, I remember Barbara saying in a very pleased way that her life felt "under control." I had no doubt that it was.

Almost three years later, when I returned to do a follow-up interview with the Merricks, I expected to find things much the same, with the possible exception of Stan's and Barbara's relationships with Brian. Because Brian was now fourteen and would be in the throes of adolescence, I assumed there would have arisen new issues for Stan and Barbara to deal with as they struggled to redefine the parent-child relationship. I knew from our past studies that teenagers asserting their independence and opinions typically changes the dynamics of a household. But I was not prepared for what I was to see and hear.

That January evening when Barbara met me at her front door, I was startled by the change in her appearance. She had her hair pulled back in a severe new style that revealed not only her graying temples, but a creased and worried expression on her face that I hadn't remembered seeing the first time. Her eyes seemed pale and distant, and there were two permanent frown marks between her eyebrows. I couldn't help but notice that there was an overall tightened look about Barbara, a tenseness that seemed to emanate from her entire body.

We sat in the living room this time—a blanket of snow covered the deck—and I accepted her offer of a glass of wine, having noticed that she had one herself. There was a fire crackling away in the fireplace, but not another sound in the house. When I commented on the stillness, she told me that Stan was in Milwaukee working and the boys were out. "It's always like this," she said. "I'm usually the only one home in the evenings." As she spoke, there was a hurt, bitter tone to her voice, a sense of pain behind most everything she said.

I began asking Barbara about the period of time that had passed since I'd last seen her. I asked her to describe any changes that might have occurred, any events that stood out in her mind. Seeming almost grateful that someone was taking an interest in her life, Barbara opened right up. She started by telling me how much Stan had changed and how disrespectful and flippant Brian had gotten. I listened to her description of each and thought that Brian sounded pretty typical for his age, especially given the reined-in personality I'd witnessed years before. But Stan didn't sound like the man I remembered. According to Barbara, Stan had become aloof and selfish, and critical of Barbara in a nasty way. She told me of specific instances when he ridiculed and embarrassed her in front of the children with comments about what she was wearing or how she was acting.

"He keeps telling me to loosen up, or lighten up, or something," she said, disgust clearly registering on her face. "He says I act like my mother." Barbara let out a snide laugh. "He acts more like a teenager than a grown man. You should see him, Larry. Every time a nice-looking woman goes by, Stan has to comment about her. He never did that kind of thing before." Barbara stared at me, her face incredulous. "And if Brian's around, Stan elbows him and gives him a look, like, 'Hey, check her out.' My God, it's humiliating," she said, shaking her head. Then, taking a sip of wine, Barbara said in a lowered voice that Stan seemed to have lost interest in her sexually. "I know how he looks at me," she said, staring down at her lap. "Especially after one of Brian's girlfriends has been over. I can see it in his face, the comparison."

Later, I learned that their sexual relations had dwindled to once every couple of months and that Barbara felt extremely uncomfortable with Stan in bed. "I feel like he's pretending I'm someone else. He says and does things that he never used to do. Most of the time he just does it automatically, with no feeling."

As I sat there and listened to Barbara, I could sense her fear and loneliness. It seemed she had few friends that she confided in, an isolation that I assumed was mostly out of embarrassment. It was clearly not her style to talk about herself or her feelings to anyone. But I could see that Barbara was unhappy with her life, that she felt as though there was nothing she could do to change it. There was a pervasive sadness about her, as though her entire world was coming apart. Even her job was not giving her the pleasure it once had. She talked about the new people in her office and their differing opinions and work styles, and the tension she was feeling as a result. Everything was changing, and Barbara was not adapting well.

When Barbara told me how powerless she felt—that she had no control over her family or work life anymore—I realized just how depressed she was.

"Brian doesn't listen to me anymore," she remarked. "I tell him to do something and he just walks away—goes into his room and shuts the door on me. There's nothing I can do about it. And Stan doesn't help either. He just tells me to leave him alone. 'He's a teenager, Barb,' he says, as though that's some kind of an excuse."

In a resigned voice she told me that everyone was going their own way, that they had very few family activities they did together. "I feel so alone when I come home from work. Nobody's here—not even Jason. He's always over at a friend's house. He says it's more fun there."

It seemed the Merricks' family dinners were a relic of the past, too. Stan's firm had taken on a large-scale project with a developer in Milwaukee, and he was frequently sent up there to oversee the job. "When Stan *is* in town," Barbara said, "he and Brian are off together cross-country skiing or working out at the gym, and I'm left behind."

Driving back to my office that afternoon, stunned by the changes in Barbara and her family, I wondered what had happened to the Merricks in that short time. What happened to the feelings of well-being and satisfaction I had seen, and to their sense of stability and security? When the Merricks' boys were in grade school, family life was manageable and satisfying for both Stan and Barbara. Each had spoken of that time fondly. And each had felt in control of his or her life, job, and family. Why had their lives become more troubled as their children grew older?

STAN MERRICK

Later that week I met Stan at his office downtown. As we spoke, his comments helped fill in a little more of the picture. It seemed that while Barbara's relationship with Brian had become more problematic and distant as he approached adolescence, Stan and Brian had grown closer. For the first time, really, Stan and Brian were doing things together separately from the family—activities they both enjoyed but had never done before, such as the skiing and weight lifting that Barbara had complained about. I could see that these new activities were rejuvenating to Stan, both mentally and physically. He looked more robust and younger than he had three years ago. There was a vibrant, eager air to him, like a horse just out of the gate, ready to take on the race. Like Barbara, he had acquired a few new gray hairs, but otherwise he looked much younger than when I last interviewed him. Quite the opposite of Barbara, I thought sadly.

As Stan talked about Brian's new way of questioning and challenging things that he and Barbara said and did, I could see that he was put off by the new behavior but that he also had a good understanding of what it was like to be a teenager. He told me he remembered very clearly butting heads with his own mother over things like cleaning his room, going out at night, his friends, and homework.

"But Barb is too strict with Brian," Stan said. "She still treats him like he's ten years old, and"—Stan let out a laugh—"the boy is taller than she is!

"I don't know," he added in a more somber tone. "Things aren't like they used to be. We try to do something, all of us together, and it always seems like someone says or does something that hurts Barb— not intentionally—but she's so sensitive to every comment we make. Then the whole thing explodes, and she ends up crying or yelling at someone, and Brian and I look at each other like, 'Who's going to apologize this time?' I don't know, it's gotten to the point where it's so volatile around here, I just keep my mouth shut. I honestly don't know what to do."

So, it was not Stan's relationship with Brian that had changed for the worse—as I had expected—but his relationship with *Barbara*. Apparently, Barbara's rigidity and her need to control everyone had pushed Stan and the boys away. Stan related an incident to me that summed up the situation fairly well. They'd all been watching TV together in the den, something they didn't do often, and Barbara couldn't stop monitoring the boys—"telling them to keep their shoes off the furniture, don't put that glass on the table, stop playing with the remote control, that kind of thing," Stan said. Then Brian had gone out to the kitchen and returned with a bag of Chee-tos.

"And before he'd even sat back down on the couch, Barb shouted that he was not to eat those things in the den, that they'd turn the furniture orange. Brian just stared at her, in disbelief almost, and said, 'All you care about is your furniture. The things in this house are more important to you than any of us.' And he turned and walked out of the room." Stan shook his head sadly. "That was the end of *that* evening of family togetherness."

After the boys had gone to bed that night, Stan talked to Barbara about the compulsive cleanliness and order that she insisted on in the house and told her it made him and the boys uncomfortable. Barbara had not responded well, accusing Stan of siding with Brian. Stan had gone back downstairs and watched television by himself, waiting for Barbara to fall asleep before he came up to bed.

Stan told me that he was concerned about Barbara, about her unhappiness. "I try to get her to come up to Milwaukee when I have to stay over, and have some fun—go out, just the two of us. But she insists on staying home to watch the kids. I don't know what she thinks would happen—they're both great kids, well behaved, responsible—but she's under the misconception that Brian is out of control." Stan shook his head in disbelief. "If Brian disagrees with her, she interprets it as bad, as disrespectful and disobedient. The boy is standing up for himself for the first time in his life—it's good to see it and to see him lighten up a bit, be more of a kid."

I could see that it was not just Brian who was standing up for himself for the first time and doing what he wanted. Stan was discovering aspects of himself that had lain dormant for years.

"I'd always tried to get Barb to go cross-country skiing with me, but she was never interested. We always had to do something she liked. So it was really nice last year when Brian got interested. Now the two of us do it every chance we get. And the weight lifting. When Brian and I are at the gym working out and talking about school and girls and stuff, I don't know what it is, but I feel like a teenager all over again. We joke around, make little comments to each other about the other people in there. It's great!"

The difference between Stan's tone of voice when he spoke about his son and when he spoke about his wife was striking. When he talked about Brian, Stan sounded confident, gratified, and rejuvenated. When he spoke about Barbara, he sounded confused, irritated, and unhappy.

BRIAN MERRICK

My interview with Brian corroborated much of what I had heard from his parents. According to him, the tension between himself and his mother had escalated considerably during the past year. I asked Brian if he had any explanation for this.

"No, not really," he said. "I mean, it's like we got along fine when I was younger, but now we fight all the time."

I asked what the fights were about.

"Oh, usually she won't let me do something I want to do. Or she tells me to clean up my room when I don't feel like it."

Did he and his mother argue when he was younger?

"Sure we did. But when I was little, I would just say, 'OK' to whatever she said. Now, I'll yell back at her if I think I'm right. And that really makes her mad. She goes to my father and complains about it to him. He and I talk about it sometimes while we're working out. He says I should be more respectful, even if I might be right sometimes.

"I don't know. I just wish she would leave me alone more. I just wish she would let me grow up."

The Merricks' story epitomizes one aspect of what happens to many families as their oldest child reaches adolescence. The balance that had been achieved when children are younger is suddenly and quite unexpectedly thrown off when the oldest child becomes a teenager. The Merricks' problems began when Brian began exerting his adolescent will. As he started testing limits, flexing his muscles of autonomy, trying on different roles and attitudes, and challenging his parents' beliefs, values, and decisions, Barbara's sense of stability and her control and authority over her tightly structured family unit began eroding. It was being chipped away at, tested and challenged by Brian's normal, healthy maturation. The equilibrium of the Merrick household had clearly been thrown off, and Stan and Barbara's marriage was deteriorating. So was Barbara's mental health.

PARENTS IN TURMOIL

When I began this study, I had expected to see this period as one of extreme difficulty for the adolescents in our sample, as they struggled to establish their independence and sense of identity. This was what adolescence was supposed to be about.

But as I analyzed the data, I saw immediately that there was something unusual and surprising going on. It looked as if the transition to adolescence was surprisingly peaceful for the children in our sample—that they were coasting through their teenage years smoothly and with little self-consciousness.

What really hit me, though, was that a large number of their *parents* were experiencing difficulty. Coping with their children's adolescence was occupying enormous amounts of their time and psychological energy. This was true for fathers as well as for mothers—and true whether they were married, divorced, or remarried.

We repeated our assessments twelve months later. We found that during the year more than half of the parents in our sample had experienced significant changes in their mental health. Two out of three who changed said they felt more depressed and anxious, more unsure of themselves, were less happily married, and more dissatisfied with their work. One mother captured the feeling painfully clearly when she said, "If my husband and son even bother to look at me these days, it's with disdain and disinterest—as though I'm in their way. They seem to have their own little club, and I'm simply there to cook and clean up after them." I thought to myself that if this was the impact of having a child in adolescence for just one short year, what toll might the entire period take on parents' mental health?

Feelings of rejection and low self-worth, and of being on the outside of life, were prevalent among both mothers and fathers. Many in our sample felt that their son or daughter was having more fun in life than they were, and that sex with their spouse had become, if not nonexistent, then certainly less pleasurable. And many reported symptoms of psychosomatic illnesses, such as headaches, insomnia, and gastrointestinal ailments.

The more I studied our findings, the more I understood why the specific issues involved in the child's transition into adolescence catalyzed a crisis for parents. As an adolescent child pulls away from his or her parents and establishes him- or herself as a separate, independent, and self-sufficient entity, parents are forced to *let go*. More than one parent in our study said it felt like an involuntary divorce. This experience, I saw, filled mothers and fathers with an array of disturbing emotions. Many felt a painful sense of loss, depression, envy, jealousy, anger, and frustration—and, often, regret. And not surprisingly, these negative emotions spilled over into other aspects of parents' lives, creating a domino effect. Many reported feeling for the first time a keen dissatisfaction with themselves, with their job and career, with their marriage, and with parenting—as we saw with Barbara Merrick.

EXCEPTIONS TO THE RULE

A teenager in the home does not automatically bring on a psychological earthquake for parents, however. A portion of our participants showed very little change in their self-esteem and life and work satisfaction, and one fifth of our sample actually reported an *improvement* in their mental health. For them, the experience reinforced their feelings of love toward their spouse and a contentment with themselves and their lives.

John and Linda Forster, another couple from our study, are an example of parents whose marital satisfaction and mental health improved during their daughter Abby's transition to adolescence. During one of our interviews, John recounted in detail the evening of Abby's first school dance: He and Linda had just dropped Abby and her two friends off at the junior high school and were parked in the faculty lot while Linda was searching the newspaper to find a movie for them to go to.

"I remember looking over at Linda," John told me, "listening to her rattle off the different movies and times, and, for some reason, I felt like we were on our first date together. It sounds funny, I know, but everything came rushing back to me, all the things I'd noticed and liked about her when we first met—her long brown hair and the way she held it back out of her face, her voice, and smile—and I realized how much I still liked being with her. Even after sixteen years. That's something, isn't it?" he asked me, shaking his head.

As it turned out, the Forsters never made it to a movie that night. They ended up "necking" in the car, as John described it, then going home, and, after making love, spent the rest of the evening in bed, sharing stories with each other of high school dances and first dates.

Unfortunately, though, the psychological distress that I saw overcome the Merricks, and the transformation that their household underwent as Brian moved through adolescence, are more common.

What is it that distinguishes those mothers and fathers who actually thrive during this period from the majority who do not? Over the three years that we conducted the study, I was able to isolate the critical variables that separate those parents who suffer, those who escape unscathed, and those who actually thrive during this transitional time.

3. PARENTS IN CRISIS

> I've got bad feet. I've got a jawbone that's deteriorating and someday soon
> I'm going to have to have all my teeth pulled. It will hurt. I've got an unhappy
> wife to support and two unhappy children to take care of. . . . I've got eight
> unhappy people working for me who have problems and unhappy depen-
> dents of their own. I've got anxiety; I suppress hysteria. I've got politics on
> my mind, summer race riots, drugs, violence, and teen-age sex.
>
> **Bob Slocum, the forty-something protagonist of Joseph Heller's novel**
> ***Something Happened***

Psychologists have long maintained that one of the most critical
times in the life cycle occurs between ages thirty-five and forty-
five—known as middle adulthood. It is a time of settling and shifting
for most people, and it carries with it enormous potential for psychological upheaval. The general public knows this, not only from the
popular press, but from daily reminders of it. Just walk through the
birthday-card section of a store and you'll find more disparaging
jokes about turning forty than about any other age:

> Some people say it's all downhill after 40. I don't think that's accurate. . . . It's
> much more like a bobsled to hell.

> Well, this is *that* birthday. The major one. The one you knew was coming. The
> big one. . . . The one that really sucks.

> What's 8 times 5? . . . . Pretty old.

THE MIDLIFE TRANSITION

The idea that middle adulthood is a transitional time first became popular in the 1950s, with the publication of Erik Erikson's theory of the life cycle. Erikson argued that there were predictable stages in adult development, as well as predictable crises during these stages. Although he did not identify midlife as a dramatic turning point, his suggestion that we have identity crises throughout life—not just in adolescence—set the stage for new ideas about middle age. In the 1970s, a series of empirical studies were published, all indicating that an identity crisis around age forty was inevitable for most adults, an idea popularized by Gail Sheehy in her best selling book *Passages*.

By 1980, the idea of the "midlife crisis" was firmly entrenched in American popular culture.

Different writers gave different reasons for the inevitability of the midlife crisis. Some, like Sheehy, maintained that adult life stages are largely inherent, triggered by some kind of internal psychological clock with a psychic alarm set to go off sometime around age forty.

Others emphasized the physical changes of middle age, such as aging skin, thinning hair, or aching muscles. According to these writers, these physical changes force us to come face to face with our own mortality. Faced with the inevitability of our own death, we begin marking time in terms of how many years we have left to live, rather than how many years we have been alive.

A different set of writers located the cause of the midlife crisis not in the adult's psyche, but in the structure of adult life itself. Following the sex stereotypes of the times, theorists looked to the workplace for men and to the family for women. Yale psychologist Daniel Levinson's seminal study *Seasons of a Man's Life*, for example, emphasized turning points in men's careers. He suggested that most men hit an "occupational plateau" in their late thirties, prompting them to look back over their young adult years and ask, "What have I done with my life?" Others saw an analogous crisis for women, revolving around the "launching" of their children. According to them, a woman's identity crisis erupts when she comes face to face with the "empty nest."

Few of the parents in our study fit neatly within these models of midlife crisis, however. Frequently, men had come to terms with any

career disappointments but were profoundly unhappy and dissatisfied with their family life or their marriage. Indeed, family life
seemed to play a much greater role in the psychological well-being of
the men in our sample than previous studies had indicated. Perhaps, I
reasoned, men had changed appreciably in the twenty years since
Levinson's study was conducted. Or perhaps our preconceptions
about men's psychological health being inextricably linked to their
work and unaffected by family affairs were simply wrong.

I was also surprised by some of the things I heard from the women
I interviewed. They were, as expected, profoundly affected by the vicissitudes of family life, but not always in the way others had pre-
dicted. Some mothers did express dread over the launching of their
children. But many mothers expressed an *eagerness*, not apprehen-
sion, for the time when their children would be grown and off on
their own. After years of caring for the family, the women we interviewed were looking forward to some free time that they could devote to themselves, their careers, and other personal pursuits that
had been neglected over the years. Far from being a cause of crisis, as
conventional wisdom held, the empty nest was anticipated as a
source of relief. If anything, it was *living* with an adolescent child, not
anticipating the child's departure, that was the cause of distress.

DIANE JACOBS

One case I remember particularly clearly was that of forty-seven-
year-old Diane Jacobs, a successful lawyer and single mother of
two—David, fifteen, and Elizabeth, twelve. When I first met Diane,
she and her ex-husband, Ben, who was almost fifty, had been divorced for over six years, and neither had remarried. Ben was a general contractor who lived on the other side of town from Diane and
the children. Diane spoke candidly about the difficulties she was experiencing.

"It starts when the alarm clock goes off in the morning—that sink-
ing feeling in my stomach—and I think, 'I don't have the strength to
go through another day of it,' of pleading with David, fighting with
Ben, putting out the fires only to have another one ignite. And then
on top of it all, there's my job, which isn't exactly stress free. Some-

times I wake up wishing I were someone else, someplace else. I wish I could rewind my life to five years ago when the kids were younger and easier and our lives were happy. I liked my life then."

I remember the night Diane confessed this to me. It was our second meeting at her home, a contemporary house in a development on the west side of town that she and Ben had bought when they were together. It was about eight at night, and Diane had just gotten home from work. She looked exhausted and apologized as she kicked off her heels and put her stockinged feet up on the ottoman in her living room, where we sat and talked.

A petite woman with a smart, boyish haircut, Diane was dressed in a fashionable business suit, large gold earrings, and a scarf draped around her neck. As she sipped her diet Coke, she told me about her daily exercise regimen, pursued in the only time during the day that she took for herself. Every day at noon she swam at the university pool or played squash or tennis with a colleague from the law school where Diane also worked, teaching an evening course. A busy and productive woman, Diane's face revealed the long days and late hours she had to keep in order to accomplish her numerous daily tasks.

"Another great day," she said, sighing loudly. "David called me at work to tell me he was heading over to the mall to get his ear pierced. That was considerate of him, wasn't it?" Before I could tell how she'd meant it, she went on to say that she and Ben had spent the previous evening arguing on the phone about David piercing his ear. "Frankly, it's fine with me if David wants it badly enough. I can't debate every single thing he does or wants to do. It's too exhausting." She continued, somewhat defensively, "I spend half my time bickering with David about his activities and the other half defending them to Ben. I'm tired of being in the middle." Apparently Ben had "hit the ceiling" over the pierced-ear issue.

"He was livid," Diane said. "Absolutely livid. 'How could a son of ours want to do something like that?' he wanted to know, and 'Why would he want to look like a woman?' and on and on." Diane looked down at her lap and shook her head. "David is fifteen. He should be allowed to make some of these decisions himself." She looked to me for confirmation. "Anyway, after Ben and I got off the phone, I told David it was out of the question, that he wasn't allowed to pierce his ear. Of course, he was furious with me then and slammed into his room."

"What did you tell him when he phoned today?" I asked.

"Well, I was shocked, first of all, that he'd call to tell me that after what happened last night. I thought I had made it very clear that he was not allowed to do it. But I was meeting with a potential client—a big one—and I wasn't about to get into it there on the phone in front of him. So I told David he had to talk to his father about it."

Looking sheepish, Diane added that she knew that wasn't the right thing to do, but that she'd wanted Ben to handle some of the problems that were continually coming up at home. It seemed that Ben had become more intrusive in day-to-day decisions and had gotten stricter with the children as they'd gotten older.

"But he leaves it to me to enforce all of his rules," Diane explained. "It never used to be this way. We used to agree on how we were raising David and Elizabeth. After the divorce, when Ben moved out, he was more laid back, relaxed about the kids and their friends and schoolwork—and he trusted my decisions, my judgment. But not anymore. He tells me I'm oblivious to what's going on with them, that I'm too lenient, and I don't keep enough tabs on them. He's constantly pushing David to try out for different things at school—like band, or the drama club, or sports—things Ben never did when he was David's age but thinks David should do. He says it's important to be well rounded, to have a good foundation. That he needs those things to get into a good college. This is from a man who went to the local tech college. And now he's starting in on Lizzy. 'Who does she hang around with? Where does she go after school?' I don't know what's changed, but I'm going crazy."

I wondered if much of what Diane was experiencing was typical for divorced parents. Under the best circumstances couples find it isn't always easy to see eye to eye on childrearing issues. Divorced couples must have an even tougher time, I thought. But while Diane admitted that being a single parent had never been easy, she said her life had *improved* after her divorce. Decisions actually became easier to make after the divorce, she remarked, "because we didn't have our resentment and anger toward each other buried in there somewhere, beneath the issues we supposedly were discussing." Her marriage had been an unhappy one, she told me—unsatisfying in the early stages, and then, later, a source of conflict and pain for both of them.

"When we split up," Diane said, "we each became happier, nicer people. We got along better when we didn't live together." And she liked her newfound freedom and the ease of coming home after work and spending time with the kids or doing whatever she wanted. "It was the little things, too," she said. "Like not having to make a big dinner every night, which was what Ben always wanted. I could come home, fix a salad or order in a pizza and not feel guilty. And the kids were just as happy. But now that David and Elizabeth are older, they're gone most of the time, with friends, or after-school things, so we don't have dinner together as often. Another thing Ben complains to me about," Diane sighed. "It sounds terrible to say this," she told me, "but I can't wait till my children go off to college. I want my life back."

THE MIDLIFE CRISIS

As a result of the scholarly work of Erikson and Levinson, and the popular writings of Sheehy, most people now associate "crisis" with midlife. Turn forty, and you are destined to have a midlife crisis. Someone tells you about a friend in his early forties who quit his six-figure job to go back to school and get a teaching degree, and your response is, "He must be having a midlife crisis."

There are different stereotypes of the forty-something casualty, depending on whether the angst-ridden individual is male or female. In popular portrayals, men *act out* the crisis; women *internalize* it. Thus, the two clichéd alternatives: *his*—the successful professional man who abruptly walks out on his wife and family, buys a flashy red sports car, grows his hair longer, and starts dating his twenty-two-year-old secretary; and *hers*—the full-time homemaker and mother, whose children have left for college and who wanders aimlessly and purposelessly through the empty rooms in her house until one day, when she has a breakdown in the middle of a department store.

Although the popular media feed our distorted visions of the midlife sufferer—in the movie *Middle Age Crazy*, Bruce Dern plays a forty-year-old who buys a Porsche, some new "threads," and leaves his wife to run off with a pro-football cheerleader—the reality is typically far less dramatic, far less drastic, and far less glamorous. And, as recent critics of the "midlife crisis" theory have pointed out, many adults—perhaps even the majority of adults—experience middle adulthood as a *turning point* without necessarily going through anything catastrophic. Nevertheless, for those who do experience something even approaching a crisis, midlife can be a very troubling, depressing, and grim time.

What separates those in crisis from those who are merely negotiating a middle-adulthood transition? Perhaps the most common symptom of a genuine midlife crisis is a pervasive sense of dissatisfaction. Nothing in life seems to provide any excitement. Individuals complain of feeling restless, bored, empty. They are frequently exhausted but at the same time unable to sleep. They are irritable, preoccupied, and short-tempered. Many also feel a pervasive sense of fear—of getting old, of not being able to change his or her life, of dying.

Joseph Heller captures the tenor of the crisis quite aptly in *Something Happened*. Through his protagonist, Bob Slocum, we see firsthand the internal suffering and anguish that grips the midlife-crisis sufferer. Unhappy with his job, his wife, his children, Bob Slocum struggles with a constant and immobilizing fear of just about everything. Similar feelings are expressed by the protagonist in Sue Kaufman's novel *Diary of a Mad Housewife*:

> What I really am and have been since midsummer is paralyzed. What I am is paranoid as a coot. What I am at times is so depressed I can't talk, so low I have to lock myself in the bathroom and run all the faucets to cover the sound of my crying. . . . What I am is suddenly afraid of most everything you could name.

This sense of free-floating dissatisfaction is usually manifested as disenchantment with something specific, like work, marriage, or parenthood.

DISENCHANTMENT AT WORK

For many individuals, the midlife crisis is experienced mainly as un-happiness about work. By the time they reach midlife, most adults have been working for at least fifteen years—some more, some less—and an internal measurement of success or failure seems to take place about this time. This personal assessment brings about some severe awakenings for many people. Some realize they have not attained the goals they set for themselves during young adulthood and that their chances of reaching them are diminishing with age. Or if they have achieved the level of success they had strived for, they realize that they didn't receive the acclaim they had hoped would accompany it.

A public relations executive from our study, for example, had de-signed many successful campaigns but complained that he had never received the coveted award spotlighting him in his state's professional organization. The same longing was echoed by a history professor who, although she had achieved tenure in her department, felt that she had failed because her peers had written more prolifically and had published in more prestigious journals.

These feelings were not limited to those in professional occupa-tions either. Mid-level managers and blue-collar workers in our study also confessed to a sense of having fallen short of their goals. During these excruciating years of reappraisal, as they reassessed their lives, they felt regret over the route they had taken and bitter about any lack of advantages they had had when they were beginning their careers.

Many individuals were prompted by this sense of dissatisfaction to guide or push their children in ways they hoped would enable them to avoid their parents' mistakes. Diane Jacobs, the divorced lawyer whom we met earlier, told me that she thought her ex-husband's pressuring their son, David, about extracurricular activities and sports so much was his attempt to make up for what he himself hadn't done as a teenager. "Ben didn't have the advantages David has, and Ben tries to make him understand that, how he shouldn't let a single opportunity go by. But Ben's looking at it through an adult's eyes. You can't convince a child of things it's taken forty years to realize. Just like we did, they're going to have to learn for themselves."

DISENCHANTMENT WITH MARRIAGE

For others, marriage was the arena in which the midlife crisis was experienced most intensely. Many reported feeling unhappy in their marriage, a sentiment that jibes with other studies of marital satisfaction in middle adulthood. These studies tell us that, over the course of time, marital satisfaction tends to follow a U-shaped curve. Soon after the wedding day, marital satisfaction begins to decline, hitting its lowest point when a couple's firstborn child is a teenager. During the remaining years of marriage, satisfaction tends to rise—somewhat. (Marital happiness declines over time for childless couples, too, although not as steeply.)

The Merricks, whom you met in the previous chapter, are a perfect example of a couple whose marriage was shaken up and redefined during midlife with an adolescent in the home. Barbara was understandably irritated by Stan's juvenile and insensitive behavior. At the same time, Stan's realization about Barbara's rigidity was pounded home by Brian's comments about his mother. While Stan may have been aware of his wife's tendency toward overneatness and her over-concern with the condition of the house, it was because of Brian's acute observations that Stan realized just how much it had dominated their activities. Stan told me he had always put up with it without much complaint because the house was Barbara's domain. But now that Brian was standing up to his mother, it was almost as if that enabled Stan to stand up to Barbara too.

When a child grows older and becomes more capable, not only in expression, but in observation and evaluation, the balanced pairing of husband and wife is tipped, as if a third party has stepped on the scale. The teenager joins the configuration, and suddenly the marriage is on stage. And the audience of one consists of someone who is exulting in his or her newfound voice and who does not hold back her or his opinions and idle comments. These critiques can cut dangerously close to parents' nerves.

DISENCHANTMENT WITH PARENTHOOD

In addition to disenchantment with work and marriage, we found a third area of discontentment among many of the midlife adults in our study—parenthood. Parenting an adolescent is different from parenting a toddler or a grade school–age child. Not only are the issues different, but suddenly you are dealing with someone who is now able to argue with more verbal and intellectual acuity.

Although it is a necessary step during the transition to adolescence that children distance themselves from their parents and establish their own identity, it is not necessarily an easy step for parents to accept. An awful lot goes on during this distancing process, and the range is broad, from trivial day-to-day matters to major ones, as we saw with Diane Jacobs, her son, David, and the issue of the pierced ear. When once a simple "no, you are not allowed to do that" sufficed (perhaps it had to be repeated a few times), you now find yourself flabbergasted at your youngster's outright refusal to obey. Once your child has reached adolescence, everything about parenting becomes less controllable.

Though we have been forewarned, we have not been prepared, nor are we used to dealing with someone confronting us in abrupt and sometimes brusque or rude ways. As you stand at the kitchen counter, making the salad dressing as you have a hundred times, your teenage daughter walks by and says in passing, "Not *that* awful dressing again—can't you make something different?" Even our husbands and wives in their cruelest, most blunt and impatient moments would fail to follow up a remark like that with a fast "I'm sorry, I didn't mean to say it that way." But your adolescent will look at you when you demand an apology, and say, guilelessly, "What for? It's the truth." And in a later, more reasonable moment, you just might agree. After all, you *have* been making that same old oil-and-vinegar dressing for as long as you care to remember.

INTROSPECTION AND REAPPRAISAL

For many adults in the midst of a midlife crisis, the overall discontentment with life increases gradually to the point that it becomes pervasive and all-consuming. There is a sense of everything being inevitable. One of the men I spoke to, who was extremely unhappy with his marriage and family, dismissed his disenchantment by saying that all couples grow apart over the years, that kids grow up and move on, and that it was all par for the course and inevitable. Social scientists have found that this overwhelming sense of powerlessness leads to increased life reappraisal, introspection, self-doubt, and a sort of existential self-examination.

An excruciating self-assessment and critical dissection of the external world occurs during the middle adult years. Prompted by acute dissatisfaction and by the realization that midlife represents the last real chance to make major changes in life—whether in a career or a family situation—many of us begin to reexamine our lives. We may question decisions we made and paths we chose and wonder with enormous self-doubt whether they were the correct ones. Where might I be, wonders the middle-level executive, had I taken that position with the small, unknown company that has now gained an international reputation? Or consider the elementary school teacher who has tired of the repetitive lessons year after year and wishes she had continued on in graduate school while she was younger. Or how about the unhappily married woman who fantasizes about what her life would have been had she married her college sweetheart?

THE CHANGE IN TIME PERSPECTIVE

Psychologists also note that in middle age there occurs a shift in time perspective, in which individuals start measuring their lives in terms of how long they have left to live rather than how long they have been alive. For some adults, this shift is gradual, for others, sudden recognition. For people in the throes of a crisis, changes in physical appearance become a daily reminder that time is slipping away. It is as if they are standing on a hill, gazing down upon their past and all the signposts that are slowly becoming dimmer but more precious. They then measure that view against the one on the other side of the hill, the future, and *that* looks frighteningly short.

George Bradshaw, a forty-four-year-old father and physician from our study, told me a story that captures this time of recognition both vividly and dramatically.

"I'll never forget the day—the moment, really," he said, "when I realized how uninvolved I'd been in just about everything but my career. It was our son's piano recital, and, which was pretty typical, I raced there from the hospital and stood at the back of the room with some other latecomers. I thought it was Johnny up on stage at the piano, and I mumbled something to the dad next to me about my son's playing, feeling proud and pretty amazed at how good he was. This guy looked over at me and said, 'That's Matt Weaver, the music teacher's son,' in a tone that conveyed all the disgust and disapproval I was due. I can't tell you how I felt—it was like I'd been punched in the gut or something. That moment was like being thrown off a treadmill."

George said he knew that med school had started a kind of momentum for him, one that increased over the years as he took on more and more at the hospital and his two offices, but that he'd also intended to slow it down one day. Like many men, he left the job of taking care of his family up to his wife. Unfortunately, like many men also, when he realized this sad fact, his children were past grade school age and into activities of their own, and his wife had a busy life of her own. George's enthusiasm for work came to a grinding halt that day, when he realized that his success had been at the expense of other aspects of his life.

This period of reassessing the meaning and value of one's life is difficult and painful. Most people experience it as a lonely struggle. This is the case particularly for men, for they are socialized to hold in their emotions and not display any signs of weakness. Levinson points out that this reappraisal cannot be a "cool, intellectual process," but is, rather, an emotionally tumultuous and debilitating time.

SYMPTOMS OF CRISIS

The midlife crisis is manifested in different ways in different individuals. For many, especially those from middle-class and professional backgrounds, the psychological struggles of midlife lead to an increase in reports of neurotic symptoms, including depression, anxiety, nervousness, feelings of loss of control, lowered self-esteem, and a diminished zest for life. Some researchers actually have tied the increase in suicide during middle adulthood among middle-class men to the prevalence of the midlife crisis.

There also are those who, though suffering through an internal crisis, have a tendency to deny that fact. In many instances, these individuals exhibit psychosomatic ailments, such as ulcers, headaches, insomnia, gastrointestinal problems, hypertension, and heart disease, rather than blatant signs of psychological distress. Some research suggests that this sort of manifestation is especially common among blue-collar adults, who are less likely to describe their experiences in psychological terms, or even to verbalize them at all. We found in our study that between 15 and 20 percent of the adults we interviewed denied that they were in any type of critical state, yet exhibited internalized distress nonetheless.

It is hard to find an adult who has not experienced at least one of the symptoms listed above. Almost everyone at one point in her or his life has had a bout of insomnia or a stress-related headache. Many in our study complained of waking up in the middle of the night with what several termed "night terrors." One woman, Rebecca Cohen, told me she thought only children experienced them, but that she awoke nearly every night at four in the morning, terrified and shaking.

"I have no idea what wakes me," she said, "but I sit bolt upright, and I feel sweaty and as if something awful is happening, or is going to happen. It takes me a minute or two to calm down, and then I just lie there for the next couple of hours, tossing and turning, my mind racing about all kinds of things. Sometimes stupid stuff, like whether the kids have a certain item they need for school the next day. But usually I worry about something that's been bothering me, like a fight John and I have had, or something I said to my mother that I feel guilty about. And more and more, I have these terrible fantasies about my dying or John dying and what would happen to the kids."

The self-doubt and disenchantment many feel during this time become manifested in feelings of anxiety, which can in turn cause people to drink too much in an attempt to numb their feelings of unhappiness. Many adults in the midst of a midlife crisis report overuse of alcohol or other drugs.

MEASURING THE MIDLIFE CRISIS

In our study, we measured the manifestations and symptoms associated with the midlife crisis by asking our parents a wide range of questions. Designed to accurately capture this emotionally sensitive and crucial time in parents' lives, the questions were posed in a number of different formats, allowing us to cross-check for inconsistencies. Additionally, through our intimate interviews with each parent, we again were able to detect signs of denial and responses that had not been completely honest. A sample of our questions is reprinted in Table 3-1 on page 45.

TABLE 3-1

Sample Items Measuring Midlife Rumination

Read the following statements and indicate how often you have experienced these thoughts within the past year or so—*Very Often, Sometimes, Not Very Often*, or *Never.*

"I find myself wondering whether my spouse and I could have developed a closer relationship than the one we have now."

"I find myself wondering what it is I really want in life."

"I find myself wishing that I had the opportunity to start afresh and do things over, knowing what I do now."

"I find myself wondering if I see myself the way I really am."

Sample Items Measuring Psychological Distress

Indicate how often you've experienced each of the following during the past year—*Never, Once, A Few Times, Many Times*, or *Very Often.*

"felt overtired"

"had a headache"

"felt nervous or worried"

"felt 'low' or depressed"

"had trouble sleeping"

Sample Items Measuring Self-Esteem

Indicate whether you (1) *Agree strongly*, (2) *Agree slightly*, (3) *Disagree slightly*, or (4) *Disagree strongly* with the following statements:

"I feel that I have a number of good qualities."

"I am confident about my physical attractiveness."

"I wish I could have more respect for myself."

"I am very satisfied with myself as a person."

Sample Items Measuring Life Satisfaction

Here are some continuums along which we would like you to rate your present life. Please place a ✓ in one of the boxes in each line to indicate your feeling.

Boring	☐	☐	☐	☐	☐	☐	☐	☐	Interesting
Full	☐	☐	☐	☐	☐	☐	☐	☐	Empty
Tied Down	☐	☐	☐	☐	☐	☐	☐	☐	Free
Useless	☐	☐	☐	☐	☐	☐	☐	☐	Worthwhile

On many items, men's and women's responses varied, with women reporting more feelings of psychological distress, especially those manifested in physical symptoms, than men. But some of the responses were divided fairly equally between men and women: Half of the men and women we surveyed said they had nagging doubts about the way their life had turned out, and half said they frequently wondered what it was they really wanted in life.

We also found, contrary to the popular belief that women feel worse about themselves than men, that men and women scored approximately equal in the area of self-esteem. But we did find an interesting discrepancy between the ways men and women experience, or at least characterize, the turmoil of midlife. Women describe it in terms of emptiness, loneliness, and unfulfilling relationships, whereas men describe feelings of frustration, disappointment, and lack of confidence and mastery.

When we looked closely at the profile of our parents and analyzed their attitudes and feelings more systematically, however, we saw that our findings departed from much previous research on the midlife crisis in some very important ways.

THE CRISIS DOESN'T ALWAYS COME AT MIDLIFE

As we saw with Diane and Ben Jacobs, some of our parents were considerably older than forty, yet many of these parents were experiencing the feelings typically associated with the midlife crisis. Did this mean that the midlife transition was getting longer? Or was it occurring later because people were delaying marriage and starting a family? Or, I wondered, perhaps the turmoil our respondents were reporting was due to other forces, not simply to becoming middle aged.

THE CRISIS ISN'T INEVITABLE

Researchers have led the public to believe that the midlife crisis is an inevitable part of middle adulthood. The magic age was believed to be forty, when, suddenly, individuals felt dissatisfied with their jobs, their marriages, and themselves. This spurred them into abruptly altering aspects of their physical appearance, as well as their careers and home lives. But contrary to this popular belief—and consistent with more recent and more systematic research—we found that not everyone has a midlife crisis in its classic form.

We looked explicitly at the prevalence of midlife crises among the parents in our study. Only 25 to 33 percent of our random sample of 360 adults exhibited intense, overt midlife-crisis symptoms. Only a quarter of our subjects expressed a desire to make specific changes in their lives. Instead, we found that most adults' midlife struggles are experienced as *internal distress*, like depression or insomnia, and that people are unable to make necessary changes to alleviate their pain.

We also found that a good number of people go into and through middle adulthood relatively smoothly and crisis free. This echoed studies by others that have found that many middle-aged adults find this time to be a period of security and satisfaction, describing themselves as more powerful and stable than when they were younger.

THE CRISIS IS NOT JUST FOR MEN, AND IT ISN'T JUST ABOUT WORK

Most of the social scientific research of the past has focused on men and the midlife transition. The researchers who carried out these studies by and large believed that men suffered through this time primarily because of career and job dissatisfaction. (Researchers Michael Farrell and Stanley Rosenberg split from popular belief in connecting men and family issues in their book *Men at Midlife*.) Our findings, however, showed that the family has just as important an impact on men's lives as it does on women's.

We found that men's home lives were as much a cause of their crisis as their work lives. In fact, some felt that work was the only good aspect of their lives, while their psychological well-being was suffering due to marital and personal problems. Stan Merrick is an example of a man whose primary source of happiness in life came from his work and whose midlife concerns centered around his marriage.

In general, men who had maintained a close, communicative marriage had relatively fewer midlife complaints. However, many men we interviewed reported feeling distant from their wives and expressed a disenchantment with their sexual relations and a general dissatisfaction with their marriage. For them, work was not the primary source of difficulty during this period of their lives.

THE EMPTY NEST IS NOT THE PROBLEM FOR WOMEN

We found that, contrary to earlier belief, women, like men, are most likely to suffer psychological turmoil during the years *before* their children leave home, not after. That is, not only do women *not* suffer from the empty nest syndrome, they adjust better than men to the launching of their children from home. Many women, while they certainly miss the presence of their son or daughter, view this time as an opportunity to pursue individual interests. Whether they worked beforehand or not, some explore new career avenues, return to school, or increase their job or community activities that they now have more time for. Diane Jacobs, the lawyer and single mother, was one of many women who said they looked forward to their children going off to college.

I remember the response of another woman whom we interviewed: "Some days it's just like the top of my head's going to blow off. *I wish that they'd be gone because I'd say it's less satisfying than when they were younger.*"

PORTRAITS OF MIDLIFE

During my interview with Diane Jacobs, she talked a lot about the feelings she'd been having, both in regard to her son David and her position as a lecturer at the university. She said that every year she would remark how much younger the students looked to her, until one year she heard several of them call her "Ma'am" instead of Diane, as she had asked them to do. "It finally clicked," she said, "when I realized "Ma'am" was *me*. That they weren't any younger looking but that it was my vantage point that was changing. *I* was the one who was changing. I'm getting older and older."

It happens in various ways, our realization that we are growing older. One father told me he knew he was getting old when his son commented that their medicine chest looked like Grandpa and Grandma's. "I have every brand of antacid that's made," he laughed.

"And a whole cupboard filled with Ace bandages and first-aid medicine for my Saturday basketball games. It's a terrible thing, what our bodies do to us. I don't feel that old inside, but after I do something strenuous, my body feels like an old lady's."

His feelings were not uncommon. Ask any forty-something man or woman how old he or she feels mentally and you're likely to get an answer that is somewhere in the twenties. It's a common feeling, and difficult to reconcile, that you still feel twenty-four as you're approaching forty-five. It's as though some internal clock stops as the external one keeps going. As the middle-aged protagonist in the popular film *Fried Green Tomatoes* put it so aptly: "I'm too old to be young and too young to be old."

And it's not only our appearance and aches and pains that reveal to us that we're getting older. One woman in our study told me it was the fact that she now flossed her teeth every day, with conviction, that made her realize she was "middle aged." Another said it was her choice of shoes—comfort over fashion—and the foundation she wore on her face, as had her mother, which she swore she'd never wear.

It happens gradually, but it seems that suddenly we start noticing all the different manifestations. From the moment we wake up in the morning and hobble to the bathroom on stiff legs and feet, to the image in the mirror that now greets us. Squinting, we notice hair growing in places we remember seeing it only on old men and consider buying a little electric implement to help remove it. Age spots and broken blood vessels that are barely concealed, even with expensive concealers. Teeth that show the years of coffee, tea, or tobacco use. There are endless signs—including perhaps the cruel fact that you can't read this typeface without your reading glasses.

And these are only some of the physical signs. You've probably shocked yourself (and sounded like one of your parents) by asking incredulously where the twenty-five years have gone since you graduated from college. Or exclaimed that it couldn't be possible for your young coworker to have been born in the seventies and not still be in diapers.

Chances are, too, that your son or daughter has outwitted you, outargued you, and outrun you; that if you haven't buried a parent yet, you've had to take care of one; and that you now think of your life as being more than half over.

Coping with these little but constant irritants isn't easy; but imagine coping with them as your son or daughter is blossoming physically and mentally, heading out the door like a fresh breeze, leaving you behind in what seems like deadened, stale air.

THE ADOLESCENT FACTOR

As we looked at case study after case study of the families we interviewed as part of the larger research program, we saw one pattern emerge time and again. And that was the fact that when the firstborn child approaches adolescence, the whole family is affected. The changes and fluctuations in the relationship between the teen and his or her parents throw the household into disequilibrium, and the aftershocks are far reaching.

As parents realize that they no longer have complete control over a child—a child, incidentally, who is no longer a child but an independent being in matters of opinion, conduct, and thought—they may have feelings of powerlessness and insecurity. Not only can you not physically control your child, for he or she may be as tall if not taller than you, but you can no longer be assured that when you tell your child what to do, he or she will comply.

As it turned out, Diane Jacobs' son, David, did not go down to the mall that day to get his ear pierced, much to his parents' relief. But several months after that incident he began defying his parents' curfew, staying out later and later at night. Ben and Diane threatened and tried to enforce punishments, but these, too, were unenforceable. Diane became even more exhausted from the daily battles and finally gave in, allowing David to come and go as he pleased.

As many of us were not prepared for parenting an infant, so we are not prepared for the changes during adolescence. One mother told me that when she first noticed her son's pubic hair, when she entered his bedroom, unaware that he was undressed, "I was so completely caught off guard, that it literally made me feel sick to my stomach." Another said she would never forget the first time she realized that, as she and her fifteen-year-old daughter were walking down the street together, men were admiring her daughter, not her. One father still remembered the moment he realized that his son looked down at him from a higher vantage point. Many of the milestones of adolescence hit parents with such force as to be almost debilitating.

One of the things that most midlife adults have in common is that the vast majority of them are living with teenage children. After months and months of interviewing and analyzing, we saw that the major underlying factor that upset the psychological equilibrium in the lives of the Jacobses, the Merricks, and many others, was not work or worries about physical decline, but the intersecting journeys of the adolescent and the middle-aged parent: It was difficult enough to face middle age and all its attendant side effects. But to face them alongside Adonis or Venus was absolutely excruciating.

4. THE TEENAGER AS TRIGGER

Although the average age at which people get married has risen somewhat during the past few decades, the majority of adults still tie the knot—at least for the first time—sometime during their mid- or late twenties. This was certainly the case among the parents in our study, most of whom exchanged wedding vows sometime during the early 1970s. At the start of that decade, the typical woman married at twenty and the typical man at twenty-three. By the end of the decade, these figures had risen only slightly, to twenty-two for women and twenty-five for men.

BOB AND LAURA PETERSON

Like the vast majority of the couples I interviewed, Bob and Laura Peterson followed the statistically "normal" timetable for members of their generation, the first wave of postwar baby-boomers. Bob, who had been born in 1947, and Laura, who was born in 1949, first met during the late 1960s, while undergraduates at the state university. Although the campus was awash in student unrest during their time there, neither Bob nor Laura was politically active. Far from it. Their social lives revolved around beer kegs and football games, rather than rolling papers and antiwar demonstrations. In fact, it was their mutual antipathy toward the drug use and political activism of many of their classmates that initially drew them together. In each other, Bob and Laura saw a potential for the sort of familial normalcy and security so many of their generation had come to expect from the television sitcoms they had watched as teenagers.

When I visited the Petersons' home in 1987, I saw their wedding picture on top of the piano in their formally furnished living room. Bob, a tall, thin young man, was grinning broadly, and Laura, dark haired, wide eyed, and pretty, was gazing at him admiringly.

Bob, who worked as an administrator in one of the city's hospitals, had as a young man managed to avoid military service in Vietnam through a combination of student deferments and good fortune. Immediately after graduating from college with a B.S. in biology, he had taken a job with the state health department as a laboratory technician. Although he had at one time dreamed of a career as a physician, Bob's long-range plan at the time he graduated was to earn a master's degree in health services administration and pursue a career in hospital administration. Unfortunately, poor finances had precluded his continuing in school at the time. He had decided to stay in the university town and work for a few years after college in order to pay off his student loans.

He and Laura had continued to date while she finished her education. Although there were periods of strain during that stage of their courtship—Laura was a bit of a social butterfly, and she was reluctant to completely let go of her undergraduate social life just because Bob had finished school and had tired of campus parties—the couple had managed to stay together during Laura's final years of college. During this time, Bob occasionally had pressed for their marriage, but Laura had resisted. She had no intention of leaving school early, for she was determined to finish her degree in early childhood education and to someday open her own preschool.

As Laura's graduation day approached, the couple had begun making plans for the future. Together, they would discuss their fantasies during long walks through the lilac groves at the university arboretum—what their home would look like, how many children they would have, how running a preschool would permit Laura to balance motherhood and a career, how Bob would return to school and complete his training.

During the final months of Laura's schooling, neither she nor Bob could wait to begin married life together. Laura had lost interest in the social events of her group of friends, whom she saw as "immature," and spent more and more time off campus at Bob's apartment. Soon after Laura graduated, they announced their engagement, an announcement that was received with enthusiasm by both of their families. One year later, they married, and within eighteen months, their first child, David, was born. Bob was twenty-seven and Laura had just turned twenty-five. When they joined our project, their son David had just turned thirteen.

Most of the couples we studied had followed a similar timetable. The majority were born during the decade immediately following the end of the Second World War. The average wife in our study had married at twenty-three, and the average husband at twenty-five, a bit older than the national average at the time, most likely because of our sample's somewhat higher-than-average level of education. (Staying in school longer tends to make people postpone marriage a bit.) Typically, they began having children within two years of marriage.

THE TIMETABLE OF ADULT LIFE

We all like to think of ourselves as individuals, charting unique paths through life, defying convention and traveling at our own chosen speed. But the fact of the matter is that most of us follow a fairly standard timetable. The timetable is as much determined by social expectations as it is by anything else, and most of us, consciously or unconsciously, give in to these pressures. Deviations from this schedule exist, of course, but in actuality, as advertisers and market researchers can attest, they are not very frequent. Psychologists even tell us that individuals whose lives follow an "on-time" schedule experience less stress over the course of the life cycle than do those who are "off-time."

The predictability with which most couples court, marry, and begin childbearing is especially convenient for social scientists, for it allows us to chart adults' development alongside the growth of their children with a good degree of accuracy. This so-called family life cycle—the series of stages in the development of the family unit over time—unfolds for most people along a well-worn timetable, and the various points of intersection between adult and child development are as familiar as are the television commercials that play on such regularities. Most husbands and wives are changing diapers during their late twenties, crooning *Sesame Street* songs as they enter their thirties, and struggling anew with multiplication tables and long division sometime around thirty-five.

And like the Petersons, most husbands and wives reach midlife around the time their firstborn child enters adolescence.

There are individuals who depart from this developmental stereotype, to be sure—those who marry very early or very late, those who delay childbearing until their late thirties, those who never marry or who choose not to have children. We all can name friends whose lives have deviated from the "normal" timetable. Although these people may stand out in our minds, it is important to remember that they are the exceptions, not the rule. Indeed, it is precisely because they *are* exceptions—the graying Little League coach or the middle-aged couple in Lamaze class—that we notice them. The next time you visit a fast-food restaurant or a shopping mall, conduct an informal survey with your eyes: Most of the parents of young children are not middle aged, but are young adults.

For most of us, then, the customary timing of marriage and childbearing impels us toward an inevitable collision between our midlife years and our children's adolescence. This collision between what we are going through as middle-aged adults and what our children are going through as teenagers is, as we shall see, often a tremendous source of psychological turmoil for the midlife adult. In order to better understand why this is so—why the teenager is a trigger of psychological unrest for the midlife parent—we need to look closely at what is happening in the family at the time the child begins the passage into adolescence.

THE TEENAGER AS TRIGGER

The notion that having a child going through adolescence might be a source of psychological difficulty for adults hardly comes as a surprise to most parents. After all, it is a part of our cultural stereotype of adolescence that the period is one of storm and upheaval, of identity crises, of introspective despair; that perfectly lovable youngsters turn spiteful, moody, and rebellious; that parents and teenagers do little other than wage war each and every day. Could this state of affairs do anything other than wreak havoc on the mental health of mothers and fathers? I remember well the words on a refrigerator magnet that a colleague of mine, an expert on adolescence with teenagers of her own, prominently displayed in her kitchen: INSANITY IS HEREDITARY: PARENTS GET IT FROM THEIR TEENAGERS.

Yet, this story is not entirely true. Several decades of research on adolescent development—including our own—has shown us that the storm and stress of adolescence is not nearly as bad as it has been cracked up to be. Adolescents' hormones do not rage, and adolescents are not much moodier than adults. Few adolescents have an identity crisis of any magnitude, and among those who do, it typically occurs during college, when they are likely to be no longer living at home. Most adolescents are not deliberately oppositional, and only a small minority are openly hostile toward their parents. Parents and teenagers squabble and bicker, but not substantially more often than husbands and wives.

Frankly, the image of adolescence that emerged during this project, as well as in the other studies I have conducted over the years, does not jibe with that fashioned by the popular press and mass media. We find few Holden Caulfields or Frankie Addamses (the protagonists in *The Catcher in the Rye* and *The Member of the Wedding*, respectively) in the random samples we study. We don't even find many Kevin Arnolds (the young teenager from *The Wonder Years*). Indeed, rather than being wrapped up in a state of existential angst, most of the adolescents in our research coast through life in a sort of pleasant fog, far more concerned with whether they have a date on Friday night or a social studies test the following Wednesday than with who they "really" are or where they are headed. And contrary to the popular image of parents and teenagers at perpetual loggerheads, the families whom we have studied rarely were embroiled in full-fledged conflict. Many, though, seemed caught on a treadmill of constant bickering and squabbling about the most mundane of issues.

DAVID PETERSON

David Peterson, Bob and Laura's thirteen-year-old son, was fairly typical of the teenagers in the Families with Adolescents project. I met with David in his family's kitchen, a pleasant room decorated with comfortable country furniture. As we talked across the table from one another, he absentmindedly rearranged the objects on the round oak table—a sugar bowl, salt and pepper shakers, and a small notepad and pencil. Slight for his age, redheaded, and on the shy side, David was a difficult interview, although not unlike many of the other seventh-grade boys with whom I've spoken over the years. Perhaps because of the braces on his teeth, David often self-consciously covered his mouth while he spoke, and I would occasionally have to ask him to repeat his answers.

I knew from David's school transcript that he was a good student, and my interview with him confirmed my expectation that he was an intelligent boy. What struck me most about David, however, was how much his world revolved around his activities with his friends and how little he thought about his parents. Some of his answers to queries about his parents were not unlike those expected from a child half his age. When asked to tell me about his mother, for example, he responded that she was "nice." When I asked for some elaboration, he could say little more—"she does nice things for me." It was as if he had never really thought much about her, one way or the other. When I asked about his father, he replied that he was "usually nice but sometimes stressed out from work." Probing uncovered little more here, either. Could it be possible that such an intelligent student would have so little of interest to say about his mother and father? After completing a number of similar interviews with other adolescents, it occurred to me that most parents would be surprised to learn how infrequently their children think about them, and how simple their images are. To many of the teenagers in our study, parents (whether your own or someone else's) were not much more than innkeepers; they were "nice" when they let you have your way and "not nice" when they did not. It rarely was more complicated than that.

It was not simply that David was inarticulate. He certainly was not at a loss for words when describing his day-to-day activities. His days were dominated by school, homework, playing basketball with his friends, watching television, and practicing the electric guitar. According to him, he and his parents seldom argued. All in all, David Peterson seemed to me to be rather unremarkable—a typical suburban teenager. As an expert on parent-adolescent relations, I saw very little in this boy's behavior that should, on the face of it, provoke any sort of psychological turmoil in his parents.

My interviews with David's parents did not reveal anything out of the ordinary, either. "David's a pretty typical kid," his father, Bob, said when asked to describe him. "Goes his own way. Spends a lot of time with his friends. Plays his guitar. I guess I'd like to see a little more initiative from him as far as school goes, but we really have nothing to complain about—his grades are good. Oh, there is the usual stuff, I guess. Dirty laundry all over his room. Talks back to his mother sometimes. But other than that, I've got no major complaints. I'm sure I've seen worse in other families."

I asked if Bob had any regrets about the way in which he and Laura had raised David. He thought for a while, and said, "Sometimes . . . not all the time . . . sometimes he seems to take us for granted—like we're just here to cook his meals and put fancy basketball shoes on his feet. That gets to me. It's expensive raising kids, and I wish he'd see that. He and his friends could go through a loaf of bread and a gallon of ice cream in a couple of minutes. It never seems as if there's any food in the house. I suppose we could have drummed that in a bit more—how he should be grateful, how we have sacrificed a lot for him. If I let myself dwell on it, I feel used, I guess—but I suppose that's what parents are for, right? You know, the give and take of parenting—we give and they take. Somehow, though, it [the sacrifice] felt better when he was younger, when he looked up to me. Now we barely see each other. He's off with his friends and we're left here, minding the fort." Bob looked genuinely bothered as he spoke.

I don't think I would have paid much attention to Bob's last few remarks had I not heard those sentiments expressed so often by the other parents we interviewed. More than a few felt exploited and taken for granted by their teenagers. Many longed for the days when their youngsters were children. Many were jealous of their children's carefree and easy life. Some missed having their children's companionship. Almost all missed having their adulation.

THE STORM AND STRESS OF ADOLESCENCE

As I thought more about Bob Peterson's interview, it struck me that the psychological discomfort that many of the parents were feeling was not the result of nattering and squabbling with their teenagers over dirty dishes and broken curfews. These arguments were irritants, to be sure, but had little lasting impact. No, the unrest had something to do with watching a child become an adult and the thoughts and feelings this triggered about oneself.

The analyses we conducted of our questionnaire data confirmed this suspicion. Regardless of the quality of the parent-child relationship (that is, whether it was high or low in conflict), parents' mental health worsened as their firstborn child moved from childhood into adolescence. During this transition, parents' self-esteem declined significantly, and this spilled over into different life domains, adversely affecting parents' feelings about their marriage, their work, their child, and themselves. The drop was especially precipitous among parents whose firstborn child was the same sex—mothers of daughters and fathers of sons—but mothers of sons and fathers of daughters were not immune.

More interestingly, though, we found that we could *not* predict this turn for the worse in mental health simply by knowing the parent's chronological age. That is, the drop in self-esteem was not tied to turning forty (or to any other specific age, for that matter), or simply to navigating the waters of midlife. If that were true, we would expect to have discerned similar patterns of change in mental health across all of the adults in our sample who shared the same chronological age. But we did not. Rather, we found that *we were much better able to predict what an adult was going through psychologically by looking at his or her child's development than by knowing the adult's age*. Given two forty-year-old mothers, then, the one whose child was further into adolescence was more likely to show symptoms of psychological unrest. Likewise, two fathers of thirteen-year-old children—one thirty-eight and the other forty-two—shared more in common psychologically than did two forty-one-year-olds with firstborn children of different ages.

In some regards, then, the constant references in the popular media to the frustrated, nagging parent and the stubborn, defiant teenager were red herrings. Not only were they not very accurate, they were hiding what was beneath the surface of the relationship and what was, ultimately, far more important. The turmoil the parents were experiencing was deeper and more profound than the annoyance that derived from daily hassles. And it was present in parents whose families did not fight and bicker, families that on the surface seemed to be functioning just fine.

It occurred to me that the turmoil was rooted not in the day-to-day stresses of childrearing, but in parents' conscious and unconscious reactions to adolescence itself. The normal, rather unremarkable passage of the child into adolescence was reverberating throughout parents' own psyches in ways that hit up against their own midlife issues.

RESPONDING TO PUBERTY

Few aspects of the adolescent passage are as noticeable or as striking to parents as are the changes in the child's physical appearance that come with puberty. Changes in the child's emotions, personality, or behavior can be dismissed as temporary stages or passing phases, but the transformation of your little boy into a man, or your little girl into a woman, provides incontrovertible evidence that your baby is really growing up. In a funny way, the very certainty of puberty is what makes it especially difficult for parents to accept. For many parents, the unshakable facts of growth spurts and facial hair, breast buds and menstrual periods, signal not only that a new phase in their child's life is beginning, but that an old phase in their own life is ending. There is no going back. This is not a phase that my child is just passing through, this is it: My child is becoming a grown-up, and I am becoming old.

A friend of mine remarked that she felt depressed and upset the moment she discovered her son's underarm hair. The way she described the feeling, though, was especially telling: "It was as if someone had died." I thought to myself that what she was referring to was not simply that her son's childhood had died (the obvious interpretation), but that a piece of her—a piece of her identity, not only as a mother, but as a *young* mother—had died along with it.

One of the ironies in all of this is that adults often believe that going through puberty is stressful for teenagers when, in fact, studies of young people find that for the vast majority, the biological changes of adolescence are not the least bit stressful—not for the adolescent, at least. If puberty is stressful, it may be far more so for the parent than for the child who is actually undergoing it. In this and in many other regards, parents probably project their own discomfort about adolescence onto their children, imagining storm and stress or difficulty in their youngsters as a way of avoiding facing the unrest they themselves feel about growing old.

The physical transformation of the child into an adult is jarring to parents for a number of reasons. At its most basic level, our child's changing appearance is a constant and perhaps annoying reminder that we are growing older—and it marks time in a way that is both indisputable and irreversible. Midlife is a time when we tell ourselves that we aren't really getting older but "getting better," that we are "only as old as we feel," that chronological age doesn't really matter very much (after all, the difference between being thirty-nine and forty-three is hardly of great practical consequence), that taking good physical care of ourselves (through exercise, diet, cosmetics, and so on) can successfully mask many of the outward signs of aging. Not all middle-aged adults have difficulty accepting being middle aged, of course, but for the millions who do and try to disguise it, walking in public with a postpubertal adolescent child is a sure sign that one has reached middle adulthood.

For some, the adolescent's sheer change in size is anxiety provoking, because it raises concerns not so much about aging, but about the parent's loss of status. Sandy Shepard was a single mother of two boys, the elder of whom, Tyler, fifteen, caused her to express a curious fear that I heard frequently from the single mothers in our sample:

"I don't feel I can discipline Tyler anymore. He is so big that I can't really control him. I mean, I can say 'Be home by 11,' but if he says

'No' and walks out the door, what can I do? He is so much bigger and stronger than me. I have to crane my neck to look up to him."

Sandy's anxiety was, of course, symbolic of something else. After all, most parents do not enforce curfews by physically restraining their teenagers, and, in any event, Sandy was not a parent who had relied in the past on physical punishment as a disciplinary tactic. In this regard, the fact that Tyler towered over Sandy was irrelevant to the issue of whether he complied with her curfew. What Tyler's height did signify, though, was that he was now big and strong, and, by default, his mother was small and weak, and the sensation this evoked made Sandy feel old, powerless, and less important.

I believe that we have underestimated the positive feelings parents derive merely from being able to physically control their children when they are younger. I do not mean this in a negative sense. The physical power they hold over their children reaffirms parents' sense of control and importance, and permits them to feel strong and powerful at home even as they may feel weak and small at work or in their marriage. The comfort that comes from this sense of dominance is lost when one's child grows taller or stronger than oneself, though, and this is an unsettling and unpleasant feeling.

The sensation of being smaller than one's child can be particularly problematic for men with adolescent sons, because physical dominance is such an important component of males' sense of power over one another, especially in our culture. Most fathers find they are left feeling ambivalent about their sons' spurt in height and strength at puberty. On the one hand, this growth symbolizes a challenge to their own sense of dominance in the household; on the other, most fathers identify closely enough with their sons to look upon their child's physical growth with pride, especially if the physical strength or size is translated into athletic accomplishment. In the healthiest of families, the end result is often a sort of friendly competition between father and son. In many homes, though, there is an ongoing tension between *social comparison* (where the parent contrasts himself with the child) and *identification* (where the parent lives through the child vicariously) that is never resolved successfully. And in families in which the father is more vulnerable, the competition can get out of hand.

This was precisely what happened to Jeff Rosenstein and his son,

Peter. Jeff had been an avid runner during most of Peter's childhood and was understandably pleased when his son expressed an interest in taking up jogging shortly after his twelfth birthday. Although Jeff could easily outpace Peter, it was clear that Peter was a natural runner who had inherited some of his father's athletic ability. After a few months of training, they were well-matched running partners, although Jeff could run farther and faster than his son if he chose to.

As Peter grew stronger, his stamina increased, and by the time he had turned thirteen he was able to maintain his father's briskest pace without difficulty. At the end of a hard run, Jeff was winded, as he normally would be, but Peter seemed little affected by the workout. After their run one Saturday morning, as they sat on the bleachers overlooking the high school track—Jeff panting and Peter breathing effortlessly—Jeff felt envious of his son's fitness. Jeff was in great shape for a forty-two-year-old—after all, he had been running regularly for the past eight years—but he was no match for Peter. Even more upsetting was Jeff's realization that while Peter was only going to get faster and stronger, his own body was not going to improve. The best he could hope for was to maintain his current condition.

Jeff's reaction to this realization was irrational. Rather than accepting his son's nascent athletic superiority with pride, he began to criticize Peter's running with a vengeance. Soon, instead of being Peter's running partner, Jeff became his self-appointed personal trainer, planning Peter's running schedule down to the smallest detail, charting the results of each and every one of Peter's runs, and riding his son about his diet.

After a few months of this regimen, Peter understandably began to lose interest in running. What had started as a way of sharing something fun with his father had been turned into work—and grueling work, at that. Peter began to find excuses for not running, and he and Jeff started arguing about the very activity that they had so enjoyed together. Finally, Peter stopped running altogether, leaving Jeff to work out by himself. In the end, Jeff had achieved what he had unconsciously desired: to maintain his status as the fastest and strongest runner in the Rosenstein household.

THE ADOLESCENT AS SEX OBJECT

Although seeing one's child grow older and larger may trigger all sorts of complicated feelings in parents, the impact of this pales in comparison to that evoked by seeing one's child mature sexually. This, we found, was one of the most distressing aspects of the adolescent passage for parents. For many, it unleashed a torrent of emotions and conflicts about their own physical attractiveness, their own sexuality, their sexual experiences as teenagers, and their marriage. More likely than not, the effects were negative, making parents feel unattractive, envious of their child's potential, longing for their own "lost" youth, and, if married, dissatisfied with their spouses.

The effect of the advent of the adolescent's sexuality on parents' mental health was more pronounced in families with adolescent girls than boys, probably for several reasons. Perhaps most importantly, the sexual aspects of puberty are more vivid in girls than in boys and are therefore harder to deny by parents of daughters than parents of sons. It is easy to forget that Johnny has sprouted pubic hair. It is impossible to overlook the fact that Sally is now wearing a bra.

Adults also tend to feel more conflicted about sexuality in adolescent females than in adolescent males because of the threat of pregnancy and the longstanding (if antiquated) view that "good" girls are not sexually active but that "good" boys can be. As a consequence of this double standard, parents may be more likely to look the other way when their sons mature than when their daughters do, which permits them to avoid dealing with some of their own conflicts in the process. To corrupt the adage, out of sight, out of consciousness.

Finally, girls mature physically on average about two years earlier than boys, and many parents are simply caught off guard by their daughter's sexual maturation. Because they have had less time to prepare for it, parents are less able to marshal the necessary psychological defenses. Not surprisingly, the decline in parental mental health triggered by their child's puberty is steepest in homes of early-maturing girls—those who have their first period before age twelve—presumably because these parents are the most surprised of all.

Mothers are bothered more by their daughters' sexual development than are fathers (in virtually all respects, parents are more affected by the development of same-sex children). As girls move through the phases of physical development, their mothers' self-esteem suffers, and their feelings of self-doubt and introspective self-awareness rise. These mothers are then more likely to long for the past, question the decisions they have made about their lives, and worry about their worthiness and physical appeal. It is as if watching a daughter come into womanhood prompts a sort of midlife crisis for many mothers. This crisis is at its most intense just as the daughter hits what is known as the *pubertal apex*—the point at which her body is changing most rapidly and dramatically.

Some parents feel so distressed by their child's sexual maturation that they try to deny it entirely. I remember once counseling a mother and fourteen-year-old daughter who were battling constantly over the daughter's weight. According to the mother, who first described their problem to me over the phone, her daughter was becoming obese, but nothing the mother would say or do seemed to motivate the daughter to lose weight. After first meeting with the two of them, I understood the daughter's reluctance entirely. She was not the least bit overweight. But she had recently completed puberty, and her breasts and hips had grown to the point where she was now more developed than her mother.

In family therapy, it became apparent that the mother was taking out her own insecurity about growing old and losing her physical appeal on her daughter. Recently divorced, the mother was single and attempting to date, and she was unhappy with her social life. Unfortunately, the more voluptuous her daughter appeared, the less attractive the mother felt. Unconsciously, she wished her daughter to return to a sexually immature state so that her own anxiety about aging would be alleviated.

Few parents go to the extreme of trying to "undo" their child's sexual development, of course. But it is not difficult to understand why the adolescent's budding sexuality could have this sort of impact on the parent, especially given the psychological vulnerability of the midlife adult to assaults (real or imagined) on her physical self-image. At a time when she may be doubting her own vivacity and sexual attractiveness, a mother's knowledge that her daughter is about to enter a phase of physical development glorified and idealized in soft-drink commercials and fashion magazines is hardly comforting. (Imagine that the proverbial "younger woman" is now sitting at your kitchen table and you'll see what I mean.) It is not so much how her daughter looks *at that moment* that is disturbing—some of us might wish to look twenty again, but few of us would choose to look thirteen—but, rather, what she has the *potential* to become.

Having said this, it is important to remember that few parents think about this issue consciously, for it is simply too dangerous to think very explicitly about one's child in sexual terms. Many, but not all, parents can talk openly and honestly about being envious of their children's freedom, or scholastic opportunities, or material possessions. Few can admit to being jealous of their bodies (this jealousy is expressed, I think, in code words, such as envy of their "youthfulness" or "energy"). In the domain of sexuality, however, most of the comparison occurs at an unconscious level, leaving parents feeling slightly out of kilter, dissatisfied, and eager for change, but without really knowing why. In our study the most psychologically distressed parents were those whose children were in the throes of puberty, regardless of their, or their parents', ages.

Among midlife men, issues of sexual comparison and identification with their adolescent sons are played out differently than women's with their daughters. Society is kinder toward men than women as far as aging goes, and men's self-esteem at midlife is less dependent on how they look than on what they've accomplished. Not surprisingly, men are more likely to feel jealous of their sons for what they might be *doing* with their bodies—what they might "accomplish" sexually—than for what they might look like. As you will read later, this is an issue that comes to the forefront when adolescent children begin dating.

EMANCIPATION AND WORRY

The adolescent's physical and sexual development provide one set of triggers for the psychological turmoil of midlife. A different set of catalysts revolves around the growing independence of the child and the fear and jealousy that this evokes in many parents.

The central psychological tasks of early adolescence revolve around becoming an independent person, or in psychological jargon, establishing a sense of *autonomy*. By the time they have turned twelve or thirteen, most teenagers want to control their own day-to-day lives, including deciding how they spend their time, how they accomplish the various responsibilities they have, whom they hang around with, and when they come and go. Most parents accept this, at least intellectually, as an inevitable part of their child's development. They recognize that their child's movement toward independence is necessary and, in the long run, desirable. After all, our children's success as adults rests on their ability to manage their own behavior without someone looking over their shoulder.

Accepting the adolescent's need for independence on an intellectual level is one thing; coping with it emotionally is quite another, however. As the adolescent becomes less dependent upon the parent and assumes greater control over his or her own activities, the parent is no longer in the role of one who governs the child's activities. The majority of parents are nervous and ambivalent about permitting the freedom that the teenager wants. Most have invested a great deal in their child, and they have a lot of hopes and dreams tied up in his or her future. Further, parents derive a great deal from keeping their child dependent—a sense of control, the security of knowing their child is safe, the child's adulation, companionship, and so on.

The paradox, then, is that the very thing that parents are supposed to be helping their child toward—growing up and becoming independent—is precisely what they deep down don't really want to happen. With each movement the adolescent makes toward more behavioral independence—acting older, more in control, and more grown-up—the parent gives up some piece of his or her authority and may feel powerless, nervous, and out of control.

These feelings exacerbate many of the concerns that are already nagging at the midlife adult but which may not be entirely conscious. Two different reactions were common among the mothers and fathers I interviewed—one characteristic of parents who felt anxious and out of sorts with their life, the other characteristic of those who felt trapped and imprisoned by their work, marriage, or lifestyle.

For parents whose midlife anxieties had gotten "out of control," the "uncontrollable" adolescent only amplified their own sense of internal chaos. They attempted to dominate the adolescent as a means of exerting some structure over a life they were feeling was either in, or heading toward, disarray. In essence, these parents were resorting to their power and security as a parent to reaffirm their sense of authority and personal control. Scuffles with his or her adolescent over issues of autonomy created diversions by which the parent's anxieties about unanswered questions about his or her own life could be avoided.

In many of these households, I saw battles between parents and adolescents over the most mundane and trivial of issues. For instance, Gray Miller, a stepfather in our study whom you'll meet in a later chapter, forbade his teenagers to lie down on the family room couch while watching television. The issue was not whether they could use the couch or watch television (both were permitted), but whether they were to sit or lie down. When pressed by the children for some rationale behind this rule, the stepfather could give none, only that, "Couches are for sitting." My interview with him revealed a bitter, angry man who was disappointed with his children from his first marriage, unhappy in his work, and anxious about his relationship with his present wife. He needed to exert some control over some aspect of his life, even if it was as minor an issue as the use of the family room couch. Doing so made him feel less anxious—despite whatever conflict his arbitrariness caused in the family.

At the other end of the continuum were parents who reacted to their adolescent's autonomy not with anxiety, but with jealousy. They were bothered by the carefree independence of adolescence, and seeing their child's freedom made them long for something similar. It was not so much the adolescent's actual activities these parents envied, but the sense of not being tied down, of having seemingly limitless possibilities, of the freedom to come and go as one pleased. In comparison to their child's life, theirs seemed stale and routine, and the security and predictability that once were comforting suddenly felt old and suffocating.

Parents react in different ways to this sort of comparison. Some become depressed and attempt to ward off these feelings by living vicariously through their adolescent's life. They appear overly interested—and overly invested—in their child's activities and live as if they have two concurrent existences: their real life, which they pursue as if going through the motions, and the fantasy life they are living through their adolescent. Unfortunately, the more they convince themselves that the adolescent's freedom is enviable, the more depressed they become about their own life situation.

TEENAGE DATING

One of the most fascinating confirmations of this envy-depression connection appeared when I examined the impact on parents' mental health of having a dating adolescent. Among mothers, having a child date dramatically increased their feelings of self-doubt, their regret over past decisions, and their desire to change their lives. Among fathers, the effect of having a child date was especially devastating if the child was a son. Fathers of sons who were dating reported an intriguing combination of more anxiety and depression but higher self-esteem, especially if their sons began dating early. It was as if a son's dating triggered both feelings of envy (which led to the anxiety and depression) and vicarious pleasure over how much fun the son was having (which contributed to the high self-esteem)—again, that tension between social comparison and identification. Interestingly, regardless of whether their child was a son or a daughter, fathers whose children were dating reported much lower marital satisfaction than did those whose children did not have active social lives.

Seeing a child date is an especially salient trigger for midlife parents, calling forth as it does a mixture of anxiety (over the adolescent's sexuality), envy (over the adolescent's freedom), regret (over the romantic choices one didn't pursue), and longing (for one's youth).

Not long ago, I was a guest on a talk show whose topic ostensibly was "early dating." I was the "expert" on a panel that included three mothers and their young adolescent children. As the show unfolded, it became clear that what the children had been doing was completely innocent—harmless stuff like going skating with other boys and girls, going to the movies in groups, going to school-sponsored supervised dances, and so forth. Many of the parents in the audience, though—eagerly spurred on by the show's host—reacted as if these youngsters were flirting with danger, on the verge of sexual activity. It was clear to me that these parents were projecting their own fantasies onto the children's behavior, turning what the children were doing into something "dangerous" to justify their own anxiety. One mother, perhaps a bit more self-aware than the others, even said, "Watching my baby date . . . it really takes me back to when I was her age."

THE JEALOUS PARENT

While some parents become anxious and depressed over their child's independence, other parents externalize their frustration and take out their jealousy on the adolescent. These parents may try to restrict the adolescent from engaging in the very behaviors of which they are envious. This often provokes bitter conflict between the adolescent and the jealous parent, since the teenager experiences the parent's restriction as arbitrary and capricious. In many cases, the other parent in the household feels caught in the middle, wanting to support his or her spouse in order to present a united front to the child, but dubious about the rationale behind the restriction.

Laura Peterson found herself in just such a bind. During our interview, she spoke at length about an ongoing conflict between her husband, Bob, and their son, David.

"David and I rarely argue," she explained. "It's just not in my temperament to fight. But he and Bob will sometimes go at it over David's guitar playing. Bob has this thing about David's homework—that it has to be done, every last page, before David can do anything else. So when he walks through the front door at the end of the day, he immediately starts in on David about how much homework he has that day, whether he's finished it, why isn't it done yet, when can he check it over. When David gets home from school, though, homework is the last thing on his mind. He'd rather go out with his friends or practice his music, or just daydream—or whatever it is he does in his room. I don't ask. The thing is, the homework eventually gets done—just on David's schedule, not his father's. David will stay up until all hours if he has to, just to finish it, but it gets done.

"Anyway, some days, especially when Bob has had a bad day at the hospital, they have it out. David tells Bob to leave him alone and Bob starts in on one of his lectures. David will stand there with this angry look on his face and then storm into his room and slam the door.

When we sit down to eat, Bob tries to pretend that nothing has happened, but David stays bothered.

"Honestly, I think Bob is making something out of nothing. But he thinks that David's guitar is a waste of time and that David could be applying himself more in school. His grades are fine, but Bob wants them to be perfect. I don't want to undermine him, but I sympathize with David. I don't know—it's weird—it's like Bob is bothered by the fact that David is having fun. I don't know, it just seems to me that that's what teenagers are supposed to do—have fun."

When I asked Bob during our interview whether he and David argued much, he talked about the same conflict, although he described it somewhat differently.

"It's not that I mind the guitar playing. It's just that he has to have a sense of priorities. Work comes first, fun comes second. Hell, I wish it was different, wish that I didn't have to carry home a briefcase full of paperwork every night, that I could just relax, fool around with my stereo, but I can't. I'm just trying to show him what real life is like. He's going to have to learn sooner or later. He might as well learn it now."

The more Bob and I spoke, the more I began to understand what Bob was feeling. *He* wasn't having very much fun. His work was time-consuming but not especially satisfying, and he resented his "home-work"—his "briefcase full of paperwork." Coupled with feeling financially strained and taken for granted by David, he had begun to transfer his dissatisfaction about his life—his dissatisfaction about not having enough "fun"—into resentment about David's leisure time. It was not at all surprising that David's homework had become the focus of Bob's irritation.

LETTING GO

The drive toward behavioral independence is one of two ways that adolescents express their need for autonomy. A second manifestation of this is emotional, and it is reflected in youngsters' pulling away from their parents somewhat. The typical young teenager wants and demands more privacy, spends more time talking with her friends than with her parents, and may even go through a phase of not wanting to be seen in public with her family, especially if there is any possibility of running into her friends.

Psychologists understand this distancing. Part of growing up is forming close emotional relationships outside the family—with age-mates—and teenagers need to withdraw some emotional energy from their relationships with their parents in order to do this. Psychologists call this *detachment*.

From the child's vantage point, breaking away feels exciting, grown-up, mature. I can remember when my own son Ben, only eight at the time, turned to me and said, out of the blue, "You know, Dad, now that I'm older (!), I like being with my friends sometimes more than you and Mom." I knew exactly how he felt.

But if the process of breaking away feels exciting to the adolescent, it leaves many parents feeling lonely and rejected. They may understand intellectually why their child is pulling away, but they experience this as an emotional loss, nevertheless. To many, it feels like going through an unsought-after divorce.

I have spoken with many parents who felt hurt and abandoned by their young teenager's emotional independence. What makes this pain especially difficult to bear is that we seldom feel free to express it. Part of the cultural stereotype is that parents and adolescents are supposed to be at war, and parents are expected to complain to one another about their battle wounds. As is the case with other losses, however, when the loss of closeness with one's child goes unexpressed and unacknowledged, it often leads to depression.

In our study, adverse reactions to the adolescent's emotional distancing were especially common among mothers with daughters. Most research on families during adolescence has shown that the mother-daughter bond is the closest of any parent-adolescent relationship, so it is not surprising that a weakening of the emotional connection in this relationship will be more painful than in others. Fathers experience this loss too, although they are more likely to describe it in terms of lost companionship ("He used to want to go fishing with me, but now he seems to prefer his friends' company") than lost intimacy.

Whether the adolescent's quest for emotional independence triggers turmoil in the parent depends a great deal on the quality of the other relationships in the parent's emotional world. For parents who are already feeling less than satisfied in their marriage, for example, the child's emotional detachment is especially unsettling, and it may leave the parent feeling lonely and empty, anxious and depressed— but not understanding why. For single parents, especially those who have become very close friends with their child during the postdivorce years, the emotional loss can be devastating.

On the positive side, however, are happily married parents who are able to redirect into their marriage some of the emotional energy previously bound up in their relationship with their child. Some couples find that the gradual emotional distancing of the adolescent has a rejuvenating effect on their marital relationship, as they discover that they have more time and energy for each other. In some senses, this is the reverse of what happens to some couples after the birth of a baby, when the investment of energy of one parent (typically the mother) in the infant leaves the other parent feeling neglected and untended. A strong marriage that has successfully weathered the emotional drain of parenthood can provide a comforting retreat when childrearing no longer requires as much psychological energy.

UNDERNEATH THE PEDESTAL

Adolescence triggers turmoil in parents for many reasons, but of all the catalysts I observed during the course of our research, none surprised me as much as the effect of losing a child's uncritical adulation. Sometime during preadolescence, most children remove their parents from a pedestal and attempt to place them underneath it.

It does little good to explain to parents that all adolescents need to "deidealize" their parents as a means of growing up and developing their own sense of identity. Psychologists call this process *individuation*: the process of becoming an individual. But simply because all adolescents need to individuate from their parents does not make it any easier for a parent to swallow. Many parents take this deidealization personally, and they feel unfairly criticized, old-fashioned, and rejected.

Many parents have a hard time brushing off this criticism. In fact, one of the best predictors of parents' mental health in our study was the extent to which their child had deidealized them—had come to see them as fallible, imperfect, at fault. Parents whose children reported seeing them through these critical lenses were depressed and dissatisfied, scoring low on our measure of self-esteem and high on our measure of midlife rumination. For some parents, their child's criticism produced intense feelings of self-doubt.

"I remember one time really well," one mother told me. "We were all about to go to a picnic at Jessica's school. It was some PTA thing, where people were supposed to dress in Western outfits—you know, jeans, boots, cowboy hats, that sort of get-up. I came downstairs dressed to go and Jessie looked at me in disbelief. 'You're not wearing that,' she said. 'Why not?' I asked. 'What's the matter with it?' 'Well, you look so big in those tight jeans.'

"Now, I didn't think of myself as fat. Sure, I know I didn't look the way I did when I was a kid, but who does at my age? But fat? No way. And I got mad at her, because now I was going to go to this picnic and I was going to be self-conscious. I've never worn those jeans since."

Why should a child's criticism prompt such reactions in parents? Do we actually depend that much on our children's evaluation? At this age, at midlife, we may—more, in fact, than we care to admit. There are three reasons for parents' sensitivity to their children's criticism. First, most parents relish the unadulterated admiration they receive from their children during the elementary school years, even though they know that the child's esteem is biased. We like it when our sons and daughters mimic our opinions, pursue our hobbies, and brag about us to their friends. Having grown accustomed to this lofty perch, many parents react to being knocked down to earth with anger and irritation. There is nothing like losing the adoration of someone who was irrationally captivated with us. And it is especially irksome to parents that their once-adoring children withdraw their idolization with such callous nonchalance. Few adolescents realize that their offhanded barbs carry as much power as they do.

Second, middle age brings with it a heightened vulnerability to any experiences that foster self-doubt. During times of intense introspection and self-examination, small criticisms and what otherwise would be unremarkable setbacks loom that much larger and, in our minds, serve to "confirm" our worst fears about our inherent weaknesses. Unfortunately, this sort of orientation easily becomes a vicious cycle—which helps to explain the frequently observed connection between midlife introspection and depressed mood. Excessive self-scrutiny invariably leads to self-doubt, which usually leads to self-deprecation and can lead to depression. This state of mind, in turn, creates a negative filter through which we view our lives, which only fuels further self-criticism and depression. The self-perpetuating nature of this process makes it a difficult cycle to break. As a consequence, critical appraisals from anyone close seem especially harsh, and they wound that much more deeply.

A third reason that deidealization hurts so much has to do with the particular nature of the parent-adolescent relationship. Most of us are well aware of the tendency for children to identify with their parents, but the reverse is also true: Parents tend to form strong identifications with their children, and this inclination is especially strong during adolescence.

At all ages, children provide vehicles onto which parents project their personal hopes and fantasies. In adolescence, however, the proximity of the child to adulthood deepens these feelings markedly, because the parent is now able to see whether these hopes and dreams are going to come to fruition. On top of this, many parents are drawn to their teenager by the strong physical resemblance between themselves and their child that appears after puberty; some describe looking at their teenager as akin to staring into a mirror from their own youth. This is why the impact of deidealization is so much greater when it occurs within a same-sex parent-child pair, since the tendency to identify with one's child is greater in this instance. Fathers seem to be able to handle criticism from a daughter, and mothers from a son, far better than when it comes from a child of the same sex.

I think it is perfectly understandable that we imbue our teenagers' criticisms with so much significance. Research tells us that the actions of those with whom we identify carry far more weight than do those of other individuals. Just as children are especially upset when criticized by the people with whom they have identified—typically, their parents—so are parents especially bothered by criticism from their adolescents. Frankly, for those parents who genuinely see themselves in their child's face—for whom looking at their child is indeed like looking at a youthful mirror image—the adolescent's critical eye feels a bit too much like self-criticism.

For all of these reasons—the child's physical transformation, emerging sexuality, drive toward emancipation, detachment from the parent-child relationship, and deidealization of the parent—a child's adolescence often is a tumultuous time for mothers and fathers.

And, in many respects, it has been our focus on the alleged storm and stress of the teenage years that has made us underestimate the tremendous impact of the adolescent transition on the psychological state of the young person's parents.

PART II

EMOTIONAL RESPONSES

5. JEALOUSY

Richard Johnson, Paula Woznicki, and Matt Johnson

Richard and Matt Johnson were so different from each other that it was difficult to believe that they were really father and son. Matt, sixteen, was the first member of the Johnson household I interviewed, and I came away from our meeting quite impressed. With his broad smile, easy manner, and athletic good looks, he was one of the most popular boys in his high school. It was easy to see why. He was outgoing without being pushy, confident without being cocky, and comfortable with who he was. I liked him immediately, and we spoke for several hours, sitting next to the swimming pool in the Johnsons' back yard.

Actually, it was hard to find an uninterrupted block of time during which Matt and I could meet. His schedule nearly warranted a full-time secretary. Matt's afternoons were jam-packed—if not with sports (he was one of the stars on the school's soccer team and played basketball as well), then with some other school-sponsored extracurricular activity. This month, for example, he was tied up most weekdays rehearsing his role as Sky Masterson—the male lead in the school's production of *Guys and Dolls*. His evenings were equally booked, divided between seeing his girlfriend, Sara, and hanging around with his two best friends, Jeff and Michael. Yet, although his social calendar was overflowing with activity, Matt managed to maintain a respectable grade average in school. He was also a terrific older brother to the Johnsons' nine-year-old son, Michael.

RICHARD JOHNSON

When I returned to the Johnsons' house the following week for my evening appointment with Matt's father, Richard, I was anticipating an interview with a grown-up version of Matt—the all-American dad to complement the all-American son. I had even remembered to bring along an extra blank cassette, just in case the interview ran longer than usual, for I assumed that Richard would be as interesting and talkative as Matt was.

My image of Matt's father could not have been more off the mark. We stood on the front porch making uncomfortable chitchat for several minutes before it occurred to Richard to invite me inside. As we sat in the living room of the Johnsons' modestly furnished split-level home, I couldn't take my eyes off his outfit: a short-sleeved plaid sport shirt that clashed with his plaid Bermudas, knee-high socks, and dress shoes. His paunch strained the buttons on his shirt.

It was hard to get Richard to open up during our interview, for he was as insecure as his son was confident, and as introverted as his son was gregarious. Sadly, though, Richard seemed all too aware of the difference between himself and Matt. One story Richard told was quite poignant.

"One Friday evening—I guess it was about a month ago—Matt and his friend Jeff were in the family room, downstairs, watching a movie. Michael was in his room playing with something. Paula was out at one of her meetings, I think. Yes, that's right, it was a meeting to help plan the neighborhood association's Fourth of July picnic.

"I didn't really have anything special to do, and I was feeling sort of lonely, so I thought I'd join the boys. I went downstairs, stuck my head in the room and asked what film they were watching. '*Revenge of the Nerds*,' Matt answered, without turning around. 'Oh,' I said, half-joking, 'that could have been my biography.' Well, instead of laughing, Matt just turned around and gave me this look, that I was embarrassing him in front of Jeff. So I figured, well, three's company, and I went back upstairs. I could hear them laughing as I left. I don't know whether they were laughing at me or at the movie. I suppose they were laughing at both." Richard looked quite uncomfortable.

"Tell me about Matt," I said.

"Gee," Richard replied. "I don't know where to begin. He's a very happy kid. Very social, very athletic. He's on top of his schoolwork. He has so much going for him, so much more than I did at his age."

I asked what he meant by this last remark.

"I did not have a normal childhood. I wasn't a social kid; I didn't do the kinds of things Matt does. I was very much a bookworm, kind of a klutz, not social at all. So I find it hard to relate to Matt, because he has what I consider to be a very normal, very nice childhood. So it's difficult for me to connect with him. I find it very difficult."

I was taken aback by this last observation. Over the years, I certainly had heard many parents complain of having a difficult time with their teenager, but rarely did they gripe about their child being too *normal*. In a funny way, however, I sensed that the contrast between Matt's easygoing sociability and his father's strained awkwardness had introduced an unusual tension into their relationship. It sounded as if the more Matt had come into his own, the more Richard was reminded of what he himself was lacking.

Things had not always been distant between Matt and Richard. In fact, Richard spoke quite warmly about how close he and his son had been when Matt was younger.

"One thing I miss with him is that we used to collect baseball cards. Boy, we used to go to card shows, to baseball-card shops. It was just a ball. We used to open the packs of cards together, getting excited." Richard looked away for a bit, as if he were trying to visualize a specific time he and Matt had spent together.

"Yeah, getting excited over getting a Ricky Henderson or a Steve Garvey or whoever," he went on, turning back to me. "I collected cards when I was a kid, so I was really reliving my own childhood." He smiled at me self-consciously.

Suddenly, Richard's tone changed from one of happy reminiscence to one that was slightly bitter. He looked irritated. "And then, as I tell some of my friends, they discovered girls and suddenly they weren't as interested in cards anymore."

I wasn't sure what to make of this. Whom was Richard referring to by "they"? Was he talking about Matt and his friends, or was he recalling something that happened when he himself had been a teenager?

"Matt didn't have much interest then," Richard continued. "I chased around to a lot of card shows, and sometimes Matt came along and sometimes he didn't. Now he's interested in girls and he's not as interested in baseball cards. But I still am, and I feel lonely because I don't have anyone to go to shows with. Michael has never shown any interest in collecting. So I go to the baseball shop every once in a while and read baseball magazines and stuff, but I'm not as active as I wish we were, but that's progress."

I asked if he and Matt had found anything to substitute for their common interest in baseball cards.

"Well, I bought a VCR and we do a lot of taping, watching movies and taping movies, but it hasn't replaced the excitement and enthusiasm that we had. Many years ago, when Matt was just a little guy, we used to write away to baseball clubs for autographed pictures of the great players. It was quite exciting, getting the mail. When Matt was much younger, you know, the excitement was there and then it went away."

We sat for a moment without saying anything.

"We don't do much together anymore," Richard sighed. "Basically, it used to be that what I was interested in, he'd follow along, like with the baseball cards. And now it has just reversed. What *he's* interested in, I tend to be interested in. He's certainly an interesting person. He sets the agenda."

Over the next hour or so, as I listened to Richard speak more about Matt's accomplishments—his grades in school, his being named to the all-state high school soccer team, his popularity with his classmates—I got the distinct feeling that Richard was more than a little bit envious of his son. No longer the "agenda-setter," Richard was feeling lost in his sixteen-year-old's shadow.

JEALOUSY

Jealousy is one emotion that is extremely difficult for parents to acknowledge feeling toward their children, much less understand and come to terms with, for it is not in keeping with our expectation of how a "good" parent behaves. We expect parents to take pleasure in their children's successes, not to feel envious of their accomplishments.

Some parents do in fact feel unequivocal happiness when their children succeed. But for many—frankly, more than one might imagine—their children's accomplishments provoke a confusing mix of reactions. On the one hand, they feel delighted when they see their child triumph, both because they empathize with their child's happiness and because they take at least some credit for their child's success. At the same time, though, these positive feelings can be mixed with envy, resentment, and feelings of competitiveness.

Sometimes, the jealousy that a parent feels toward a child has its basis in an implicit comparison between what the adolescent has, or is, and what the parent lacked as a teenager. For example, one mother in our study could not bear to watch her daughter getting dressed for a date because the mother herself had been extremely overweight and self-conscious as a teenager and had spent far too many weekend evenings alone in her room. Whenever the daughter would ask her mother's opinion about an outfit she was planning to wear, the mother would act as if the daughter were being overly vain and give her a lecture about being too concerned about her appearance. One father I spoke with said that whenever he sees his son win a wrestling match, instead of feeling overjoyed at his son's success, he thinks first of the matches that he himself did not win as a high school wrestler.

RICHARD JOHNSON'S CLUMSY ADOLESCENCE

Richard could not help but think back to his own adolescence—his "abnormal" adolescence, as he put it—and contrast it with what he perceived to be Matt's storybook youth. An asocial, shy, and interpersonally clumsy teenager, Richard, who had grown up in an affluent suburb of New York City, was throughout his adolescence envious of the boys in his school who were comfortable and self-assured, especially around girls. These boys, members of the popular athletic crowd, poked fun at Richard and the other socially inept members of his class. As a consequence, Richard's youth was spent alternately despising himself and the boys he so envied. He spent a lot of time alone as a teenager, occupying himself with his various collections—stamps, coins, and, of course, baseball cards.

The fact that Matt had abandoned Richard's passion for baseball cards in order to spend time with girls stung like salt rubbed into Richard's emotional wounds. Card collecting had been a source of comfort to Richard during his lonely adolescent years, an activity he held on to while many of his classmates turned their attention and energy to dating and socializing. His extensive collection (and the impressive body of baseball knowledge he had amassed along the way) was one of the few "accomplishments" he felt he could pass on to Matt. When Matt was younger, Richard took pride in impressing Matt with his command of baseball statistics. Now, it felt as if his own son, who had once shared his father's enthusiasm for this hobby, was rejecting him for an interest that was more mature. Like the popular boys Richard had grown up resenting, his son Matt was now "setting the agenda," and it was an agenda that reminded Richard of his own unpleasant youth. Once again, Richard was left behind. Card collecting was out, and girls were in.

Now, twenty-five years later, it was hard for Richard to look at Matt without feeling a mixture of complicated and unpleasant emotions. There was a big part of Richard that was proud that his son had not turned out like he had—an outcome that he credited to the efforts of his wife, Paula. According to Richard, Paula had enjoyed "a regular childhood" and knew how to "associate with a socially inclined son." This was a relief to Richard, who felt as awkward around his own son as he had among his popular classmates when he was a teenager. But because Matt was precisely the type of boy whom Richard had resented as an adolescent, it sometimes was hard to hear about Matt's achievements without being reminded of his own teenage shortcomings.

Most of the time Richard was able to squelch his feelings of envy and take pride in Matt's accomplishments. But occasionally, Richard's old adolescent anger would bubble up out of unconsciousness, and Matt would bear the brunt of his father's irritation. During these periods, Richard would become unfairly restrictive of Matt's social life, insisting that his schoolwork take precedence over his sports and social activities. Interestingly, I would learn from Richard's wife, Paula Woznicki, that, as Matt had moved into adolescence, she and Richard had increasingly disagreed over how to raise their son, with Richard attempting, in her view, to place far too many restrictions on Matt's social life. Indeed, Paula felt that Matt had turned out as well as he had because she had "protected" him from Richard's "ignorance" as a parent.

It was not clear to me, though, how much of Richard's behavior toward Matt was genuinely due to a lack of parental knowledge and how much of it was passive-aggression directed toward a son of whom he was quite jealous. Each soccer award, each telephone call, each Saturday-night party invitation was a reminder to Richard of the adolescence he had not had but had desperately wished for. Even Matt's girlfriend, Sara—whom Paula described as a delightful girl who was just like a member of the family—was a source of irritation for Richard. Sara was one of the prettiest and most popular girls in the school—the very type of young woman whom Richard had never had the courage to approach as a teenager. Naturally, there was a side of Richard that was thrilled for his son. Like many of the fathers in our study, Richard derived vicarious pleasure from his son's social successes. But there was also a side that was quite jealous, and it was difficult for Richard to handle these feelings.

Paula's behavior toward Matt only exacerbated Richard's jealousy. Each of Matt's achievements was a source of great pleasure to Paula, and she would eagerly listen at dinner as Matt regaled her with stories about his days at school, his escapades with his friends, and his dates with Sara. As I learned during our interview, she would turn at these moments to Richard and say, "Isn't that great?" but Richard would barely be able to muster a smile. Not only was Matt becoming the adolescent Richard had always wished *he* could have been, his own wife was paying more and more attention to Matt and less and less to him. Michael looked up to Matt more than to his father.

I imagined that even when Matt was not around, Richard must have felt his older son's presence, for Matt's presence in the Johnson household was very strong. It must have bothered Richard that his conversations with Paula were dominated by discussions concerning Matt.

PAULA WOZNICKI

When I interviewed Paula, she hinted that there were strains in her relationship with Richard, especially around his reluctance to socialize with other people. I could see in Paula where Matt had gotten his exuberant personality. A seasoned instructor in the university's nursing program, Paula was talkative and poised, like her son. When I asked how things were going with Richard, she frowned.

"To tell you the truth, this is not a good time for us," Paula said. "Richard feels I nag him about his antisocial personality, and I suppose I do a bit. He was never the social type, even when he was younger. He was a loner."

I asked Paula what she had been like as an adolescent.

"Oh, I was more like Matt, real extroverted—always going out, always involved in this thing or that thing. I loved being a teenager.

"You know, when Richard and I started dating in college, my friends had a hard time understanding why we got along—we seemed so opposite. I always thought that deep down, Richard just needed a push, and I guess I saw myself as the person to push him. It wasn't as if I was trying to make him over or anything—I was just trying to help him get out of his shell.

"Early in our marriage, Richard went along with me just to be a good sport. We'd have dinner parties, bridge club, community events, lots of fun things. We were always doing something, which I think is good for a couple—it keeps that spark going. But during the past three or four years, Richard has started complaining about everything we do. He says he's tired, that our friends are boring. He's content just to stay home every night and watch television. He bought a VCR and started this collection of movies that he tapes—he must have two hundred by now. I don't know, I can't sit still long enough to watch television night after night.

"Finally, I said, 'Look, I can't do this anymore. I need to get out, to be more active. If you don't want to come along with me, fine. But I'm going to get out more often.' He said, 'Fine.' It was fine with him, so I started playing bridge again, got involved in the PTA, and I joined a women's group that meets once a week. I'm out several times a week now. I miss doing things with Richard, but he was driving me crazy. I mean, his idea of a big time out is to go to the baseball-card shop on the mall."

I made a note to examine Richard's questionnaire responses. It sounded like he might be somewhat depressed.

I asked Paula if she thought that things in their marriage had changed in any dramatic way since Matt had become a teenager.

"It's hard to say," she replied. "It's true that Richard started becoming more withdrawn about the time that Matt turned thirteen, but I don't know if it was a coincidence or not. Now that you mention it, though, it was around then that Richard and Matt started arguing a lot."

"What did they argue about?"

"Oh, Richard did not like the fact that Matt was going out so often with his friends. Richard wanted him to help out around the house more. Matt felt that as long as he was making good grades, he should be allowed to come and go as he pleased—within reason, of course. He had his curfew. Frankly, I was sympathetic toward Matt. I said to Richard, 'It's normal for a boy his age to want to go out with his friends. Don't make him miserable. Don't make him miserable like you were at his age.' I think it was hard for Richard to hear that. But I think it needed saying."

JEALOUSY VERSUS JOY

The vast majority of the parents in our study were delighted with their adolescents' accomplishments, at least on the surface. Some were happy because they viewed their adolescents' achievements as a reflection of their own talent as parents. Others were overjoyed simply to see the pleasure that these achievements brought their child. John Forster, for example, who, with his wife, Linda, had ended up sharing love and reminiscences on the night of their daughter's first dance, talked about the joy he felt when his daughter had won an important race at a statewide track meet:

"I never pushed Abby to compete—it was something she wanted to do. And she worked awfully hard at it, the training, the practices, the long days. She had finished second a couple of times but had never won a big event, and it bothered her. So, when she won the half mile at the invitational last month, we all just about died! You should have seen the look on her face after it was over and she found out she'd won. She was *so* happy, *so* proud. And Linda and I felt so delighted for her. Not just happy that she had won—happy that she was happy."

For some parents, it was not the obvious achievements of the classroom, the playing field, or the high school auditorium that thrilled them, but the more subtle and sweeter accomplishments of development itself. Vicki Dobson, one of the single mothers in our sample, spoke with great emotion about the pleasure she experienced simply watching from a distance her daughter, Melanie, interacting and laughing with her classmates.

"I was so happy that she was able to enjoy herself with her friends," Vicki told me. "Able to hold her own, to carve out her own relationships, to make good friendships. I never had any doubts that she would be able to do this, but seeing it made me overjoyed. And I was genuinely happy for her. She had grown up and had turned out to be an interesting, funny, well-adjusted kid. I think knowing that has given me almost more pleasure than anything else."

Not surprisingly, I heard many more stories of parental joy than parental jealousy over the course of the interviews. But the number of parents who were envious of their adolescent was not at all trivial, and for many, the emotion was quite strong.

PARENTAL SACRIFICE

A different type of jealousy that arises during adolescence comes from the fact that some parents view their child's success as having been purchased at their own expense and sacrifice, thus fanning the fires of their resentment. When Richard Johnson spoke about Matt "having more going for him" than he did at his son's age, he wasn't simply referring to the fact that Matt was a more capable child than he had been. Richard was also alluding to the advantages that Matt enjoyed because of what Richard and his wife, Paula, had provided. The sentiments expressed in the Johnson household were ones I heard frequently: Matt enjoys advantages of time ("When I was a teenager, I had to work every day after school; I didn't have time to see my friends"), money ("He has his own stereo, television, and telephone in his room . . . I wish I lived as well as he does"), and, ironically, even parental attention ("My parents were too busy to take much of an interest in my life; I go to every single one of Matt's soccer games and cheer from the sidelines").

This sort of envy is quite difficult for parents to admit, again, because it goes against our expectation of what a "good" parent is supposed to feel. "Good" parents sacrifice willingly for their children and take pleasure in knowing that their children are enjoying themselves, even if it means that the parent is doing without something. "Good" parents do not envy the advantages their children enjoy, especially those the parents themselves have provided.

Even "good" parents sometimes feel jealous of their children's privileged lives—although it is difficult for them to admit this. When pressed, however, most will confess to occasional pangs of envy. Jack DeAngelo, a reasonably successful dentist in his mid-forties, put it this way:

"I look at Jason's life, and I think, boy, has he got it made! This winter, he's off on a weekend skiing trip with his friends—male friends *and* girlfriends, if you can believe it—and here I am snowblowing the goddamn driveway while it's 20-below, and I can't stop thinking of him and how much fun he's probably having. I'm imagining him and his girlfriend cuddling up in some ski lodge someplace. And I start getting angry. I'm thinking, great, I can't afford to hire somebody to plow our driveway—not at the rates these guys charge—because I'm paying for Jason to go off for the weekend and have a ball with his friends. It was different when he was younger, I guess, because how he spent his leisure time wasn't appealing to me. It wasn't as if I envied his Little League games or pizza parties. But this was different. I could picture *myself* in that ski lodge as easy as I could picture him there. And then it dawns on me: *We have reached a point in our lives where Jason is having more fun than I am*!

"It's as if you could graph it," Jack continued. "My 'fun line' is heading downward," he said, drawing an imaginary downward-sloping line through the air with his index finger. "And his is heading up," he continued, with an upward-sloping line. "A couple of years ago, those lines crossed for good—you know, 'never the twain shall meet.' I will never again have as much fun as my son. Now *there's* a depressing thought."

The realization that one's "fun line" is on a downward trajectory while one's child's line is climbing is especially difficult to accept for parents who are working hard and who find little in the way of fulfillment or pleasure. Many parents mentioned this, but this sentiment was expressed particularly frequently by single mothers, many of whom were struggling to make ends meet on a tight budget. Some had a "what can you do?" attitude about the "fun" problem, but others were quite angry about, and resentful of, their adolescents' freedom from responsibility. For example, one single mother, Eileen Brown, when asked to describe a typical summer day for her thirteen-year-old daughter, Becky, said:

"Her typical day? Sleeping until 10:30, 11:00, or later. Getting up and taking an hour or so to wake up. Watching TV. Getting on the phone and disappearing as fast as she can. Do you want to hear about *my* typical day? Up at 6:30, fold a load or two of laundry, straighten up the kitchen, unload the dishwasher, make sure the kids have something to eat for lunch, write the kids a note to remind them to start dinner, drive to the [travel] agency, finish up yesterday's paperwork, cover the phones until noon, try to drum up some new business, pay bills during my lunch break, cover the phones again in the afternoon, stop at the store on the way home and walk through the door, only to discover that the house is a mess again and dinner hasn't been started. That's my day—six days a week, fifty-two weeks a year."

THE ADOLESCENT AS THE PARENT'S FOIL

Jealousy that results from comparisons between one's adolescent and oneself as a teenager, while sometimes disheartening, is often dismissed as "spilt milk." Many parents feel that there is no sense in crying about what happened to them—or did not happen to them—twenty-five years earlier.

And parents' envy over the advantages their child enjoys as a result of the parents' own sacrifices is often offset by the satisfaction they take in knowing that they had done the "right" thing. Some parents actually seem to enjoy complaining about how easy their teenager's life is, as if this were a sort of testimony to their own hard work and diligence as parents. "My child spends her summer doing nothing but swimming and playing tennis" sometimes means "My *lazy, ungrateful* daughter has a great time while I slave at the office" (see Eileen Brown's response to my question about her daughter, Becky), but it often signifies "I am hardworking and successful enough to be able to give my child a privileged life." It is easy for some parents to defend against this sort of jealousy by transforming their envy into a badge of honor.

It is more difficult, however, for parents to deal with the envy that inheres in comparisons they make between their child's life and their own as *middle-aged adults*. This was by far the most interesting kind of jealousy I saw, and in many regards is the most difficult for parents to defend against. For many parents, comparing themselves with their adolescent reinforces their own unhappiness and tempts them to change something in their present situation. In a way, the adolescent becomes a living symbol of the parent's own frustration.

SEXUAL ENVY

A few of the parents in our study were aware of the nature and extent of their jealousy. Peter Rosenstein's love affair with a girl he met at one of his track meets was a tremendous source of frustration for his father, Jeff. Jeff, as you may recall, was already envious of his son's physical ability. He was even more jealous of the fact that Peter walked around in a lover's daze, whistling and grinning to himself and talking on the telephone with his girlfriend for hours on end. It bothered Jeff that those days were part of his past and that his marriage to Peter's mother, Amy, had grown stale and sexually uninspiring. Seeing Peter and his girlfriend together reminded Jeff of what he and Amy had once had but had lost years before.

"It's not that I'm jealous of what Peter has in any concrete sense," Jeff explained. "It's not like I look at his girlfriend and feel attracted to her—I mean, my God, she's only fourteen. But when I see Peter and Christy together I start to think about what he's feeling, about how good it feels to be young and in love, and about how that is a part of my life that is over, dead. Amy and I still have sex, of course, but it's not the same as when you're a kid, just discovering how good it feels. I've talked to a couple of other guys about it. They all say the same thing: 'Ah, to be fifteen and in love again!'

"I'll tell you a story. The other night I accidentally walked in on Peter and Christy while they were making out on the back porch. I don't like to admit it, but seeing them with their hands all over each other was a turn-on; it was like seeing myself when I was younger. Now, you'd think that somehow, it would have made me interested in having sex with Amy. But even though it made me feel a little horny, I didn't feel it for my wife. It wasn't like I felt it for Christy. Actually, I'm not sure what I felt. Just general randiness, I guess. It's something, though. A friend of mine said the other day, '*Since my son started dating, all I can think about is sex and food.*' I guess eating is a sort of sublimation, right?" Jeff asked me. I nodded. He smiled and continued.

"Anyway, after I saw Peter and Christy, I went upstairs and there was Amy, in bed—she had fallen asleep reading with her bedside lamp still on. I considered waking her up but then I thought, she's not going to understand, this is a man's thing. She's going to say it's childish, joke that I'm a "dirty old man," that sort of thing. So I kissed her on the forehead and tucked her in and turned the light out. Then I went back downstairs, pulled a carton of milk out of the fridge, and sat at the kitchen table, chugging it from the carton.

"I thought back to what it was like to come home from a date when I was Peter's age, all hot and frustrated and hungry—and, of course, so thirsty from all those hours of making out. Everyone else would be asleep and the house would be real quiet. After one of those dates, I would sit at the kitchen table and grab some cookies and drink some really cold milk out of the carton. I'd sit and replay the night in my mind, over and over again. And here I was now, married, with a teenage son who was out on the porch with *his* girlfriend, while my wife was conked out upstairs. I was happy for him, but I was feeling sorry for myself. I thought, there he is—he's got so much to look forward to."

Sexual jealousy was common among the fathers of sons in our study, many of whom echoed Jeff's feelings. Most were quick to point out that they did not consciously desire their son's girlfriends, but, like Jeff, they envied their teenager's freshly discovered sexuality. Several mentioned that they missed the variety of sexual partners they had had in late adolescence. Although the existence of AIDS was known at the time of our study, its threat to the non-drug-using heterosexual population was not yet fully realized, and many fathers at the time said they were jealous of their son's sexual "opportunities." This, of course, would change drastically over the next few years.

Ironically, by 1990, most of the parents I met felt sorry that their children would not be able to enjoy the sexual freedom they themselves had enjoyed as adolescents.

Wives were less inclined to feel jealous of their teenager's sexual relationships (or were less inclined to confess it) but several did admit that they were envious of the *romantic* aspects of their adolescent's social life. Amy Rosenstein, Jeff's wife, also talked about their son's girlfriend, but in a different tone than her husband. Whereas Jeff came away feeling sorry for himself after seeing Peter and Christy, Amy's reaction was more upbeat.

"When I see Peter, I see a young version of Jeff. It reminds me so much of what he and I were like when we started dating. Sure, we don't fool around often like Peter and his girlfriend do—I wouldn't expect to, not after sixteen years of marriage. Frankly, I'm not even sure that I would want to. At the end of the day, I'm exhausted, and I'm content just to have Jeff hold me as we fall asleep. But seeing Peter and Christy does make me wish that Jeff and I could put some of the romance back into our marriage. It's more that than the sex that I miss."

JEALOUSY OVER THE ADOLESCENT'S ACCOMPLISHMENTS

Although the jealousy that parents feel toward their children—especially, fathers toward their sons—typically begins in the child's adolescence, it often continues well into the child's young adulthood years. One of my former colleagues, psychologist Carol Ryff, has been studying the mental health of parents whose children are in their mid-twenties. She began this research because little is known about the dynamics of parent-child relationships once children are grown.

How do our relationships with our grown children affect our psychological functioning? Ryff expected to find that having a child who was successful, either scholastically or occupationally, would be a boost to parents' well-being. After all, this would reflect positively on the parent's childrearing talents.

Surprisingly, Ryff has found that the opposite is true. That is, parents whose children were highly successful as young adults reported *more* depression and *more* difficulty than did parents whose children had accomplished less. The explanation: Parents cannot help but compare themselves to their children, and when a parent does not measure up to his or her child's level of accomplishment, the parent's self-esteem falls. This was already beginning to happen to Richard Johnson.

RICHARD JOHNSON'S DISAPPOINTMENT

Although Richard felt somewhat envious of his son's social life, it was his jealousy over Matt's success more generally that was at the root of his unhappiness. His work as a laboratory technician at the university, managing the day-to-day operations of a research program for a prominent biochemist, had grown unfulfilling, and he was getting tired of carrying out studies designed by someone else. Fifteen years earlier, as a graduate student in plant pathology at Cornell University, Richard had shown great promise as a research scientist. But lacking the confidence he felt was necessary to pursue a high-powered career in academia, he decided to stop his training at the master's level and declined Cornell's offer of admission to the Ph.D. program. It was a decision that he now regretted.

Richard explained that, at the time, this seemed like the safe thing to do—he had known his graduate advisor well and knew what it took to succeed as a faculty member in a science department at a major research university. Richard could not envision himself having to hustle grant money and play the tenure game. But he knew he had technical skills that would be in demand at medical schools, university research centers, and in the world of corporate research. He decided to trade the potential glory of a successful academic career for the quieter, less demanding pace of a nine-to-five research position. This would enable him to work in a scientific setting with the latest, most sophisticated equipment without the strain of having to design and maintain his own research program. The idea of being able to leave his work at the office each day was particularly appealing, for it left him more time for Paula and their family.

At that point in their relationship, Paula did not have a strong opinion about Richard's career decision. Paula was finishing up a nursing program at Syracuse, and she was thinking more about her own career than Richard's. When he discussed the options with her, Paula could see the costs and benefits of each approach. She knew that Richard was not a go-getter—that he was pretty much a homebody with fairly modest aspirations. That was fine with her; in some regards, that was part of Richard's attractiveness. Her own father, a successful Milwaukee attorney, worked long hours and was seldom home during Paula's childhood. Richard would be a more devoted father. When his advisor put Richard in touch with a colleague at a major research university in the Midwest, Richard jumped at the opportunity.

During Matt's elementary school years, Richard was indeed a model father. He was always available to watch Matt's baseball games, help with Matt's homework, and drive Matt from one weekend activity to another. Occasionally, he and Matt would take a weekend off to travel to a baseball show in another city. All in all, they spent a great deal of time together, and Matt looked up to his father. Richard looked back on those years—his early and mid-thirties—as some of the happiest in his life.

As Richard entered his late thirties, however, he became less and less satisfied with life—with work, with marriage, and with fatherhood. His job seemed repetitive, boring, and, he felt, far less interesting than Matt's whirlwind of academic, athletic, and social activity. He felt that Paula had little interest in him—that all her energy was tied up in Matt and his brother Michael.

Paula's lack of interest in Richard was compounded by the fact that Matt seemed to need Richard's attention less and less. Matt's emotional distancing was probably amplifying Richard's unhappiness, making him even more difficult for Matt to take. When Richard tried to give Matt advice, they would end up bickering. My guess was that Richard's jealousy of Matt had begun to undermine their relationship, and that Matt was pulling away because Richard was becoming increasingly difficult to be around. In my interview with him, Matt complained about his father's irritability.

MATT JOHNSON

"I don't understand him," Matt said. "He gets really ticked off easily. Really ticked off about really stupid things. Like the other night he had Xeroxed this article on Japan that he wanted me to show to my friend Jeff, and when I told him that I wasn't going to be seeing Jeff that night, he was really mad. He was holding a pack of gum, and I asked if I could have a piece, and he said, 'No.' We fight a lot about stupid things that aren't worth fighting about."

Matt also complained that his father had stopped coming to watch Matt's soccer and basketball games, which I found intriguing in light of the interest Richard had taken in Matt's sports in the past. "I don't really expect him to come," Matt said. "But it's a letdown when he doesn't."

Richard had his own version of this, of course. During our interview, I had asked him if his emotional relationship with Matt had changed.

"Well, he doesn't confide in me as much as he used to. He doesn't come to me with his problems, like with girls. He talks to his mother, so I don't feel as if he's out there handling this all by himself. But we used to talk more when he was younger. I think it's just a passing thing. I think as he gets older, he'll come back."

I had the feeling that Richard was trying to convince himself of this as much as he was trying to convince me. I was not optimistic that Matt would "come back" until Richard changed his posture toward him.

Back in my office, I pulled up Richard Johnson's data file on my computer. His profile on our questionnaire battery indicated pervasive dissatisfaction—across marriage, work, and parenting. His self-esteem was extremely low, and he reported frequent bouts of tension, nervousness, and anxiety. He was experiencing strong feelings of self-doubt. There was no question that he was in a state of turmoil.

I was curious to see how Richard had responded to several of our questions about parenting. One item, from our midlife rumination scale, concerned regrets that individuals might have about their careers as parents: "I find myself wishing that I had raised my children in a different way." A second, from our parent orientation scale, assessed the extent to which fatherhood was a source of satisfaction: "The satisfactions I get from life come mostly from my role as parent." A third, also from our parent orientation scale, concerned the adult's anticipation of the "empty nest": "I will probably feel a little empty when my children all leave home."

Considered together, Richard's responses to these three questions were revealing. Although he reported few misgivings over the way Matt had been raised, he disagreed both with the statement that being a parent was a major source of satisfaction and with the notion that he would feel a little empty when Matt left home.

At first, I thought this odd, since it seemed to me that most parents would have been quite satisfied to have a son as interesting as Matt, and if they did, would surely miss his company when he had left home. It seemed from Richard's responses, however, as if he could hardly wait for Matt to leave.

The more I thought about this, the more I understood that the issue was not whether Matt was an exceptional or interesting son, or whether his accomplishments were impressive. No, the issue was whether Richard was going to be able to grow beyond the feelings of inadequacy he felt in comparison to Matt. Somehow, Richard was going to have to find genuine joy in Matt's happiness and success, or they each would suffer.

I felt sorry for both of them; for Matt, because his successes would always at some level be diminished by his father's ambivalence, and for Richard, because his son's impressive achievements—which, ironically, *did* reflect Richard's earlier investment in fathering— would always taste more than just a little bittersweet.

The issue was affecting more than the father-son relationship, however. As we shall see, Richard's jealousy of his son was also beginning to take its toll on his marriage.

6. ABANDONMENT

Cynthia and Jessica Garrison

CYNTHIA GARRISON

When I first rang the Garrisons' doorbell and was greeted by Cynthia, my initial inclination was to check my notes and make sure I had the correct address. Dressed in her jogging clothes, Cynthia, an attractive woman with short, stylishly coiffed blond hair and a youthful face, easily could have been mistaken for a thirty-year-old rather than the forty-four-year-old she was. She certainly looked too young to have a fifteen-year-old daughter.

Cynthia invited me into their house, which was tastefully decorated with expensive but comfortable furniture in a Southwestern style—the sort one might see featured in a magazine like *Metropolitan Home*. It was unusual to see this sort of furnishing in our town, where tastes tended to run more toward the traditional. We sat in the family room, and I admired the Native American objects that were placed around the room.

"Oh, we picked those up last summer on vacation. Jessie and I had driven down through the Southwest, and we spent my two weeks of vacation traveling through New Mexico and Arizona. We just fell in love with all of the artwork and the Indian crafts. That was a fun time. We try to take some sort of trip every summer. This year, we're probably going to fly out West and go camping in Washington and Oregon."

We talked nonstop for the next two hours. Cynthia seemed especially eager to open up, and rarely did I have to probe for more detailed answers. But it took some time for me to form a coherent picture. At first, I found it difficult to put my finger on what it was about her that seemed so sad. On the surface, she was cheerful enough, talkative and energetic. But every so often during our interview I got the sense that her outward sunniness was somewhat forced, a veneer the Cynthia put on not so much for my benefit as for her own. Beneath the surface, I sensed that she felt a deep sense of longing.

A few days after our interview, I looked back over Cynthia's responses to our questionnaire, and in particular, to her scores on our measures of midlife rumination, life satisfaction, self-esteem, and internalized distress. Sure enough, her profile was one that suggested denial: few conscious midlife concerns and above-average life satisfaction, but very low self-esteem and a good deal of psychosomatic distress. According to her responses to our distress inventory, Cynthia was suffering from frequent insomnia, headaches, and a loss of appetite. Something was clearly upsetting her, but she herself did not know what it was.

I learned from our interview that Cynthia was no novice when it came to denying her feelings. Her nine-year marriage to her ex-husband, Michael, had given her plenty of opportunities to cut herself off from her innermost emotions. Although Michael's persistent criticism—about her spending too much money on their home, about her "excessive" attentiveness to their daughter, Jessica, and about their unsatisfying sex life—had bothered Cynthia, she had bottled up her anger. She had grown up with parents who fought bitterly in front of their children, and she had vowed not to do the same to her daughter. So, when Michael complained, Cynthia listened patiently, even though she felt that his criticism was unfair. Unfortunately, Cynthia's inner rage made her feel resentful toward Michael, and over time she found herself turning more and more to her job as the chief staff assistant to a state legislator, her home, her hobby—gourmet cooking—and, most of all, to her daughter for satisfaction and self-affirmation.

To her surprise, when Michael announced that he had fallen in love with another woman—a twenty-two-year-old physical therapist who worked in the hospital where he practiced internal medicine—Cynthia's initial reaction was one of relief, not remorse, or so she told me. She and Michael agreed to part amicably, and Michael offered to take an apartment in town while they "sorted things out." Cynthia felt as if a weight had been lifted from her shoulders. Although she did not relish the thought of going through a divorce and worried about how Jessica would react to the situation, Michael's constant complaining made her feel tense much of the time, and having him out of the house felt cleansing—"like opening the windows on the first warm day of spring," as she put it.

Jessica was eight when Michael moved out. Like most girls of this age whose parents divorce, her initial reaction, as Cynthia described it to me, was one of depression. "She cried a lot," Cynthia told me, "and she became quiet and withdrawn, which was not like her at all. She had been a happy, enthusiastic child. It was a good two, two-and-a-half years before she became herself again. I think she's fine now." Cynthia laughed and shook her head. "Well, as fine as any normal fifteen-year-old can be."

I asked what she meant.

"Oh, she's moody. Forgetful. Self-absorbed. You know, a typical teenager."

Could she give me an example of something that happened recently?

"Sure. Last Friday night, we had planned to go out for dinner. Friday night out had become sort of a routine for us—at least when she wasn't staying with Michael for the weekend. We'd try a different restaurant, pretend we were food critics. I've taught her a lot about cooking, so she knows a good meal when she's had one. If we had something that we really enjoyed, we'd try to figure out how it was made and cook it ourselves sometime the next week.

"Anyway, six o'clock rolls around, and no Jessica. I wasn't really worried, because she often stops at a friend's house after school. I assumed that she had gotten tied up for a while, and I jumped in the shower to get ready to go out. Finally, close to seven, the phone rings. It's Jessica. She had gone to the mall with some friends and they had decided to have dinner there, at Friday's. She was calling to let me know that she would be home by nine.

"I wasn't going to get into it with her over the phone then, but I was really annoyed. I guess I was looking forward to going out, and I felt like I had been 'stood up.' This is the third time she's done this in the last two months. It's funny. I feel like I'm being dumped by my best friend—like she's moving on with her life and I'm being left behind."

I found her phrasing revealing.

ABANDONMENT

Feeling left behind—feeling abandoned—was an important source of distress among many of the parents in our sample. Initially, I viewed this feeling as synonymous with loss, as a slightly different version of the same experience. But as I came to a better understanding of what parents like Cynthia Garrison were feeling, I realized that there were subtle, yet important, differences between these two reactions. Parents who experienced their child's maturation as a *loss* were grappling mainly with the loss of a role and of the self-definition that accompanies it. As we saw in the case of Barbara Merrick, for example, her son Brian's emotional independence filled her with uncertainty about what her day-to-day life would be like without having a child to care for. Her loss was not so much the loss of her relationship with her son, but rather, a loss of purpose and a loss of a piece of her own identity. The experience struck me as being akin to having to cope with an unwanted, yet mandatory, retirement from one's occupation.

Parents who experience their child's maturation as *abandonment* also experience a loss, but for them it is the loss of the relationship, not the role, that is significant. These parents have usually had a very intimate emotional connection with their child and have come to depend on their child as a companion and confidante—actually, a more common phenomenon than popular portrayals of the inherently antagonistic parent-adolescent relationship would lead one to expect.

In our sample, as has been found in other studies of adolescent-parent relationships, the vast majority of parents and teenagers say they like each other a great deal, admire each other, and enjoy each other's company. Fewer than one fourth of parents and teenagers have terribly strained or unhappy relations. Oddly enough, though, studies of the changing dynamics of the parent-child relationship in adolescence are skewed toward research on the troubled minority. As a result, we know far more about strained parent-teen relationships than we do about harmonious ones. And we know very little about the substantial number of parent-teen relationships that are truly emotionally intimate.

Although adolescents fare better when they are close to, rather than distant from, their parents, intimacy between parents and children has its costs. One significant cost is the sense of emotional abandonment, even rejection, that parents feel as their children begin to detach from the relationship and form close emotional attachments to peers. These feelings of abandonment are most intense, as one would expect, among parents who have few other sources of support and companionship in their life.

One can see this quite clearly in Cynthia Garrison, whose feeling of abandonment stemmed simultaneously from her dependence on Jessica for companionship and friendship and from the absence of other intimate relationships in her life. Like many of the single mothers and daughters in our sample, Cynthia and Jessica had established an exceptionally close and intimate bond during the years following the divorce. Although they had always been close, Michael's leaving brought Cynthia and Jessica closer still, initially for mutual comforting, but over time, for emotional support and companionship as well. As they adapted to Michael's absence and emerged from the initial shock, they turned increasingly to each other. And as Jessica matured, Cynthia found her company more and more satisfying.

"I was always struck by her maturity," Cynthia said when we discussed her relationship with her daughter. "I guess from the time she was eleven or so I would start to confide in her—nothing major, just things at work or with my parents, or about my childhood, when I was her age. We spent so much time together, just the two of us, especially in the first couple of years after Michael left. Jessie was depressed, and I was in a state of shock, so we didn't get out much. Jessie seemed to lose interest in her girlfriends, and I had absolutely no interest in dating. So we spent a lot of time at home, lazing around, being together. I mean, I was relieved in a way when Michael left, but I had no idea what to do—so much of my energy had revolved around being his wife. It was nice to have Jessica there. I don't know what I would have done if I had been alone. Being busy at work helped a lot, sure. But I guess I really relied on Jessie to pull me through."

GOING IT ALONE

I asked Cynthia if being a single, working mother had made being the parent of an adolescent more difficult in any way.

"I don't know. I guess I haven't really given it much thought. I suppose if I had to say, I'd say it was *easier*, not harder. Michael and I disagreed a lot about how to raise Jessie—he's always been much stricter than I was—and that was always causing problems. A lot of my married friends complain about the same thing. When you have a baby, it's nice to have someone else around to help, because raising small children really is a lot of work. But later, there's much less to do in raising them. And it's easier to do it your way than to have to negotiate every little decision with someone else."

I heard this sentiment over and over from the divorced mothers in our sample, contradicting my stereotype of the harried, overwhelmed single parent trying to cope with an independent-minded teenager. But by far the most common complaint among the single parents I interviewed concerned finances, not childrearing. A substantial percentage of the single mothers in our study, as in others, saw their standard of living drop after the divorce. When economic circumstances were dire enough to force a dramatic upheaval in the family's living conditions, the financial stress sometimes spilled over into the parent-child relationship.

Overall, however, we saw little evidence that adolescent-parent relations were habitually strained in single-parent homes, as long as adequate financial resources were present. In some respects, we actually found that the *reverse* was true, especially in families of single mothers and daughters. In many of these families, parent-child relations were particularly warm and intimate. I heard dozens of stories from mothers and daughters about the fun they'd had together as "buddies."

"The divorce really made us a lot closer," Cynthia told me when I asked how it had affected her relationship with Jessica. I think that it released something in me, let me relax more. When we were with Michael, I was always nervous about what he was thinking, whether I was paying enough attention to him or paying too much to her. I think that after he moved out, Jessie and I felt freer to be ourselves. Sometimes it felt nice to have a more feminine household. You know, just the girls.

"That's the other thing about Jessie—she's a lot of fun to be with. Oh, we would get silly sometimes, the two of us. One time, I remember, we were over at Hilldale [one of the city's shopping malls] and we were at the cosmetic counter in Marshall Field's. Jessie was about twelve at the time. Anyway, there we were with this very serious salesperson, and we kept trying on the most hideous makeup we could find, and each time, we would laugh so hard that we could barely catch a breath of air. Honestly, the people behind the counter must have thought we had lost our minds. But it was sure fun."

In many respects, the Garrisons' bond sounded more like that between sisters than between mother and child.

JESSICA GARRISON

When I interviewed Jessica a week after I met with Cynthia, I asked her how she thought their relationship had been affected by the divorce. I was taken aback by her candor and insight. I was also struck by how much she resembled her mother. We were sitting in the family room, where I had interviewed Cynthia. This time I noticed that pictures of the two of them were placed throughout the room. I was drawn to one in particular. In it, Jessica and Cynthia were standing at a campsite, side by side, their arms around each other's shoulders. They looked invigorated and enormously happy. I guessed that the photo had been taken during last summer's Southwestern vacation.

"When I was younger," Jessica said in response to my question, "I felt really lucky. I mean, all of my friends were *so* jealous. They'd say how young my mom was, how she and I could talk about anything, how I got to spend so much time with her, how she wasn't afraid to do crazy things with me. And that made me feel good.

"Lately, though, it seems like we're *too* close. It's hard to explain."

I asked her to try. She frowned and groped for just the right words, as if she were phrasing something delicately.

"I don't know. It's just that I've been feeling like I don't want to spend as much time with her as she wants to spend with me. It's weird. I mean, it's like she's started to rely on me, instead of the other way around, and I'm starting to feel sorry for her. And I don't think that this would have happened if my parents hadn't gotten divorced, because they would have each other.

"I wish she had more of a life, you know, outside of me? I mean, she doesn't date or go out unless it's something we're doing together. When I was in junior high school, it was fun. But now I'd rather be with my friends. Isn't it normal for kids my age to want to spend time with their friends?"

I said that it certainly was. Then I asked if her mother tried to limit how much time she spent with her friends.

"Not really, I guess. I mean, no, not in that way. It's more that she sort of tries to compete with them or something, like she gets jealous of me for going out with someone other than her. And then I feel guilty."

I asked her what she felt guilty about.

"Well, when my father left, my mom was really hurt. I was pretty young at the time, so I didn't really understand a lot of what was going on, but I can remember my mom standing in the kitchen a lot, looking out the window and crying. Now, I think of her when I go out, all alone here at home. I imagine her standing in front of that window again, waiting for me to come home."

I thought to myself that it was interesting that Jessica had remembered her mother as being quite sad about her divorce from Michael. Cynthia had described herself as having been relieved. I assumed that in some senses, both were telling the truth. The difference was in what each recalled most vividly, and it was not surprising that Jessica would have remembered her mother crying, since this would have been a strong and salient image. As well, I imagined that Cynthia would have been reluctant to communicate her sense of relief to her daughter, out of fear that this would turn Jessica against her father.

"My mom would say things like, 'It's just the two of us now,' or 'We've got to help each other through this.' And I guess we did. I mean, it was hard getting used to not having my dad around—hard for both of us. And, like, when we would have dinner, it would just be me and my mom, and at first you couldn't help thinking about what was missing. You know, like 'What's wrong with this picture?' But after a while, it started to seem not so bad. We had these things that we would do, like going out on Friday nights, and we spent a lot of time together, talking, shopping, watching television, cooking—we both like to cook. When I was younger, I just sort of figured that she was doing this stuff for me, to make up for my dad not being around very much. But now I realize that she was also doing it for herself, because she was lonely. And I guess over the years she got more and more used to me being there for her, and now I'm not as much."

"What about you?" I asked. "Do you miss your father?"

"At first I did. And I would call him a lot and try to see him on weekends, but after a while he seemed to sort of lose interest in me. You know, he'd call at the last minute and say he was tied up when we were supposed to be doing something, or he would seem rushed on the phone when I called. I guess that had a lot to do with having another baby. He and Jane—that's his wife—started their own family, and he got really involved in that, I guess. I never got along with her and she was never very interested in me, so we sort of drifted apart. My dad and me, I mean. I barely see him now."

I asked Jessica if she was hurt by this.

Her expression hardened. "Not now. Not anymore."

Initially, I took this reaction as an indication that Jessica had acquired some of her mother's capacity for denial. Of course she would have to have been hurt by her father's disengagement—what child would not have been? And of course she would cope with this by telling herself—and telling me—that she no longer felt hurt by what had happened.

The more we talked, however, the more I came to see that the strong affection that developed between Jessica and her mother had provided a substitute, of sorts, for her relationship with her father. This was not to say that Cynthia by herself was providing everything to Jessica that she and Michael could have provided had they stayed together. But in many respects, Jessica probably enjoyed a closer relationship with her mother because of the divorce than she would have had her parents remained together. I wondered if this in fact was the source of the problem that she and her mother were now having—that is, because Jessica and her mother had come to depend on each other so much after the divorce, the normal pulling apart that occurs at adolescence must have been all the more salient and difficult for each of them to fully understand.

I asked Jessica to tell me about her relationship with her mother now. Were they less close now than before?

"Less close? Oh, no. It's not like that. We're still real close. It's more that I just need to be with my friends. I can't explain it. It's not the same when I'm with her as it is when I'm with my friends, no matter how close we are. She's—I don't know—*she's my mother*." She looked at me as if what she said were self-evident.

"I don't know," she continued. "It's starting to get on my nerves."

"What is?"

"Just that she's *there* all the time. I mean, I'll be talking on the phone with one of my friends and she'll want to know everything. Or I'll come home from school and she'll have made all these plans to go out together. It just isn't as much fun anymore."

THE ADOLESCENT'S NEED FOR EMOTIONAL DISTANCE

Jessica was describing something that psychologists understand but that parents have difficulty accepting: that there arrives a time in the child's development when she comes to feel that there are certain emotional needs that her parents simply can not satisfy, not because of anything in her parents' behavior, *but simply because they are her parents*. It is not, as some might suspect, merely a "generation gap"—a difference in viewpoints between teenagers and their elders. Many adolescents form perfectly fine friendships with other adults, such as their teachers, their friends' parents, or other relatives, during this time. Thus, the adolescent's movement away from parents has nothing to do with age differences or differences in values. Rather, the central issue revolves around the adolescent's growing sense of emotional autonomy and the need that this creates for some emotional distance in the parent-child relationship.

Because popular writings about adolescence focus disproportionately on the sources of strain in the parent-child relationship, we tend to underestimate the strength of the bond that develops between some parents and their adolescent children. Many parents, especially those with a firstborn child of the same sex, find that their adolescent child can become a good companion and valued confidante, a situation that is enhanced when intimate companionship is lacking or limited in the parent's life, either because of being single or in an unhappy or unfulfilling marriage.

THE MIXED BLESSING OF CLOSENESS

An exceptionally close relationship between parent and child is a mixed blessing. On the positive side, closeness in the parent-child relationship has been shown to be associated with psychological well-being among both parents and children. In our study, for example, we found that mothers who reported feeling close to their children enjoyed higher self-esteem, reported more life satisfaction, and experienced less psychological or somatic distress than did mothers who described their relationship with their children as more distant. (We find a basically similar pattern for fathers, although the effects of a close relationship with a child on men's mental health is not as strong as it is among women.)

Similarly, adolescents from homes in which they enjoy close relationships with their parents do better in school, score higher on standardized tests of psychological adjustment, and generally have more positive overall mental health than do youngsters who do not get along well with their parents. Thus, with respect to the immediate benefits to individual mental health, closeness in the family is by and large a good thing.

During the childhood years, few problems arise as a consequence of closeness in the parent-child relationship, as long as emotional closeness does not become confused in the parent's mind with disciplinary laxity. If the parent maintains a sense of authority in his or her dealings with the child, a close, friendly relationship generally will have positive effects on the child's well-being, and this in turn will have beneficial effects on the parent.

At adolescence, however, emotional closeness between parent and child can clash with some of the child's normal developmental needs. When this clash occurs, as it almost always does, the child will pull away from the relationship somewhat. And when the child pulls away, the parent may suffer emotionally.

It is important to understand the psychological origins of the adolescent's desire for more emotional distance and what this distance does and does not signify. In order to do this, we need to look back at what has been happening to the parent-child relationship over time and how this relationship is used as the building block for the child's developing sense of identity.

THE ORIGINS OF INDIVIDUALITY

During infancy, the child does not really have much of a distinct sense of self—of the psychological boundary between who he is and who his primary caregiver, typically his mother, is. He is, in essence, defined entirely by the relationship. He only begins to develop a sense of self by distinguishing himself from this other person. In other words, from the outset, the process of forging a sense of self is achieved through separating from those we are close to. This is what psychologists call the *separation-individuation process*: by separating, we assert our own individuality.

The child's attempt at self-definition first becomes apparent during the toddler years, when children often become insistent on doing things their own way. As most parents will attest, the three-year-old's favorite word often is "No!"—expressed forcefully and unhesitatingly. Even the most compliant child usually goes through a phase sometime between the ages of two and four when he demands to have things done his way, and no amount of reasoning or cajoling on the part of the parent does any good whatsoever. Although many parents see this as "oppositional" or "negative," it rarely is either. Instead, it is the child's first attempt to say, "I am my own person, separate from you."

THE DANCE OF INDIVIDUATION

Our needs to separate from others are complemented by our needs to connect with them. In each of our relationships—not only in our relationships with parents or children, but in romantic relationships and friendships as well—we seek a comfortable balance between connecting and separating. More often than not, though, in a relationship, one person's "comfort zone" differs from the other's, and the degree of distance between them changes as each partner asserts new emotional desires. In order for the relationship to survive when this happens, the partners must negotiate a new equilibrium that is comfortable to each of them. Psychologists refer to this process, this emotional dance, as *distance regulation*.

Over the course of the child's development, the parent-child relationship undergoes several important periods of distance regulation, mainly due to the child's growing needs for separation. The child's need to assert his individuality is especially intense during adolescence as well as during toddlerhood, and many experts have pointed out that the adolescent's drive for autonomy shares much in common with that of the three-year-old. Once again, the child is driven to separate in order to individuate. This time, however, the child achieves this not simply by asserting his will, but by emotionally distancing himself from his parents. In adolescence, as in early childhood, the young person must pull away from his parents in order to establish and solidify his own sense of self. Much of this process goes on at an unconscious level—that is, few adolescents are consciously aware that they are pulling away, nor would they describe it in these terms. For them, it just seems natural to want to be with friends and to want to spend less time with parents.

Unfortunately for the parent, no parallel need arises at this time: Parents do not "need" more distance in their relationship with their child in the way that their child needs this distance. Indeed, parents, especially those who have been close to their child, want the relationship to remain close and perhaps even crave more intimacy as the maturing adolescent becomes a more interesting companion and a potentially better friend. As a result, what the child experiences as a normal desire to be more independent and somewhat more emotionally distant, the parent often experiences as a problem—as personal rejection or abandonment. It is not unlike a romance in which one of the partners announces that she needs more "space" while the other is trying to hold on to the existing level of intimacy. The partner wanting space is likely to feel suffocated, whereas the one wanting intimacy is likely to feel neglected.

In essence, this was what was happening to Cynthia and Jessica. Jessica was feeling suffocated and was "asking" for more space in their relationship. Because of their history of intimacy, Jessica could not bring herself to ask for more space directly. Instead, she tried to make her needs known indirectly, by "forgetting" her dates with her mother. Cynthia was too invested in the relationship to take the hint. Instead of looking at the situation from Jessica's point of view—after all, nothing Jessica was asking for was extraordinary—she interpreted her daughter's behavior as a sort of rejection.

Cynthia had touched on this during our interview. "I had read that there is usually a time when kids begin to pull away, but I guess I told myself that our relationship was going to be different," she had said. "Because we always were so close. And we rarely struggled over the usual things. So I assumed that things would continue just as they had been. But Jessica has changed. At least, I *think* she has changed. She's more private, more moody, more self-absorbed. Sometimes I think she forgets that I exist."

I can't tell you how many times I've heard *that* from parents of teenagers.

At a deeper level, though, Cynthia's sensation of being abandoned by Jessica reopened some of the emotional wounds that she had received when she was rejected by her ex-husband. Although she had told me that she was relieved when Michael left, I suspected that she actually was far more ambivalent about the divorce than she would admit. Michael's criticism of her over the years had shaken Cynthia's self-confidence, and his leaving her for another woman had only exacerbated her feelings of insecurity and self-doubt. Despite her outward attractiveness and cheeriness, Cynthia was not at all confident. One of the few sources of emotional happiness in her life was her relationship with Jessica, and now she was facing being "dumped" again.

I thought also that Cynthia might be upset, if only unconsciously, by the fact that Jessica was, in a funny way, leaving her for someone who was younger and more exciting—just as Michael had left her for a younger woman several years earlier. Thus, in addition to her feelings of being left behind by her daughter, Cynthia was also feeling old and no longer "with it." Given Cynthia's shaky sense of security, it was no wonder that Jessica's perfectly natural inclination to spend more time with her friends, and less with her mother, was having the effect it was.

ABANDONMENT VERSUS REJUVENATION

I noted earlier that feelings of abandonment were more common among parents who, like Cynthia, had invested a great deal of emotional energy in their adolescent partly as a means of compensating for an otherwise unfulfilling emotional life. What about those parents who were close to their adolescent but who also had a satisfying emotional relationship with a spouse or friend? Did these parents feel left behind as their adolescent began the distancing process?

Generally speaking, they did not. These were parents who remained close to their child but at the same time permitted the adolescent to grow apart emotionally. More important, because these parents had other sources of emotional satisfaction, they were far less likely to view the child's movement away in a negative light. Many, in fact, had quite the opposite reaction, finding a sense of rejuvenation and excitement in watching their child's social life take off.

VICKI DOBSON

Vicki Dobson was one of the women in our sample who fell into this category. The contrast between her and Cynthia Garrison is particularly instructive, because each was a single mother of an adolescent daughter. Yet, unlike Cynthia, Vicki reacted to her daughter's emotional growth with interest and enthusiasm.

"I don't know, maybe it's this child psychology course I'm taking now at MACC [the local community college], but watching Melanie become a young woman is just so interesting," she told me. "It sure takes me back. The other night, while she was out with her boyfriend, I got out my old annual, and I spent the evening looking through it, looking back at the boys I had dated when I was her age. That was sure a nice time in my life."

I asked how things were going with Melanie now. "Oh, I'd say very well. No surprises. We've been on our own for quite a while now—Melanie's father left when she was three—and we've worked out a comfortable routine. To tell you the truth, it was almost getting a little too comfortable—oh, what's the word?—claustrophobic. You know, two people together all the time. No matter how well you get along, you need breaks from each other, and you need other people in your life. And so, when Melanie started dating I was thrilled for her. And I've had a ball watching it from the sidelines. She'll have her friends over and I'll joke around with them—they're great kids—fun, clean-cut, polite, you know, really *nice* kids. And so full of energy, with their music and dancing and all the talking. I like having the energy around here. It makes me feel younger just to be around them."

I asked her to explain why.

"Oh, I try to take an interest. I ask questions, about their clothes, about their music, about what they're learning in school. And their excitement is contagious. Melanie doesn't know it, but I even play some of her tapes when she's out of the house. Some of the stuff they listen to is awful, but some is better than you'd think."

And then Vicki said something that I wish Cynthia Garrison could have heard.

"I look at it this way. You have a choice. You can either sit around and watch them grow up and feel sorry for yourself, or you can go along for the ride. And I've never been one for self-pity. There are too many things to do in life. And I don't think it would be good for Melanie. I want her to go out and have a good time without worrying about her mother back at home. I didn't want her to feel responsible for me, like I did with my mom. My father died at a young age, and my mom never remarried. I spent most of my adolescence feeling guilty about her.

"It's not Melanie's fault that things didn't work out between her parents. I want her to have as much fun as a teenager as possible."

"Do you miss Melanie, now that she's out more often?"

"Sometimes, sure. But not all that much. I have a pretty full life. I have this circle of women friends—gosh, we've known each other for years—and we see a lot of each other. We'll play cards or go out to the movies, or just gab on the phone. So I always have people to talk to and to do things with. And I have my job—I sell real estate—which keeps me running around. And I'm a big reader. I'm always working on two or three books. And I try to take courses at the college, not for credit or anything, but for fun. So, believe me, my time is pretty well filled up."

As I drove home from this interview, I couldn't help but compare Vicki Dobson and Cynthia Garrison. I imagined each of them home alone on a Saturday night, Vicki treating herself to something interesting—a good mystery, a long telephone call, a rich reminiscence—and Cynthia standing and staring out her window, too distracted to enjoy her own company, just standing and waiting for Jessica's return. Deep down, Cynthia must have recognized that she was waiting for something that simply was not going to happen.

7. LOSS

Amanda, Jonathan, and Paul Spencer

AMANDA SPENCER

"I can remember Paul's thirteenth birthday so vividly," recalled Amanda, a thirty-seven-year-old homemaker whose son was now nearly fourteen. Amanda and I were sitting in the Spencers' living room one evening, finishing up our interview while Jon, her husband, and Paul, her son, played Ping-Pong downstairs in their basement family room. The living room was tastefully furnished, although the copy of Sunday's newspaper strewn about suggested that it had not been straightened up for at least a few days.

"I'd knocked myself out getting together a birthday party for Paul and his friends," Amanda told me. "I felt sort of bad, because he has some Jewish friends and they were all having these elaborate bar mitzvahs—I mean it seemed like he was invited to one every other week—and I was thinking that maybe we should do something special for Paul, so that he wouldn't feel left out." Amanda looked very tired that evening, even a bit depressed, and the long expression on her face was in marked contrast to the laughter and joking shouts emanating from the basement.

"It was the first party he had at our house where there were boys and girls. You know, dancing, the whole thing. Anyway, it was a Friday night, and I had gone out that morning and bought all this food and had put up some decorations and rearranged the furniture in the rec room. I even carried down the stereo from the living room and set that up, too. Jon, of course, hadn't lifted a finger. But that was all right. He was in a faculty meeting at school all afternoon, and I don't work, so I had the time to do it.

"Anyway, Paul came home after his soccer practice—I guess it was about 4:30 and the party was supposed to start at 7:30—and he headed upstairs to shower and change. I was excited about the party and I just really wanted him to see how I had fixed things up, so I dragged him downstairs to see. And he took one look at the decorations and then gave me this really disgusted look, like I had done something horrible, just terrible. And he stared at me and said, very matter-of-factly, 'I'm taking all this junk down. This isn't how my friends and I party.' And then he just climbed the stairs and headed up to the bathroom. Just like that. I just stood there and watched him climb the stairs. I guess I stood there for a while, just thinking, listening to his shower water run down the drainpipes.

"You know, I was furious, but I didn't want to say anything, not then at least, not right before the party. But I can't imagine ever saying something like that to my mother when I was his age. So disrespectful. So unappreciative. I mean, I had really knocked myself out for him. And for what? For nothing."

As the interview progressed, I learned that Amanda had been feeling this way for some time now—that what she did for Paul was unappreciated, unnoticed, even disparaged.

"I know it's not a big deal, and I probably should have let him plan his own party," Amanda had said, "but I really wanted to do something special for him. A lot of moms really don't care, they let their kids run wild all over the place. But I'm not that way. He thinks he's more grown up than he is. He still needs someone to be there for him. That's what I'm here for, right?" She said this with some hesitancy, as if she wasn't certain exactly what her role was any longer.

I find myself wondering if I've put too much emphasis on certain things in life while neglecting other important things.

This item, taken from a questionnaire we called the midlife rumination scale, captured Amanda's current psychological state to a tee (see page 45 for other items from this questionnaire). When Amanda had enrolled in our study and had first completed our standardized assessment battery, she had reported experiencing this thought only rarely. Now, one year later, she said she felt this way very often.

Amanda Spencer's scores on the battery of psychological tests we had administered clearly identified her as one of the "decliners" in our sample—parents whose mental health took a significant turn for the worse during their child's transition into adolescence. Over the previous twelve months her complaints of depression and anxiety had risen, along with her reports of headaches, insomnia, and fatigue. Her score on our self-esteem inventory had dropped significantly, as had her score on our measure of life satisfaction. Her score on our midlife rumination scale had shown a dramatic increase.

Although she worried that she was slipping into a depression, Amanda felt unable to stop the slide. In the past, she had looked to her family for affirmation of her competence and importance. She held their world together, or so she felt. Now she was beginning to doubt just how central she was in their life.

When Paul was born, Amanda had chosen full-time homemaking happily and enthusiastically. During Paul's elementary school years, while her friends were complaining of the drudgery and boredom of being at home full time, Amanda pressed onward cheerily, throwing herself into PTA activities, cub scouting, and making their home as close to a *House and Garden* photo spread as she and Jonathan could afford on his salary as a high school social studies teacher. Amanda's activities were not some elaborate sort of denial—for her, they genuinely engendered feelings of accomplishment and pride. These days, though, she found these sorts of feelings hard to come by. She felt Jonathan and Paul pulling away, and, as they did, taking away something from her sense of self.

"I know that Paul has to grow up, has to become his own person," Amanda said pensively at one point during our conversation. "But it's hard for me to stand by and watch it happen. It just feels like . . . like I'm losing something that I will never get back." She started to sigh sadly, then caught herself, laughed a little, and shook her head. "So many of my friends couldn't wait for their kids to get older, couldn't wait for the freedom, couldn't wait to retire their chauffeur's license."

She picked up a key ring from the coffee table and showed me the metal tag with MOM'S TAXI imprinted on it.

"Honestly, I can say that I was never happier than when I was shuttling Paul back and forth between school, friends' houses, music lessons, and soccer games. I would ask him about his day, and he would chatter on and on. Now, if I dare ask him anything, he just about bites my head off. If I offer him a ride somewhere, he insists on riding his bike instead. Whatever I do, he thinks I'm prying."

The majority of mothers in our study went through a difficult period with their child sometime during the early adolescent transition. In families with an oldest son, this usually happened between the child's eleventh and thirteenth birthdays; in families with an oldest daughter, it occurred earlier, between the ages of ten and twelve. (In general, most events in adolescence follow an earlier timetable for daughters than for sons, mainly because puberty, which triggers so much of the psychological change of adolescence, comes earlier in females than males.)

During this difficult period, mothers and children find themselves battling more frequently than usual, and over the most mundane issues—household chores, homework, back talk. Their arguments begin fairly innocently, but soon spiral out of control and end only when one or both parties storm out of the room. Often, the teenager comes away from these bouts feeling unfairly accused and overcontrolled, the mother feeling misunderstood and frustrated.

Although most of the mothers we interviewed complained about the relentless nature of this squabbling, not all of them were depressed by it. Part of what distinguished those who suffered from those who did not had to do with the extent to which the mother experienced her child's growth toward independence as a sort of loss.

Seeing the child's adolescence as a time of loss versus seeing it as an opportunity for one's own freedom and rebirth was one of the core dimensions along which parents in our study differed.

LOSS VERSUS FREEDOM

Psychologists tell us that most instances of depression are linked to some sort of loss—the loss of a relationship (e.g., after a divorce), the loss of a role (e.g., after being laid off), a loss of health (e.g., after an injury), even a loss of self-esteem (e.g., after some sort of failure). The "loss" of a child to adolescence is enough to trigger feelings of depression among some parents.

Coping with the loss of one's child to a new phase in his or her development is unlike coping with most of the other losses we experience in life, however. For one thing, the losses that result from divorce, unemployment, or illness are both real and easily identified. We can put our finger on the cause and, in most instances, on the cure: a new relationship, a new job, feeling healthy again. In contrast, when we "lose" our child to adolescence, it is not immediately clear just what it is that we have lost, if anything at all. Many parents who, deep down, feel a sense of loss when their child reaches his or her teens have a hard time putting their finger on just what the feeling is all about. And without understanding the origins of the feeling, they have no clue as to what might alleviate it.

Losing a child to adolescence is also different from other sorts of losses, because we are sent so many mixed messages about whether our child's maturation is supposed to be greeted with despair or celebration. When someone divorces, is fired, becomes ill, or fails in some way, we expect the individual to feel down in the dumps for a time. In fact, we worry if individuals do *not* show signs of sadness under these circumstances, and we may accuse them of denying their true feelings.

Our expectations about how parents *should* feel when their children become teenagers are not so clear cut—perhaps because there is no one "right" way to feel. Some parents, like Amanda Spencer, feel a profound sense of loss and emptiness. Others, however, feel an uplifting sense of freedom. Both reactions are common, and both are normal. Some parents feel a mixture of loss and freedom, and may find their feelings vacillating between the two ends of the continuum.

Sarah Fein, like Amanda Spencer, in her late thirties when her firstborn reached adolescence, was one of those parents for whom the transition was liberating. Although she had enjoyed raising her son Douglas and had been, by most indicators, a very active, involved mother, Sarah could not wait for Douglas to reach an age at which he no longer had to rely on her each afternoon for entertainment. A free-lance editor of manuscripts for a scientific textbook publisher,

Sarah had decided to try her hand at writing a science-fiction "tech-nothriller" about a genetic-engineering project gone awry. Glued to her word processor in her attic office, Sarah liked nothing more than hearing Douglas come home from school and call upstairs that he and his friends were heading over to the park to play basketball, for that meant that she had two additional hours to work on her book before her house became noisy. Nor did she feel the least bit guilty about the pleasure she took in her work:

"I was starting to feel tied down and at loose ends," she told me. "Frankly, I feel happier now, and I think I'm a better parent because of it. Believe me, Doug would be the first to agree."

By contrast, Amanda Spencer could not find any relief in her son's growing up. And in Amanda's case, her sense that she was losing something by Paul's becoming a teenager was creating psychological turmoil within her. Not only was she feeling the sense of sadness that accompanied her feelings of loss, she was beginning to question who she was, what she had done with her life, and what the future held for her.

I find myself wondering if I've put too much emphasis on certain things in life while neglecting other important things.

As Amanda struggled to cope with her feelings about losing Paul, she began to think seriously for the first time that perhaps she had made a mistake by having chosen some years earlier to forsake her career in journalism in order to be home full time for her son. She had always had strong domestic interests and had discovered during college at Ohio State that she had a talent for writing about the things she herself so enjoyed—interior design, gardening, cooking, and home crafts. She had even written a few pieces on quilting for one of the Columbus newspapers.

When Jonathan was offered a job teaching at a Columbus high school, Amanda was delighted to discover that the university had a formal program in what was called home economics journalism, and she made plans to return to school and take courses in the area. As often happens, though, Amanda put her occupational plans on hold when Paul was born, and the years sped by. Wrapped up in the day-to-day demands of childrearing, Amanda channeled her interests in domestic activities into her own family's life—through decorating, canning vegetables from their garden, and working on her quilts. Now, her family seemed to need and want less and less from her. Amanda worried whether she had the energy to start writing again. She certainly had no interest in returning to school.

As she watched Paul grow, Amanda began to worry that perhaps she had placed too much emphasis on motherhood and had neglected developing her interests outside the home. Now she worried that maybe it was too late to do anything about this predicament. She found herself feeling more and more insecure about who she was and where she was headed. She began to fear that things would only worsen as Paul got older. Unfortunately, there was no way to stop *that* from happening.

The more anxious Amanda felt about her situation, the more she reacted by refusing to acknowledge that what Paul was going through was a normal part of adolescence. The more he pulled away, the more Amanda panicked. The more she panicked, the harder she tried to keep Paul from pulling away.

Amanda carefully monitored Paul's activities, queried him each afternoon about his day at school, and planned all sorts of family outings. In her mind, she simply was being a good mother, making sure that Paul had the attention and guidance and affection she had always provided. But to Paul, whose needs for independence were developing at a normal pace, Amanda's attention was suffocating.

PAUL SPENCER

In his interview, Paul described his relationship with his mother in very different terms from those used by Amanda. She presented herself as well intentioned and caring, but misunderstood and greatly unappreciated. Her son saw her as intrusive, inflexible, and simply unwilling to let him grow up.

"She babies me," Paul complained. "Or if she doesn't baby me, she's on my back all the time." When I asked Paul one of our standard questions about how day-to-day decisions are made in their house, he hesitated. "It depends on whether it's my mom or my dad who's involved," he said. "My mom, you know, she and I usually argue until somebody gives in. My dad pretty much lets me go my own way." I asked for an example.

"OK, there was this time when me and my friends wanted to take the bus to West Town [a shopping mall], you know, to hang around, get something to eat, check out the stores. We weren't going to leave until after school got out, and I asked if it was OK if I had dinner at the mall. And she said, 'Out of the question,' like I was asking for something really outrageous. She said, no, I had to be home for dinner and we had to have dinner as a family. I mean, we have dinner together every night. I don't see what the big deal is if I miss dinner one time to be with my friends. So we had this fight and she made me stay home. It ended up that dinner was ruined anyway because I just ate as fast as I could and went up to my bedroom."

"Would your father have reacted differently?" I asked.

"I guess."

"Tell me how."

"I don't know. He's a lot looser about things. He probably would've said, 'Fine, just be back before 9:00,' or something like that. He would definitely have let me go."

I made a note to myself to look back over the Spencers' answers to our childrearing questionnaires, which would give some indication of how strict Paul's parents actually were, relative to other families in our study. I knew from years of interviewing teenagers that each believed that his or her parents were the strictest ones on the planet. Sure enough, though, on our measures Amanda was among the strictest mothers in our study. Her husband, Jonathan, while on the permissive side, was well within the average disciplinary range for fathers in our sample.

TYPES OF PARENTAL CONTROL

Amanda's excessive strictness was manifested in a particular way, which psychologists call *psychological control*. Rather than attempting to control Paul's behavior by having a lot of rules and regulations, Amanda attempted to control Paul by making him feel guilty for having his own opinions, by withdrawing her own affection and love when Paul didn't comply with her wishes, and by making Paul feel that it was wrong to have an emotional life outside the family. Adolescents whose parents use a lot of psychological control often experience their parents as intrusive and overprotective, which is exactly how Paul felt about Amanda. When children are subject to too much psychological control, they begin to feel ambivalent about becoming autonomous and may feel anxious and depressed, instead of excited and confident, about growing up.

At my university's psychological services clinic, we see many over-anxious children whose parents are very psychologically controlling—so much so that the normal, healthy psychological boundaries between individuals in the family have begun to break down, and relationships have become overly enmeshed. In some of these families, for example, when the child is asked by the therapist how he is feeling about something, one of the parents will answer the question before the child has had a chance to respond. When a child grows up in this sort of environment, it becomes difficult for him to tell which feelings are really his, and which are his parents'.

Actually, there are two different forms of control that parents use with their children. In addition to psychological control, which is aimed at controlling the child's sense of individuality, parents can also use what we call *behavioral control*, which is aimed at controlling the child's activities. Behavioral control is exercised by having a lot of rules, regulations, limits, and so on. Many adolescents react to excessive behavioral control by rebelling.

Parents who have been close with their child throughout childhood and who experience their child's maturation into adolescence as some sort of loss often react by becoming more psychologically controlling during the transition. Whereas controlling the child through excessive rules and regulations—that is, through behavioral control—maintains the parent's sense of authority over the child, controlling the child psychologically is a technique that parents employ in order to maintain the child's emotional dependency on them. Since it is the loss of this dependency—rather than the loss of authority—that parents like Amanda fear most, they resort to parenting practices that try to keep the child emotionally dependent.

JONATHAN SPENCER

I pursued the issue of the Spencers' disciplinary differences in my interview with Amanda's husband a few weeks later. He was a friendly, handsome, expansive man, youthful in his blue jeans and denim work shirt, and I could imagine that Jonathan Spencer was a favorite among the students at his high school. He was animated and expressive as we spoke over glasses of ginger ale at the Spencers' kitchen table.

"Oh, there's no question that Amanda is the disciplinarian around here," he said, taking a sip and smiling. "But early on we sort of divided the labor that way. It was kind of an unspoken thing, I guess. Being a teacher, I'm with kids all day long, trying to keep my classroom running smoothly. It takes a lot out of you, working with teenagers. Don't get me wrong—I love it. I love teaching, and I love my kids. But it's draining. I am beat at the end of the day. Hell, if Amanda wants to play cop around here, that's fine with me. I play cop all day long."

I asked Jonathan whether he and his wife had conflicts over discipline.

"Well, I'm basically a pushover with Paul, and that bugs her. I suppose it is mostly my fault, but I think she's too hard on him. I see a lot of kids at school with problems, big problems, and I know how lucky we are to have Paul. He's a good kid—a very nice kid. Actually, as Paul has gotten older, I've become more lenient and she's tightened the reins. I guess we sort of balance each other out in that way. I just can't see placing too many restrictions on a boy Paul's age. This time should be fun for him. I keep telling Amanda to sit back and enjoy things more. I don't know why she can't. I keep telling her, 'No wonder you're so down in the dumps all the time.' "

It was clear to me that part of the difficulty Amanda was having in accepting Paul's maturation inhered in the obvious contrast that existed between her response and her husband's. Jonathan viewed Paul's transition into adolescence as an opportunity—for a closer and better relationship with his son, for a sort of invigoration. His wife saw it as a loss—of purpose, of affection, of identity.

"I've always liked teenagers," Jonathan told me. "And I've always looked forward to the day when Paul would be old enough for us to be good friends, real buddies. Now that this time has come, I'm having loads of fun. I'm a sort of sports nut, and I've pushed Paul in that direction, too. When we're not playing something, we're watching something. Now, instead of heading over to the stadium alone on a football Saturday, Paul and I head over together. It's nice to have company after all those years of sitting by myself. Amanda hates going to the games." Jonathan was referring to the university's football games, which were major events on the town's fall calendar.

When I asked Jonathan about his own adolescence, he responded that he did not have much of one. "I grew up outside Cleveland. My father left us when I was very young. I have one brother and one sister; I'm the youngest. I don't really remember him—my father—at all. My mother had a tough time of it raising us alone. She worked in a bakery. Never remarried. She died last year, actually, and we all drove back [home] for the funeral. Anyway, when I was a kid, money was always tight, and we never had much to go around. I always worked after school to help out—so did my brother and sister—and I never really had much time for fun, for the normal teenage stuff. I guess that's why I've tried so hard to be pals with Paul."

What had started as Jonathan's desire to provide Paul with the adolescence that he himself had been deprived of had turned into a genuinely close friendship between father and son. There was nothing inherently wrong with this. As sometimes happens in families of only children, however, the developing closeness between one parent and the child may begin to feel isolating to the other parent, who may feel jealous of the relationship and neglected by both child and spouse. When this occurs, the "unified front" that the parents had presented toward the child begins to break down, and conflicts over discipline frequently arise.

The Spencers reminded me a lot of the Merricks, the family you met in the second chapter. In many regards, the issues each family was struggling with were similar. I was not surprised, because the two families shared in common a firstborn adolescent son, a mother who had invested a great deal in childrearing, and a father who tried to use his son's adolescence as a means of holding on to his own youth.

THE SPENCERS' CONFLICT OVER CHILDREARING

Over the course of our study, I saw conflicts over childrearing erupt in many families. Sometime in their child's early adolescence, one parent would begin to become increasingly strict, while the other would become more and more lenient, almost in response to the strict parent. In many such homes, conflicts over whether and how much to rein in the adolescent took their toll on the marriage. Indeed, one of the things that single mothers almost universally expressed satisfaction over was not having to fight with a spouse about childrearing.

I came to understand that differences between parents over how, and how much, to control their adolescent often reflect differences in their individual experiences of midlife. Parents like Amanda, who over the years have invested their time and energy exclusively in the parental role, feel confused and threatened by the changing nature of the parent-child relationship and, in particular, by the adolescent's developing sense of autonomy. In response to these feelings, the parent frequently reacts by trying to exert more control over the adolescent. For these parents, holding on to the adolescent is tantamount to holding on to their own identity. Because of this, the imminent "loss" of the adolescent looms that much larger.

Most adolescents, however, resist their parent's attempts at control and respond by distancing themselves even further. This, of course, only feeds the parent's worst fears, and exacerbates his or her feelings of internal turmoil. In Amanda's case, Paul's normal growth toward emotional autonomy left her feeling purposeless and empty. Instead of trying to find new ways to connect with Paul, Amanda continued to try to re-create their old relationship. This strategy was doomed to failure, though, since it clashed with Paul's needs to feel grown-up and emotionally mature. Ultimately, because he did have one parent who was willing to accept his autonomy—his father—Paul was able to develop along a reasonable emotional timetable. But in the process, Amanda's mental health suffered.

In many other families with similar dynamics, the spouse who is having an easier time of things is able to come to the aid of the spouse who is having difficulty, either by helping the struggling partner face the midlife issues constructively or simply by devoting special attention to the marriage. In the case of the Spencers, however, Jonathan's own developmental history—specifically, his desire to create a sort of adolescence for himself through bonding with Paul—clouded his ability to see how Amanda was really feeling. It was not that he was angry with her—he had long ago accepted that Amanda was stricter and more "uptight" than he was. Unfortunately, the worse Amanda felt, the more Jonathan felt aligned with Paul and withdrew from Amanda, which only exacerbated her sense of isolation. Not fully aware of where this isolation stemmed from, Amanda began to view Jonathan's relationship with Paul disparagingly. It was almost as if she felt that her husband and son had teamed up against her.

When we spoke about her husband, Amanda cast Jonathan's permissiveness in a different and unflattering light. "Oh, it's like he's found his own lost adolescence, or something," she said sardonically. "Honestly, sometimes he seems more excited about Paul's life than Paul does. Jon had a very tough time with his own mother when he was a teenager, and I think he's eager to see Paul have the adolescence he never had. Jon's afraid that if he lays down the law, Paul won't be his good buddy anymore. So he pretty much leaves the discipline up to me. And, naturally, I get labeled as the Wicked Witch of the West by everyone around here."

It was clear to me that Amanda had been thinking a lot about these issues and, moreover, that she was irritated with Jonathan for boxing her into this disciplinary corner. I knew that it wasn't worth trying to determine what had occurred first—whether Amanda's strictness had led to Jonathan's permissiveness or vice versa. All that mattered was that once the cycle had begun, one spouse's behavior pushed the other one's buttons in all the wrong ways.

"Oh, I don't know," said Jonathan when I asked if their marriage had changed at all as Paul had moved into adolescence. "We disagree more about how to raise Paul, as I was saying before. But in other ways, it seems pretty much the same. Maybe we're a little less close now than we have been at other times. Marriages have their ups and downs, I suppose."

I was always thankful that we had collected "hard" data on people's marital relations, because this was a topic that many husbands and wives felt difficult to discuss openly in interviews. I had learned over the years that a statement like "marriages have their ups and downs" often means "our marriage is going through a bad time."

The Spencers' scores on our standardized measures of marital satisfaction and marital cohesion bore out my hunch. On both indices—the first, an index of how happy each was in the marriage, the second, an index of how close each felt to the other—the Spencers appeared to be a couple whose marriage was in decline. Their satisfaction and cohesion scores had dropped over the last year—Jon's by a modest amount, but Amanda's by quite a bit.

As it turned out, Amanda, in her interview, was less sanguine than Jonathan about the state of their marriage. "It's not just that I feel I'm losing Paul," she said, "it's that I feel I'm losing Jon along with him. It's almost as if Jon is pulling away at the same time Paul is. To tell you the truth, I think Paul's growing up would bother me less if Jon and I were doing better. It's not that we have a bad marriage. It's just that . . . that you might expect, well, I guess, *I* expected, that as Paul grew up and moved away, Jon and I would grow closer together. I'm not sure why, but the opposite seems to be happening."

Actually, Amanda's intuition was partially correct. Some couples do become closer as their child moves into adolescence. Sarah Fein, the aspiring science-fiction writer, and her husband, Dan, an insurance salesman, actually reported increases in both satisfaction and cohesion as their son Douglas grew into adolescence. As Doug matured, his parents spent more time together and enjoyed each other's company more and more. I saw this pattern emerge often in families in which both parents responded to their child's adolescence with a sense of freedom or rejuvenation. They were able to channel these positive feelings into their marriage.

The Feins, for example, would take advantage of their son's maturity—and the fact that he enjoyed spending more time with his friends—by doing more things for fun as a couple. When Douglas went out after dinner for a neighborhood basketball game, his parents would often take the family dog out for a walk, or stroll arm in arm up to the corner shopping area for ice cream.

In the case of the Spencers, however, their child's adolescence had clearly taken a toll on their marriage. The couple's differences over childrearing were real on one level, but symbolic on another. Discussions over whether one was too strict or the other too lenient reflected and symbolized the different ways in which Amanda and Jonathan Spencer defined their son's entry into adolescence. For Amanda, this transition was one of loss—a loss of role, a loss of identity, a loss of relationship. She responded by trying to hold on out of fear. For Jonathan, the transition was positive, even, perhaps, a bit of a second chance for himself. He responded with energy and enthusiasm. This clash of viewpoints drove a wedge between them.

ADOLESCENT INDIVIDUATION AND PARENTAL REJECTION

As I pieced together various parts of the Spencers' puzzle, I began to discern a pattern that was all too common in the families we studied. The trigger is the adolescent's press toward emotional autonomy. As the child attempts to define a separate sense of self—to individuate—one of the parents begins to panic, fearing being left behind. As the child begins to pull away from the parent, by seeking privacy, by being less physically affectionate, by deidealizing and criticizing, the parent may begin to question his or her own identity: *What is going to happen to me once my child grows up?*

In the Spencers' case, this dynamic was intensified both by the fact that Amanda had invested so much of her adult life in being home full time and by the fact that Paul was an only child. She had no idea what her life would be—actually, what *she* would be—in the context of a changing mother-child relationship. Rather than face the unknown, she attempted to stop the process from happening.

Over time, Amanda's doubts began to churn themselves into a personal crisis—she became despondent and anxious, and regretful about having chosen full-time homemaking. Her response to Paul's growing up—to tighten the emotional reins—was an understandable attempt to exert control over a situation that was making her feel out of control. Unfortunately, her attempts at psychological control had just the opposite effect on Paul from what she wanted; as she tried harder to keep him close, he only pulled away more aggressively.

Jonathan's stance aided Paul while at the same time making Amanda's situation worse. Paul, through his relationship with his father, was able to find some relief from his mother's psychological control and avoid the internalized distress that adolescents often feel when both parents are overprotective or overwhelmingly intrusive. Amanda's intrusiveness made Paul pull away from her with more urgency, and this only contributed further to Amanda's despair and anxiety. What Amanda needed—the support and understanding of her *husband*, not her son—was, unfortunately, not forthcoming. If anything, over time, the Spencers' marriage was weakened by the situation.

Although Amanda's being a homemaker and Paul's being an only child exacerbated the Spencers' situation, I saw similar dynamics unfold in families with employed mothers and in those with several children, like the Merricks. I also saw similar patterns in some fathers' relationships with their firstborn child, particularly among men who had invested a great deal of energy in fatherhood. The critical factor in this process did not seem to be whether the parent worked or whether the parent was male or female, but, rather, whether the parent experienced the child's development as some sort of loss. As we shall see, how parents define the adolescent transition profoundly affects how events in the family unfold and what impact they have on the family's mental health.

8. POWERLESSNESS

Gray Miller, Ellen Hansen, and Cindy Hansen

Dealing with the adolescent's developing sense of independence is one of the hardest struggles—perhaps *the* hardest struggle—that parents and teenagers face in their changing relationship. Whenever I speak to a group of parents about raising teenagers, their main concerns invariably touch on questions of the adolescent's growing desire for autonomy: Why is my child challenging my opinion all the time? How much freedom should I grant? When should I hold my position, and when should I give in to my adolescent's demands?

Over the course of our study, I came to understand that parents' concerns about how to deal with issues of adolescent independence really needed to be considered on two different levels. On the surface, these questions often reflected parents' legitimate anxieties about their child's well-being. They were genuinely worried about whether early dating would compromise their child's social development, whether granting a late curfew would endanger their child's welfare, whether permitting attendance at a party without adult supervision would tempt their child toward risky behavior.

The more I probed these issues in interviews with parents, however, the more I saw that for many of them the adolescent's drive toward independence touched a raw nerve that was not really related to concerns about the child's welfare. Too many parents seemed too concerned about issues that were obviously too trivial to worry so much about. Why would a parent struggle—and I mean really struggle—with a teenager over whether she did her homework at four in the afternoon or eight at night, especially if she was performing just fine in school? Why did so many parents spend so much time grappling with their children over such mundane things as the way they styled their hair or the music they listened to? Why did parents invest so much energy in battles over their teenager's wardrobe? *These* confrontations were certainly not motivated by concerns about the child's welfare.

As I thought further, I realized that, on another level, parents' concerns about adolescent autonomy also were concerns about power—or, more accurately, powerlessness. Many of the parents in our study, like Gray Miller, were having trouble coping with feeling out of control.

Gray was one of the thirty or so stepfathers who participated in our study. At forty-nine, he was also one of the older fathers in our sample. At the time of our interview, Gray, who was employed as a fleet-lease manager for a Ford dealership, had been married to Ellen Hansen, a forty-year-old medical secretary, for about three years. They lived with Ellen's three children: Cindy, fifteen; Michael, thirteen; and Betsy, twelve. Gray also had four children from a previous marriage who were in their twenties and living on their own.

The Miller-Hansen household was one of the most conflict-ridden in our sample. According to their own reports on our questionnaires, family members fought frequently and bitterly. My interviews revealed that arguments over power and authority had been raging steadily in the household for the past year or so. At least one argument had resulted in physical fighting, with Gray shoving Cindy against the wall of her bedroom while Ellen watched, horrified. Fortunately, the Millers entered into family therapy immediately after this incident, and things had calmed down somewhat.

Had I met the Miller family two years earlier, I would have come away with a different picture. At that time, one year into the marriage, things were going very well. But problems had surfaced after Cindy went through puberty, shortly after her thirteenth birthday. For the Millers, Cindy's and Michael's adolescence was a period of storm after one of surprising calm, a pattern that I saw in several stepfamilies. In our study, as well as several others, stepfamilies were having a great deal of difficulty adapting to a child's adolescence.

Gray had entered the family expecting to be a white knight, rescuing Ellen from her postdivorce poverty, providing Michael with the male role model he felt the boy needed, and restoring order to a household that he perceived had become far too lax. Initially, Gray's arrival was accepted by Ellen's three children. But as Cindy and Michael, the two older children, moved into adolescence, problems in the family began to erupt over relatively trivial issues.

In our questionnaires, we make independent assessments of how frequently and how angrily family members fight with one another. We do this because we have found that it is the *intensity* of conflict, and not the frequency, that harms people's mental health. In fact, some of the healthiest families in our sample report having very frequent—but very calm—arguments. As I mentioned before, full-out conflict was rare in our sample.

I was worried about the Millers, though. Not only did they argue often, the conflicts were exceedingly angry, especially those between Gray and Cindy.

GRAY MILLER

Gray Miller greeted me warmly when I came to the front door. "Here for a little head-shrinking, Doc?" he joked. "You've come to the right place. Just show me where the ticket dispenser is and I'll take a number." I laughed.

"Why don't we sit out back?" Gray offered. "It's such a beautiful day." I followed Gray around the side of their house and into their back yard. We sat in facing Adirondack chairs in the Millers' small but neatly tended garden.

Gray was a large, powerfully built man, and he looked as if he could have been a professional athlete at an earlier age. He wore a tight-fitting knit shirt that emphasized his muscles. He was balding, and his face was tan and deeply lined from years in the sun. While we spoke, he fiddled with a yellow, plastic Whiffle bat. Occasionally, he would hit the bat against the leg of his chair to punctuate his answers. I wondered what it felt like to have him as a stepfather.

Based on what I had seen in the Millers' questionnaires, I wasn't surprised that our conversation quickly turned to the topic of fighting. I asked him to tell me about a recent argument.

THE SOFA STRUGGLE

"I had been in the kitchen, finishing up the dinner dishes," he began. "The kids had gone off to watch TV. I can't remember where Ellen was at the time—I think she went upstairs to fold the laundry. Anyway, after I finished I came into the living room and found the kids sprawled all over the sofa, watching some stupid game show. I said, 'In this house we sit on the sofa, we don't lie down on it.' Michael looked up at me and said, 'Mom always lets us lie on the sofa.' I stared at him and said, 'Well, I'm not your mother, and I don't like it.' Then Cindy looks over and she says, 'Well, you're not our father, either.'

"I stood there, waiting for them to sit up. I said to Cindy, 'What's that supposed to mean?' But nobody said anything back—they just ignored me and turned back to their program. I'll tell you, I was furious. So I walked over to the television and turned it off and said, 'That's it, then, no television. Everybody up to their bedrooms.' Before they could start their back talk, I said, 'You guys don't like it around here? Tough. What I say, goes.' They all gave me dirty looks." He banged the Whiffle bat against the chair.

I asked what happened next.

"The usual," he said. "Michael ran to Ellen and complained that I was being 'unfair'—that's the word of the month around here, 'unfair.' Then Ellen called down and said she wanted to talk to me, so I went upstairs and we stood in our bathroom, talking. I told her that she was too loose with the kids, that they had to learn some discipline. We discussed it for a while, and at first she disagreed, but in the end, she came around to my side, like she usually does. Then she went downstairs and into the living room and told the kids that she and I had talked things over and that we had agreed that from now on, the sofa was for sitting. Case closed. End of story."

GRAY MILLER'S FRUSTRATION

I surprised Gray by what I asked next. "It must have hurt your feelings an awful lot when Cindy said that you're not her father. After all, you've invested a lot of time and emotional energy in trying to be a good father to them."

Gray paused before responding. "Yes, I have. A real lot. It was easier when they were younger," he said, avoiding my question. "Now, everything is some sort of power struggle with them. These days, nothing seems to work, even when I really put my foot down. The problem, in my opinion, is that Ellen never had any rules for them. After the divorce, things became very loose around here. Not that I blame her. I mean, her ex wasn't giving her much in the way of support, and she was always fighting with him to make his payments. So she was working as many hours as she could, working overtime, working some weekends, and the kids were left to fend for themselves. You should have seen this place when I moved in. You couldn't tell *who* was in charge.

"We went through a good phase at the beginning—I guess you'd call it a sort of honeymoon. Everyone wanted things to work out. Oh, Cindy was a little jealous of me at first, but I had expected that and I knew it would pass. Mike, I think, was glad to have a man around the house again. I would spend a lot of time with him, playing ball and so on, which I think he enjoyed. Betsy—she's the youngest—was no problem at all.

"I got Ellen to see that she had really let things get out of hand and we sat down and discussed having some rules around the house. So we had a family meeting and we explained that things were going to change—nothing major, I said, but some small changes in the way that things were done. Honestly, I don't think the kids minded at all. At least, no one said anything to me at the time.

"For the first few months, I was feeling pretty good about how things were going. A lot of friends warned me about how tough it was going to be, being a stepfather, and I worried quite a bit about it. Also, things hadn't gone so well with my own kids, and I didn't want to go through that again."

I asked what he meant by this.

"The only real tragedy of my life was my divorce from my first wife. . . . Not so much that, but missing out on my children's growing years. I feel very guilty about that."

Gray was divorced from his first wife when his own children were still small, and he rarely saw them after the divorce. None of his children had graduated from high school. One of his sons had been in and out of trouble with the law; the other worked as a janitor. In her senior year of high school his older daughter had gotten pregnant, dropped out of school, married, and moved away; Gray hadn't heard from her in years. He considered his youngest child, who drifted from job to job and boyfriend to boyfriend, a lost cause.

Gray told me that he blamed himself for the way they turned out, but said, "I'm a realist. I can't wave a magic wand and make things different. What's done is done."

He was determined not to make the same mistakes again, though, and that agenda affected everyone in the family, as Gray admits. "Seeing my own children going through their teens, all the problems they had, all the trouble they got into, I expected more of the same from Ellen's. Sometimes I think I'm not doing her kids justice. That I'm not giving them the freedom they deserve because of that shadow. . . .

"Anyway, about a year ago, all hell broke loose around here. It started with Cindy. All of a sudden she started questioning me, on every little thing. I'm not her real father, she would say. She didn't have to listen to me if she didn't want to. She wasn't a child anymore. I couldn't force her to obey me. That sort of thing. I could see it coming. I had been there before with my own. I told Ellen, 'It's time to tighten the reins.' Frankly, I couldn't stand the worrying. It was really eating away at me." Gray frowned and stared at the ground. "It still is."

I suspected that it was the loss of power, not the worrying over Cindy's welfare, that was eating away at Gray—this was a man who looked angry, not worried. Cindy was asserting her will and challenging his authority, and this really irked him. From his viewpoint, the family should have been grateful to Gray for rescuing the household from disciplinary disarray. Instead, he was being cast as an evil martinet. Unfortunately, the more Cindy asserted herself, the more threatened Gray felt, which only prompted him to be more dictatorial in his approach, since he believed that showing Cindy who was "really" in charge would restore his position of power. This strategy backfired, however, because it merely strengthened Cindy's resolve even further. I could see that the two of them were caught in an ever-spiraling battle of wills.

CINDY HANSEN

When I spoke a few weeks later with Cindy, I heard a different side of the sofa story. She had asked that we meet at her school, rather than talk at her home, because she felt uncomfortable talking about her family with them around. This was something that few teenagers in our study requested, and I took it as a sign that things were not going well at home at all. We sat in an empty classroom during one of her free periods. Clean-cut, attractive, and athletic-looking, Cindy looked like she had been sent by central casting to play the part of a high school cheerleader. Her fashionable, but conservative, clothes marked her as a member of the school's "preppie" crowd.

"We call him the dictator," Cindy said, referring to her stepfather. "I really think that something's wrong with him. Really, I do. I mean, he blows these little things up way out of proportion. It didn't bother me so much at first, the way he was, because I really wanted things to work out for my mom. So I would go along with whatever he'd say. And then I'd go to my mom when he wasn't around and complain. But whenever I would complain to her, she'd remind me that we really needed the money and that we wouldn't be able to live as well as we did if it wasn't for Gray. She would even say that she disagreed with him but didn't want to contradict him in front of us, because she was worried that if he got unhappy, he'd leave. But you know what? I'd rather be poor and not have to live with him. Him and all of his idiotic rules. We were much happier before he moved in."

I asked Cindy to give me an example of something they had argued about recently. "OK, here's one. Last week Mike and Betsy and I were watching TV and Gray barges in and yells at us for lying on the couch while we were watching and before we could say anything, he just goes and turns the television off and storms out of the room. I mean, we didn't have shoes on or anything, so it wasn't like the couch was going to get dirty. He is so *unfair*."

How did her mother act when she and Gray disagreed?

"She always takes his side. That's the thing that really bothers me. I mean, for all those years before Gray came, it was fine to lie on the couch. Now all of a sudden, it's not. It's like she doesn't have an opinion anymore. It's like she's a different person. I don't understand it. It makes me wonder, well, what does she *really* think is right, the way things were around here before Gray, or the way things are now?"

I got a partial answer to Cindy's question in my interview with Ellen.

ELLEN HANSEN

Like her husband, Ellen Hansen Miller was also trim and athletic. In fact, they had met at a health club and had continued to work out together over the next several years. We chatted in her kitchen over coffee one Saturday morning. Ellen was wearing a sweatshirt and sweatpants. I remembered that when we had scheduled the interview, she had told me that she would have to leave promptly at 10:30 for her regular tennis game. A tennis racquet and gym bag sat on the floor next to the back door.

After some preliminaries, we got to the subject of Gray and the children. Ellen told me that she felt caught between her husband and her children. "There is a lot of competition between him and the kids for my time and attention." She said she doesn't want to have to choose between them, but often the choice was forced upon her. Ellen felt that Cindy didn't appreciate how much Gray cared for her, and that hurt. "If she only knew how much he loves her, how he brags about her. . . ."

But it was clear to me that Ellen still was feeling somewhat uneasy about having remarried, even though it had been three years already. I felt that at some level, she needed her daughter to approve her decision to remarry, by accepting Gray into the family.

At the same time, Ellen admitted that sometimes Gray was overbearing. "He means well, but he comes off a little too hard, a little too suspicious of anything that doesn't seem quite right. He gets very upset about something that doesn't seem like a big deal. I'm much more easygoing. You know, this is really a new thing for Gray—having children to take care of. He and his wife split up when their kids were very young, and he didn't have all that much contact with them. So all of this is unfamiliar territory. With time, I'm sure he'll relax, take things a bit easier. He's going to have to, or he's going to drive us all crazy."

Ellen saw her role as that of peacemaker, but it was not a position she enjoyed.

"It's awful to be in the middle and try to make both parties understand that you're not taking sides. I feel I always have to get Gray's approval and then I have to defend him to Cindy. What's really hard is trying to make him seem good to her when, in fact, I don't totally agree with him, either."

Ellen had worked out a partial solution.

"I've learned that there are some things that are better left just between the two of us, between me and Cindy. I try to include him as much as possible. But I don't want to cause any more uproar, upset, than there needs to be. I remind myself how hard things were when we were on our own." She pointed to the tennis gear. "Believe me, I wasn't off playing tennis on Saturday mornings when I was single."

Most of the time Ellen felt she was caught in a no-win situation, however. If she didn't include Gray in discussions, he felt betrayed; if she did, Cindy felt betrayed. The big loser, in Ellen's mind, was her marriage. She said that the honeymoon was over far too soon. "I wish there was some way we could put some of the sparkle back." She talked wistfully about the way it used to be, when they were dating and had time for just the two of them, without the kids; Gray thought nothing about paying for a babysitter so that he and Ellen could go out alone. But Ellen also missed the time she and the children spent doing things together, without Gray.

DEFINING THE LINES OF AUTHORITY

The Millers' struggle to define the lines of authority was a common one in remarried families. Having seen similar situations many times before, I could sympathize with each member of the family. More often than not, the children in this situation had grown accustomed to a relatively more lenient atmosphere; our studies, as well as many others, have shown consistently that single mothers are, on average, far more permissive than married mothers. The arrival of a stepfather—especially one who, like Gray, sees his task as the imposition of order into a family system that has gotten out of hand—clashes with the child's understandable desire to retain the looser, more relaxed climate that had prevailed.

But research also has shown that the impact of remarriage depends a lot on the child's age and sex. If the remarriage occurs during the child's elementary school years, he or she is more likely to accept the newly imposed structure in return for having the attention of a second parent in the home; this is especially true for boys. If the parent's remarriage occurs in the child's preadolescent or early adolescent years, however—as it did for Cindy Hansen—the child is likely to perceive the costs of living within the new order as far outweighing the benefits of gaining an additional parent. In this context, struggles over authority are virtually inescapable, and they are often most bitter between stepfathers and stepdaughters. Daughters perceive that they have even less to gain, and more to lose, by the entrance of a stepfather into the family. The family may enjoy a brief honeymoon right after the marriage, but this rarely lasts through the child's puberty.

Although power struggles are common in stepfamilies with young teenagers, they are by no means limited to remarried homes. Many parents' sense of authority is threatened by their adolescent's drive toward autonomy, even in homes in which no divorce has occurred. Bob Peterson, for example, the hospital administrator whom you met in an earlier chapter, struggled with his son David in a way that was reminiscent of Gray and his stepchildren. The Petersons' battles over whether David would do his homework before or after practicing his guitar were struggles over power, comparable to Gray's argument with Cindy and Michael over whether they could lie down on the sofa while watching television.

In neither case could the parent articulate a good reason for the regulation in question. For Bob, it was simply "a matter of making sure that David had his priorities straight," even though David's academic record should have been ample evidence that he took his schoolwork seriously. In Gray's case, no rationale for the sofa rule was provided at all. All he could say when challenged was that reclining on the sofa simply was something that wasn't going to be permitted in his household.

In each family, it appeared on the surface that the parent's desire was being imposed just to show the child who was in control. I wondered as well whether the regulation wasn't also being put into place to counter the parent's own feeling of powerlessness. I came to see that the critical factor in understanding the genesis of power struggles between adolescents and parents was not whether the adult in question was the child's biological parent but, rather, the degree of importance the parent placed on his or her role as an authority figure. If this was a crucial aspect of the adult's definition of what it means to be a parent, he or she was going to have a tough time of it during the child's adolescence.

POWERLESSNESS

Powerlessness is a difficult state to accept for many midlife adults, particularly midlife men. Middle adulthood is a period during which many men achieve the highest level of power they will enjoy during their work career. Although a few more rungs may remain on the occupational ladder, by their mid-forties, most men have climbed high enough to be able to judge how far they will ultimately go—what psychologists call the *occupational plateau*.

For the minority who indeed have achieved their dreams, being challenged at home by a teenager feels irritating and unfamiliar. As one business executive told me, "I sit in meetings making fairly important decisions all day long. People pay attention to me. They respect my judgment and listen to what I say, and when I ask for something to be done, it gets done. I worked hard to get here, and, to tell you the truth, it feels damn good. Sometimes, when I get a moment to myself at the end of the day, I look around my office and just smile to myself. And I think, the stress and all the long hours really have paid off. I get in my car, turn on some nice music, and drive home. And then what? I have dinner across the table from a fourteen-year-old who tells me, in so many words, that I have my head up my ass. I'm supposed to be calm and communicative? It's hard not to lose my temper. If anyone at work acted that way, he'd be out the door in no time flat." He laughed. "Believe me, there are days when I wish I could fire my own kid."

Maintaining one's composure in the face of a challenge to one's authority is difficult for individuals who are accustomed to being in complete control at work. But being questioned or even belittled by one's adolescent is even more irksome for those who have little authority in the workplace, because their sense of powerlessness at home only reinforces their feeling that there is no place, no situation, in which they are at all in control.

Gray Miller fell into this latter category. He scored quite low on our measure of occupational satisfaction and quite high on our measure of midlife rumination. I learned during our interview that work had never been especially satisfying to him—that he had always felt underemployed. In combination with his regrets about his first marriage, Gray's dissatisfaction with his career left him feeling like a failure. He had resigned himself to having a career that wasn't all he had hoped for. For Gray, though, marrying Ellen and moving in with her children was a second chance in the marital arena—an opportunity to start over, to right the wrongs he had committed in his first family, to raise the kind of children and enjoy the kind of happy family life he had missed the first time around.

When things got off to a good start, he felt proud. But now that things had turned rocky, Gray was beginning to doubt himself again. He was asserting his authority over his stepchildren partly as a means of reassuring himself of his own competence. What he did not understand was that this approach to childrearing was not going to succeed, especially with children who had gotten used to a relatively more permissive environment. Now he was feeling that things were beyond his control.

One of the most interesting questions we asked parents came at the end of our interview. After we had covered all of the scheduled topics, I asked "Knowing what you do now about being the parent of a young teenager, what advice would you give to someone with a six-year-old, in order to prepare them for their child's adolescence?" I had included this question in order to give the interview a feeling of closure, not realizing before the study began that it would elicit different and, in some cases, revealing answers from our respondents. Many parents responded by saying something like, "Spend time with your child," "Make sure your child knows you're always there for him [her]," or "Let them be themselves."

Gray responded with two words: "Good luck."

POWERLESSNESS AND PARENTAL DEPRESSION

Psychologists have known for many years that feelings of powerlessness can have adverse effects on our mental health and well-being. Over time, the experience of powerlessness can lead to feelings of worthlessness ("If I were really a competent parent, this wouldn't have happened to me"); helplessness ("There is nothing I can do that will make a difference"); and hopelessness ("Things are just going to get worse"). All of these feelings can lead to depression and other forms of internalized distress, such as anxiety, insomnia, and psychosomatic problems. Unfortunately, the more depressed we become, the more worthless, helpless, and hopeless we feel, and this only exacerbates the situation.

Feelings of powerlessness are especially debilitating if they persist despite our attempts to establish or maintain control. Doomed to failure, continued attempts to assert control over an uncontrollable situation necessarily lead to ill feelings—and literally, to feeling ill. On the other hand, when we are able to look realistically at a situation over which we have no control and say, "There's really nothing I can do about this—I might as well stop banging my head against the wall," we typically feel relieved. By attributing the difficulty to the uncontrollability of the situation, rather than to our failure to have controlled it, we protect our self-esteem and maintain our confidence in our abilities. It is not the same as "giving up" or "giving in"—it is more like "going with it."

Most of what we have learned about individuals' responses to powerlessness comes from laboratory investigations in which individuals are studied after they have been made to feel helpless. For example, a researcher might ask a subject to solve a problem that looks easy but that in reality has no solution—completing an impossible maze, for instance—and measure his mood before, during, and after the task. Even in these short-term and artificially constructed situations, powerlessness has been found to have deleterious consequences for people's mental and physical health. Over time, individuals become tense, depressed, and irritated.

There has not been a lot of research on the consequences of powerlessness in the parent-child relationship. But we can assume that because adolescence inevitably involves an increase in the child's drive toward autonomy, it almost invariably entails a decline in the parents' feelings of control, and that the consequences of trying to maintain control in the face of an uncontrollable situation will be similar in real life to what has been found in laboratory-based studies.

Parents who persist in attempting to maintain the same level of power over their teenage child as they had when the child was younger will nearly always encounter difficulty in doing so. The natural progression in the parent-child relationship at this time is toward a more equal balance of power. Very few adolescents will tolerate increases in their parents' power over them; most, in fact, will feel that they are *entitled* to more autonomy and freedom with age. Thus, to the extent that adults evaluate their own competence as parents in terms of the degree to which they control their child, they are more than likely to come away feeling frustrated and powerless. As a consequence, they will feel agitated, irritated, and depressed.

POWERLESSNESS VERSUS ASSURANCE

Not all parents see the parental role in this way, however. In order to better understand the ways in which parents differed in their definition of the parental role, we included on our questionnaire a series of questions that asked mothers and fathers to rank twelve different aspects of parenting, from most to least important. Some had to do with providing guidance (e.g., "Being an example of a person with admirable values."), others had to do with providing support and affection (e.g., "Supporting my children when they feel troubled or upset."), and others had to do with setting limits and maintaining authority (e.g., "Being able to develop some rules to ensure smoother family functioning.").

Although each of these three dimensions of parenting—guidance, affection, and authority—is important to some degree to all parents, and although children need a certain amount of all three, parents differ in their relative emphases. Gray Miller was one of those parents who ranked authority and limit setting well above affection or guidance. Not surprisingly, conflicts between parents and teenagers were most common in households in which parents placed relatively more emphasis on authority, and relatively less on other parts of being a good parent. And, not surprisingly, it was the adults in our sample who emphasized authority as a key component of parenting who were most vulnerable to feelings of powerlessness when their child hit adolescence.

Parents who emphasized their roles as providers of guidance or affection were, in contrast, far less likely to experience their child's independence as a loss of power. Interestingly, their children were no less insistent on seeking autonomy than were adolescents whose parents placed special emphasis on obedience and authority. One important lesson I learned from this study is that differences in parents' experiences during their children's adolescence have just as much to do with differences in parents' perceptions and beliefs as they do with differences in their adolescents' behaviors. In some regards, then, the adolescent's drive for independence is common across families—a given. Some parents, like Gray Miller, took this as a threat to their authority. But others, like Ed O'Hara, reacted to their adolescent's autonomy with confidence and assurance.

ED O'HARA

Ed was a city police officer and the father of a fifteen-year-old girl who, as it happens, attended the same school as Cindy Hansen. Although one might expect that someone from his occupation would have emphasized power and authority in his relationship with his child, nothing could have been further from the truth in Ed's case. If anything, Ed was relieved not to have to play "cop" at home. I asked him what type of child his daughter was.

"She's a great kid," he told me, beaming. "She's sweet and responsible, she has a great sense of humor, and she's a good student.

Frankly, we have had very few problems with Sally, knock on wood. We don't have to keep close tabs on her because we have faith that she'll do the right thing. Oh, I'm sure she'll make mistakes, but that's what growing up is all about. I don't see my job as making her decisions for her. I'm here to give her advice and to give her a shoulder to cry on if she needs one."

I asked if he thought that raising Sally was more difficult now that she was a teenager. "More difficult? No, I wouldn't say that. It's different, but not more difficult. It was never hard with her, but if anything, it was more time consuming when she was younger. My wife and I spent a lot of time with her growing up, making sure she got a lot of love and a lot of structure. I suppose you would have called us strict. But looking back, I think it was a good investment. Now that she's a bit older, we sort of sit back and watch our investment pay off.

"The other night, she came to me with a problem. She had been babysitting for some people down the street on Friday evenings, which she enjoyed. Well, they liked her so much that they offered her a regular babysitting job after school during the week. It was going to tie her up every day. She wanted to take the job because she wanted the money to buy clothes, but if she took it, she'd have to give up her team sports—she plays sports most afternoons. I had my own opinion—I thought that playing sports was more important than buying clothes at this age—they all spend far too much on clothes. But I wanted it to be her decision, so I kept my mouth shut. I told her that she should think through her options and decide for herself—you know, weigh all the pros and cons.

"Well, she thought about it for a couple of days and one night announced that she was going to take the job. Now, that's not what I wanted her to do, but I thought it was more important for her to make her own decision and live with the consequences than to do what I said just because I saw it a different way. It wasn't like it was a matter of life and death, right?"

At the end of our interview, I asked Ed the usual closing question—what advice would you give to the parents of a six-year-old?

"Spend a lot of time with them when they're young. Teach them what's important. Then you'll be able to relax more when they're teenagers."

POWERLESS PARENTS AND OUT-OF-CONTROL TEENAGERS

Although many parents feel powerless in the face of their teenager's strivings for independence, they do not all respond to this feeling in the same way. Some parents experience such intense feelings of powerlessness that they disengage from their parental responsibilities. For these parents, the feeling of being out of control is so overwhelming and so frightening that they persuade themselves that no attempt at authority is possible. In these families, the parent's complete abdication of authority more often than not leads to unfortunate consequences for their teenager—behavior problems, run-ins with the law, difficulties in school. Ironically, the parents then use these problems to rationalize their own negligence, as if to say, "My child is so out of control that there is nothing I can do." Although this is true in a small minority of cases, in general, it is the absence of parental control that leads to children's problems, not the reverse.

It is more common, however, for parents to react to feelings of impotence with increased attempts at control—convincing themselves that the problem is that they are not trying hard enough, just as Gray Miller did. This is a response that is far more common among fathers than mothers—not surprising, in view of the fact that men in our culture face strong socialization pressures against being seen as "quitters." For them, "going with the flow" of their child's adolescence without putting up a good fight is tantamount to "giving in." Because they frame the issue as a battle of wills, they cannot escape seeing the conflict as involving a "winner" and a "loser." Some fathers are able to accept battling and losing, but few are willing to concede the match without even trying.

I have yet to see a parent who frames the parent-child relationship in terms of winning and losing emerge from his or her child's adolescence as a winner. Invariably, such a parent comes away feeling frustrated and either angry or depressed. Often, so does the child.

9. REGRET

Theresa, Frank, and Maria Rossi

THERESA ROSSI

She recounted the time she had run away from home.

She had not gone far, and she had only stayed away for three days, but, of course, her family had worried. They did not understand how things could have gotten so bad that a grown woman, a wife and mother of three, would actually pack her bags and run away from home. That was the sort of thing that only happened in made-for-TV movies.

Theresa Rossi spoke at length about the incident during our interview. "I was fed up with all of them. Frank was always complaining about this or that, how I was too easy on the kids, especially Maria. *She* was driving me crazy, running around with her friends, in trouble at school, always on the phone with her boyfriend. And Richie—he's eleven—he was starting to get real mouthy. The baby—that's what I call Linda, even though she's five—was always coming down with something. Everyone was fighting. We couldn't get through a single day without some sort of blowup."

A few days later, I was listening to Theresa Rossi's interview in my office at the university. I paused the tape for a moment and stared out the window. I could see the throng of well-dressed students crossing the grounds on their way to midmorning classes. As I was watching the students laughing and talking cheerfully with each other as they walked, their backpacks slung casually over their shoulders, I couldn't help thinking how different Theresa's life was from that of most of the people who were fortunate enough to spend four years on this beautiful campus. There was very little physical beauty in Theresa's life. The Rossis lived on the other side of town, in a depressed and worn-down neighborhood.

I thought back to Theresa's story, of how it came to pass that she had run away from home.

"Anyway," Theresa told me, as we talked at the kitchen table that day, "I knew that my parents—they live down in Rockford—they were going on vacation, and I called and asked if I could stay at their place for a few days, while they were away, just until things cooled down. I guess I should have discussed it first with Frank, but I just had to get out of there. I called him when I got to Rockford. Boy, was he pissed." Theresa paused at this point to light a cigarette. She stared off for a few seconds and then smiled. "I can still remember pulling on to the interstate that morning, driving back to Illinois. I waited until everyone had left for school, and then I just packed my bag and took off. It was like I was a kid again, going back to my old house.

"It was good to get away, to get some distance. I did a lot of thinking down there, about my life, about different things. Frank. The kids. My job. How things have turned out. Anyway, when I came back, everyone was a lot nicer, at least for the next couple of weeks. Frank, Maria, Richie, even Linda, I think they all appreciated me more. Everything I do around here. Now things are back to the way they were, though. Back to being the slave and chauffeur." She laughed as she tapped the ash from her cigarette. "Maybe I'll have to hit the road again."

I asked Theresa to tell me about her childhood. The question took her by surprise. "I don't know, I was pretty wild when I was a kid, you know, during high school. My parents couldn't tell me anything. They sure as hell tried, but I wouldn't listen. Like a typical teenager. Like Maria is now. I ran around until all hours of the night, never paid much attention to school. All I cared about was having fun. Until Frank and I got together and we got married. Then everything changed. I was only eighteen."

. . .

More than one third of the adults in our study were, like Theresa and Frank Rossi, from blue-collar backgrounds. Like many of the working-class adults we studied, Theresa, thirty-four at the time, looked significantly older than her middle-class counterparts. The financial strain of making ends meet on the salaries she and her husband earned clearly had taken its toll on her appearance. I tried to picture her as she had described herself—as a wild, party-going teenager—but I had difficulty reconciling that characterization with the image of the woman who sat across from me that afternoon. Heavyset and hard edged, with tightly permed dark brown hair and eyeglasses whose frames had long been out of fashion, Theresa was hard to imagine as a free spirit. Quite the contrary: She seemed beaten down, resigned, embittered, angry. I would later learn that the Rossis' modest kitchen, where we sat and talked, with its yellowed Formica counters and worn linoleum floor, had seen its share of angry arguments—between spouses, between siblings, and between parents and children. Each of the Rossis whom I interviewed spoke about the high level of conflict in their household.

The psychological literature on middle age has not had much to say about the Theresa Rossis of this world. Surprisingly little has been written about the midlife concerns of working-class adults, as if to suggest, if only implicitly, that self-awareness and introspection are self-indulgent luxuries that only the affluent can afford. Popular portrayals of the midlife crisis, with their emphasis on the frustrations and emptiness of living on the fast track—the "crises of the rich and famous"—have helped to perpetuate the myth that only members of the professional class experience intense bouts of anguishing self-doubt and trepidation. However, while it is true that educated adults are more verbal and facile with the language of popular psychology when they are asked to describe their midlife experiences, feelings of internal turmoil are neither less prevalent nor less intense among blue-collar adults than among their more advantaged counterparts. Working-class adults merely speak about these concerns in different words.

If anything, the occupational routinization, the physical strain, the unpleasant living conditions, the relentless financial pressure of blue-collar life—all of these add even more stress to the inherent emotional difficulty of middle age. These stressors amplify existing feelings of dissatisfaction, rather than providing a distraction from it, as some middle-class adults mistakenly believe. Many middle-class individuals who are unfamiliar with blue-collar life romanticize its apparent simplicity, its putative freedom from "difficult" or "complicated" psychological struggles, as if the working-class adult never has time or energy to think about his or her life. Actually, nothing could be further from the truth. With few intellectual demands, manual labor actually permits a great deal of rumination. The next time you are folding laundry, chopping vegetables, or raking leaves, see for yourself.

Middle-class adults in the midst of psychological crisis at least have the means to pamper or divert themselves, if only for temporary relief: dinner out at a fancy restaurant, a "getaway" weekend without the children, a shopping spree at a favorite store, an aerobics workout and massage at the health club. They also may turn to psychotherapy—which is frowned upon by many working-class adults—as a possible means of coping.

In contrast, when psychological turmoil hits at midlife, blue-collar adults have fewer resources and, therefore, fewer options for alleviating it. When the turmoil of middle age hits, they have few places to turn. Theresa Rossi turned to the familiar and the affordable—the house in which she had grown up. Although her choice of destination—her parents' vacant house—was influenced mainly by price and proximity, I came to understand that it also symbolized her desire to return to her youth.

REGRET

I find myself wishing that I had the opportunity to start afresh and do things over, knowing what I do now.

Few items from our midlife rumination scale were endorsed as rousingly as this one. Nearly two thirds of all the women we studied said they had this feeling frequently, as did more than one half of the men in our sample. Look closely at the wording of the item, however. It does not say "I wish I were young again," nor does it simply say "I'd like to have a shot at another life." Rather, individuals who feel this way fantasize about combining a chance at a fresh start with the benefits of their accumulated wisdom ("knowing what I do now"). Despite what their spouses might shout in moments of angry frustration—barbs like, "Stop acting like a teenager"—midlife adults in the throes of a crisis are *not* interested in having a second adolescence; what they want is a second adulthood. Filled with misgivings about their choice of career, spouse, or lifestyle—or all three—they want a chance at another life. This time, though, they believe they will get it "right." Even many of those who are moderately satisfied still want another chance, if only to see if they can come closer to perfection the second time around.

Among the adults in our study, having a child enter adolescence frequently triggered feelings of regret, feelings which were often accompanied by a longing for another opportunity at building a different, and presumably more satisfying, life.

It was not until her daughter turned thirteen that Theresa Rossi began feeling this way. Before that time, Theresa had pretty much tolerated her life for what it was; although she missed feeling excited, the way she had when she was younger, she would never have described herself as unhappy. She knew that she and Frank did not have a perfect marriage, but she had grown to accept it. She certainly knew friends who had it worse.

As her daughter Maria grew into a young woman, however, Theresa began thinking more and more that her own life had not turned out the way she had hoped. She and Frank were arguing frequently, and Theresa was growing more and more disenchanted with their all-too-contentious relationship. Believing that her pervasive sense of dissatisfaction stemmed ultimately from their financial struggles—Frank earned only a meager salary as a repairman for the local telephone company—as soon as Linda, the Rossis' youngest, started preschool, Theresa took a job as a part-time data processor. She was able to work out of her home on a computer terminal provided by her employer, a large market research firm. Although the work wasn't especially interesting—in fact, it was downright tedious—it brought in extra money that the Rossis sorely needed, and Theresa felt some satisfaction every time she deposited her paycheck. She also felt good when her boss, pleased with Theresa's speed and accuracy, asked her to increase her work hours.

After six months on the job, however, Theresa's enthusiasm began to wane; the tedium of the work and the social isolation of being home alone for much of the day was getting to her. Rather than alleviating the pressure around the house, Theresa's work was only making her feel more tense. About the only positive thing she could say about her job was that the work had become so automatic that she no longer had to concentrate very hard while she did it—it was almost as if the numbers she was entering jumped off the data sheets and into her fingertips, bypassing her brain entirely.

The mindless work of data entry gave Theresa a lot of time to think. As she would type, Theresa's thoughts wandered from Frank, to the children, to her parents, and back to Frank. She found herself worrying a lot about Maria, ruminating about the problems she was having in disciplining her daughter.

Often while thinking about Maria she would find herself taken back to her own adolescence, replaying scenes from her high school days. Occasionally, an hour or two would pass while Theresa was lost in time, fifteen years earlier, before Maria was born.

THERESA ROSSI'S YOUTH

It was not surprising that in her daydreams Theresa's thoughts would shift so easily from her daughter to herself. As Maria had grown into a young woman, she had developed a striking resemblance to what Theresa had looked like when she had been that age: dark, pretty, and shapely. When her thoughts of Maria would be transformed into reminiscences of her own youth, though, Theresa would become progressively sad, then angry, then bitter. She found herself filled with regret over how her life had turned out. The more she thought about Maria, the more she ruminated about her own adolescence, the more upset Theresa became. Sometimes she would become so angry that she would explode at Maria the moment her daughter walked through the door at the end of the school day.

Theresa had grown up in a working-class section of Rockford. Her parents had both been factory workers in a nearby plant. During her senior year of high school, Theresa had started dating Frank, who was several years older and was working as a salesman at a local Ford dealership. Theresa had enjoyed the fact that Frank always had a new car to drive, and they frequently would spend Frank's days off from work on long drives through the Illinois countryside.

About two months before her high school graduation, Theresa discovered that she had become pregnant. She was in a bind over what to do. She did not feel ready for marriage and was unsure about her feelings for Frank. Nevertheless, Frank suggested that they marry, and Theresa's mother and father, Catholic and conservative, pushed for this resolution. That June, before she had begun to show any signs of the pregnancy, Theresa walked down the aisle with Frank. Maria was born the following spring, when Theresa was only nineteen. When Maria was four, Frank was laid off from work. The Rossis left Rockford and headed out of the state. One of Frank's friends had said that job opportunities were likely to be better outside of Rockford's depressed industrial economy.

It would be an exaggeration to say that Maria's inauspicious arrival had disrupted any well-reasoned plans that Theresa had made for her own future. She had not taken school very seriously and had not thought much about a career. She had assumed that, like many of the other girls who had grown up in her neighborhood, she would find some sort of office work in Rockford and spend young adulthood playing the field and having a good time with her friends. Her plans, however vague, certainly did not include early motherhood. Now, as she watched Maria begin to "run wild," as she put it, Theresa worried that her daughter was headed down the very road that Theresa wished she herself had been able to avoid. Unfortunately, Theresa felt paralyzed, unable to do anything about it.

THE LIFE REVIEW OF MIDDLE AGE

Psychologists who study the elderly describe a phenomenon they call the *life review*. According to these experts, in later adulthood we spend considerable time looking back over our life course in an attempt to make sense of the life we have led. Although most individuals engage in a life review, not all reach the same conclusions. Some emerge from the life-review process feeling satisfied and at peace, whereas others look back with disappointment and despair.

For many adults, watching a child become an adolescent also prompts a life review, albeit a far less exhaustive one than that in which we engage during late adulthood. Nevertheless, when we look at our child on the verge of entering adulthood, some of us begin to reconsider the important life decisions we made during this time in our own development. For many individuals, adolescence was a period of hard choices and momentous decisions. This is especially true among those from more modest backgrounds, who are more likely to have to make occupational and marital commitments earlier in life. As parents think back to their own youth, those who made bad choices when they were adolescents—or who simply had bad fortune—may be overcome by profound and intense feelings of regret.

Theresa found that she could not stop thinking about the spring of her senior year—she could still remember the anxiety she felt when she discovered that her period was late and the sickening sense of dread that filled her as she received the positive test results from the clinic nurse. She told Frank about the pregnancy a few days later but agonized over whether or how to break the bad news to her parents. After a few weeks of terrible morning sickness, she felt she had no choice but to tell them what had happened. Angrily, her parents told Theresa that marriage was the young couple's only option. Theresa told Frank this, and he reluctantly agreed. Theresa felt that she was trapped inside some vehicle that was being driven by someone else. If only she had never met Frank. If only they had been more careful.

Many early marriages like the Rossis' end in divorce. But somehow, Theresa and Frank's survived. Over time, Theresa even came to accept her lot. Although she knew that Frank was far from an ideal mate—he insisted on always having the last word and was prone to aggressive outbursts, especially after he had been drinking—she told herself that he was better than many of her friends' husbands. He was steadily employed and was a reliable provider. And while their marriage certainly had its bad times, the Rossis had worked out an acceptable, if unexciting, relationship. During the early years of marriage, between tending to young children and trying to keep their checkbook balanced, Theresa had not had much time for long reflections on what might have been had she not gotten pregnant at so early an age.

Now, though, with time on her hands, she was consumed both with worry over how Maria was turning out and with regret over her own past. She was beginning to question how long she could continue on with things as they were.

THERESA'S DISAPPOINTMENT

Although Maria was indeed giving her parents some things to worry about—she occasionally failed to keep her curfew and her grades in school were slipping—I sensed that Theresa's disappointment in herself was tainting her view of her daughter. During our conversation, Theresa spoke several times about how "let down" she was by Maria, but when I pressed for details, the examples Theresa gave of Maria's shortcomings seemed like typical adolescent fare to me. Theresa described one incident in particular with what I felt was unusual emotion.

The previous Christmas, Maria, who found that she did not have enough money to buy her parents a present, had planned on putting together a scrapbook for them. Evidently, Maria had a great deal of artistic talent, and her plan was to make a hand-bound, cloth-covered book of family photos that was to be illustrated with her own original cartoons.

Unfortunately, Christmas arrived and the scrapbook was not quite completed. Maria presented the book to her parents in its incomplete state, to show them what she had done so far. Although Theresa said the book was "delightful," she expressed her disappointment to Maria over the fact that the project wasn't finished on time. "I'm big about meeting your obligations," Theresa explained to me. In the five months that had passed since Christmas, Maria had not returned to the scrapbook and it was left unfinished. This annoyed Theresa a great deal: "It really rang home," she told me, angrily, "really rang home." Without any further prodding from me, Theresa went on to tell other stories about Maria's "irresponsibility."

"Oh, she wanted me to take her someplace. She has a boyfriend who lives about an hour from here. And she wanted me to drive her to see this boyfriend and I said, 'That's a long way to go. I don't want to do it.' Then I said, 'I'll tell you what. If you do some of my work, I'll take you there.' It was a two-hour trip, so she was supposed to do two hours of work. And she has not done that two hours of work, and it's been three weeks," she said, slapping her hand on the table for emphasis and looking to me for a sympathetic reaction.

While I understood why Theresa might have been a little irritated over Maria's failure to come through—both with the scrapbook and with the household work she had not yet done—it seemed to me that her anger with her daughter was far out of proportion to Maria's failings. As almost any parent will attest, most teenagers' rooms are littered with half-finished projects, and virtually all children occasionally fail to deliver on a promise of household work in return for a parental favor. By the time their child has turned Maria's age, most parents have learned that responsibility develops in fits and starts. Most parents are irritated by their child's lapses, but few take it so personally. I tried to understand why Theresa had reacted so strongly to what was, after all, fairly typical adolescent behavior.

As I thought further about the Rossis, I came to see that the answer had to do with Theresa's identification with her daughter. Maria's behavior reminded Theresa of her own "irresponsibility" as a teenager; the half-finished scrapbook was, in some regards, symbolic of Theresa's interrupted, half-finished youth. Although Maria's lapses were far less serious than her mother's had been, the path Maria seemed to be headed down reminded Theresa enough of her own adolescent mistakes, and watching Maria filled Theresa with regret about her own past and fear for her daughter's future. Because of this, what otherwise would have been easily excused mistakes on Maria's part became imbued with special significance for Theresa. The fact that Maria had let her mother down specifically over going to see her boyfriend did not help matters.

One might think that under these circumstances, that is, given Theresa's own history, she would have cracked down on Maria in an attempt to limit her daughter's "running around." But rather than stimulating her to provide more restrictions on her daughter, Theresa's obsession with her past thrust her into a sort of disciplinary paralysis. She wanted to be a more vigilant mother, but she was so immobilized by regret that she could not seem to motivate herself to act on her wishes. I examined the Rossis' questionnaire data. By most of the measures in our battery, Theresa was a disengaged, overly permissive mother.

The disappointment that some parents feel toward their adolescent is frequently blurred with regrets they have about their own lives, especially when there is a strong identification between parent and child. In Theresa Rossi's case, the identification was made especially salient by her daughter's physical similarity to Theresa. The frustration Theresa felt over her own developmental history was being transformed into unwarranted anger toward her daughter. Ultimately, this anger distanced Maria from her mother, which only intensified Theresa's anxiety that her daughter was heading for trouble. Unfortunately, the more anxious Theresa became, the less effective she was as a mother. Maria pulled further and further away, staying out later and later and disengaging from her family. She had never felt especially close to her father. Now, though, the emotional gulf between her and her mother had also become very wide.

MARIA ROSSI

Maria made no attempt to hide her irritation with her mother in our interview. About to enter her sophomore year in high school, this girl carried herself with the sort of pseudomaturity that often accompanies early dating and a fast social life. She wore a good deal of makeup, and, like her mother's, Maria's clothes smelled of cigarette smoke.

By her account, Maria and her mother had been close when she was younger, but as she had matured physically, her mother had "changed," and their relationship had deteriorated. Now, they rarely communicated at all.

"How would you say you get along with your mother?" I asked.

"OK, but not great."

"Would you say you're close?"

"Not really."

"Do you ever do anything together?"

"No."

"Was there ever a time when you did?"

"We used to do stuff together when I was little. We used to make things and stuff like that."

"What about talking to her? Did you feel more comfortable talking to her when you were little?"

"I guess so."

"Have you ever been able to talk to her about your inside kind of feelings?"

"Not since I've had any inside feelings."

Because Theresa did not want her daughter to know that she had been conceived outside of marriage, she could not speak openly about her own youth and felt unable to share the "lessons" she had learned along the way. Instead, she would make only vague references to her early marriage to Frank and tell Maria that she hoped her daughter would "make something of herself." Maria, of course, could not truly understand just what it was that her mother was so worried about. She just wished that they were closer and that her mother and father would stop fighting so much. As we shall see, Theresa's paralyzed permissiveness was countered by Frank's authoritarianism, and Maria was caught in the middle.

SOURCES OF REGRET AT MIDLIFE

Theresa Rossi's regret over her lost youth was deep and substantial. I also saw parents whose child triggered midlife regret that was over something less dramatic, although in some cases this too caused more than a little discomfort. Dan Fein, whose wife, Sarah, was writing the technothriller, provides a good example of this sort of situation.

When his son Douglas began bringing home trophies for his outstanding play in the city's basketball league, Dan found himself feeling surprisingly depressed, rather than elated, over his son's success on the court. In fact, the more accolades Douglas accumulated, the more despondent Dan became. It was all he could do to hide his feelings from his son, who, fortunately, was sufficiently caught up in his team's triumphs not to notice his father's ambivalent reactions.

Sarah knew what was going on, though, and she explained this to me while we were talking about her husband. As an adolescent, Dan had decided to quit his school's basketball team in order to take on an after-school job, a choice he had always regretted. Now, more than twenty years later, Dan found himself reminded of his decision whenever Douglas donned his uniform. Fortunately however, Sarah was able to tease Dan out of his worst moments, and she even was able to persuade him to direct his adolescent passion for basketball into coaching in the city's youth league.

Dan, of course, was not able to reverse the past and become, at thirty-nine, the college basketball star he might have been had he stayed with the sport as a teenager, just as Theresa Rossi was not able to undo her early pregnancy and marriage. These parents had to find a way to come to terms with their feelings of regret mentally, rather than by doing anything concrete. But there were some instances in our sample of adults who actually were able to channel their feelings of dissatisfaction and disappointment into healthy change. Some parents used the opportunity to reassess their own life situation and alter the structure of their lives.

For example, one father in our study, who for most of adulthood had been a highly successful business executive in the electronics field, had as a young man always wanted to teach history at the college level, but he had stopped short in his education in order to get a job and make money. One evening, after helping his fourteen-year-old son decide on which school subjects to take, he began to fantasize about becoming a student himself. After some serious discussions with his wife, and with the comfort of the financial resources he had accumulated over the years, he decided to go back to school to earn his Ph.D. When we spoke, he was busy mapping out a topic for his dissertation research.

"I've never had so much fun," he said, "although it sure is a lot of work. There is so much to read—sometimes I think my eyes are going to give out. But I'm more organized than a lot of the other students. I guess that's one advantage of going back to school when you're older and more experienced."

I asked if he missed his work.

"A little bit, I suppose, at first. Because I was good at it, and it felt comfortable. But this was something I had always wanted to do. I just couldn't actually bring myself to take the plunge. And then when Jimmy and I began talking about his plans for the future—now he's thinking about going into medicine, but I'm sure that will change. Anyway, it got me thinking, 'Hey, why not? Why not just go ahead and do it?'

"And so one afternoon, instead of returning to the office after lunch, I went over to the history department at the university and picked up some information about their graduate programs. Let me tell you, now that I've actually started in on it, I can't understand why

I waited so damn long. I don't know where this is going to lead, but I'll face that when I have to. It's funny. This never would have happened if Jimmy hadn't asked for my advice about what classes he should be taking. That's what really got me going."

REGRET VERSUS SATISFACTION

Not all parents looked at their teenager's nascent life and wanted to start over in their own, of course. I also met many parents who, after some serious reappraisal, looked back with strong feelings of satisfaction, sometimes even relief, that life had turned out better than they had expected. More than a few parents looked at their teen's life and felt happy not to have to relive adolescence, especially in today's world.

One mother, a social worker who had been divorced for three years at the time we talked, put it this way: "Have I had disappointments? Sure. But overall, I'm basically satisfied with the way that things turned out. I don't look back with regret or anything like that. I mean, I wish that my marriage had been better, but, honestly, I'm happier being single than I was in that relationship. I have a lot of good friends, two great kids, and a job I look forward to on most days. How many people our age can say that? I look at my daughters now, facing all of the pressures of growing up, and wonder how they cope with all of it. There is so much pressure on kids today. I wouldn't want to be that age again, even if you paid me. I was a mess when I was their age—depressed, unsure about who I was, nervous about fitting in. I might not have everything I want in life, but at least now I know who I am. I'm much happier as an adult than I was as a teenager."

FRANK ROSSI

Unlike his wife, Theresa, Frank Rossi no longer spent a great deal of time thinking about how his life might have been different had they not been forced to marry so young. But Frank was not happy either. He was merely resigned. We sat in their kitchen and talked one Saturday afternoon while he nursed a can of beer.

"My wife, she lives in the past. She's always daydreaming. I don't know, I think that's a bad kind of attitude, to be wrapped up in how things might have been, could have been, should have been. Like now, she keeps harping on this thing that happened with her sister and brother-in-law two years ago. They had run into some real hard times, moneywise, and we loaned them some money. Really quite a bit of money, for us. Well, you know what they say about lending money to relatives. They haven't paid back any of it, and I don't think we're ever going to see it. It eats away at Terry. That's why she started working. I tell her, 'Forget about it. It's only money. What can you do? Worrying isn't going to bring it back.' You don't dwell on problems. You count your blessings and you muddle on through. Sleep on it and hope it will be better in the morning."

I asked Frank if he ever wished that his career had turned out differently.

"I'd like to work for myself someday—be my own boss. I hate punching the clock, which is what I do now at the phone company. And it's tiring work. Before Terry and I got married, I was selling cars. I liked that. I kept thinking that some day I'd buy my own lot, manage my own place. But we had kids early and couldn't seem to save a cent. After I was laid off, we moved up here and I started with the phone company. It's not what I wanted to be doing, but, hey, that's the way it is. I've tried to make the best of it. We were saving that money for something better, but . . . " His voice trailed off.

Like many of the working-class men in our study, Frank's stoicism prevented him from openly admitting his discontent. Although Frank's score on our midlife crisis scale was not high, he was reporting higher than average psychosomatic complaints: headaches, stomachaches, problems sleeping. This was a common pattern I saw in the psychological profiles of blue-collar men, who generally are less likely than men in professional or white-collar occupations to express their internal distress verbally but who experience the physical symptoms of tension nevertheless. If pressed, Frank would admit to feeling disappointed. But most of the time he would try his hardest to keep a lid on those feelings.

Frank was not always successful at keeping his emotions in check, however. Rather than surfacing as disappointment, his dissatisfaction would come out as anger, and he would have it out with his wife and children. Frank was especially sensitive to any threats to his authority around the house, a fairly common response among men who feel a lack of power in the workplace. It is often observed that men who desire but do not enjoy power at work typically seek it at home, in their marriage, with their children, or, usually, both. Often, these men have an especially difficult time of it when their children hit adolescence and begin challenging parental authority. And they are dealt a double whammy in homes in which their children's adolescence prompts changes in their wives' demeanor. Theresa's running away from home not only upset Frank but directly challenged his authority as the individual in charge. It was Theresa's way of having the last word.

I asked Frank if, looking back, he would have done anything differently as a parent.

"I don't think that I would have given Maria as much latitude as I did. The way I was brought up, my parents used to say, 'This is the way it is. It's because I'm your dad. Because I said so. That's the way it is. End of conversation.' I can remember when I was a freshman in high school. I had to be home at 9:00. At home in the house. Not at somebody else's house. Obviously, things have changed. I don't think I was as prepared for raising a teenager as I would have liked to have been. But then, it's an unknown thing."

Frank continued. "One night Maria ran away from home." Like mother, like daughter, I thought to myself. "It turns out she spent the night sleeping at one of her friends' house. But she didn't want this other girl's parents to know that she was there, so she slept in the closet, standing up all night. One of those weird things. We thought, 'We're doing something wrong here,' so we got some books. My wife went to the library and got a bunch of books on child development. I read a few pages of Dr. Spock and took the book and threw it across the room and said, 'I ain't gonna read this garbage!' My wife read it from cover to cover, so I blame her in that manner."

"I'm 'Mister Mean' around here," Frank told me, in a voice that revealed both pride and pain over this moniker. "They accuse me of being a dictator and power hungry and all that other stuff. I think it was a lot easier when Maria was younger. If she asked, 'Well, why do I have to be home at 10:00?' I'd say, 'Because I'm your father' or 'Because I said so.' She'd accept it. Now she questions everything."

On some levels, Frank was talking about his wife as much as he was about his daughter. Theresa, too, was beginning to question everything.

In the Rossis' story we see how a child's adolescence can trigger feelings of regret in a parent and how these feelings can reverberate throughout the family. Maria's transition into adolescence reminded Theresa of the circumstances surrounding her own unplanned pregnancy and ambivalent marriage, which unleashed in Theresa deep-seated feelings of dissatisfaction. Unfortunately, Theresa was not able to channel these feelings in a constructive way. Instead, her bitterness over the way her life had turned out began to work itself into disengagement from the maternal role.

As we shall see, parental disengagement during adolescence often provokes problem behavior in the child, who interprets the disengagement as apathy or even hostility. As Theresa withdrew from the maternal role, Maria began to disengage from the family, spending more and more time away from home and challenging her parents at any opportunity. This, in turn, angered Frank, whose heightened needs for power and authority were especially vulnerable to both his daughter's rebellion and his wife's refusal to do anything in response. Theresa accused Frank of being a hot-tempered autocrat. Frank insisted that the family's problems stemmed from Theresa's permissiveness. Each was partially correct.

By the time I met the Rossis, fighting had become a pervasive part of life in their home, with each parent pointing the finger at the other. Their house was like a boxing ring, with each parent sulking in his or her own corner between rounds of angry accusations. Maria was caught in the middle. As we shall see in a later chapter, she was beginning to show the signs of being caught in her parents' conflict.

PART III

REVERBERATIONS

10. THE SPILLOVER INTO MARRIAGE

As a rule, a married couple is never again as happy with their relationship as they are on the day when they walk down the aisle. When social scientists chart changes in marital satisfaction over time, they invariably find that individuals' happiness with their marriage suffers a precipitous drop during the first few years of matrimony. And with each passing year, marriage partners grow ever more disenchanted.

This over-time decline in marital happiness afflicts both husbands and wives, although there are important differences between the genders. Men and women start off at different points and follow different trajectories. Generally, women begin marriage more satisfied than men, but they report an earlier and much steeper drop in happiness than their spouses. Men, on the other hand, begin married life less happy than women, but they report a more gradual drop in satisfaction over time than do their wives. Although women may look forward more than men do to getting married, in reality, marriage treats men much better than women.

The drop in husbands' and wives' marital happiness over time is probably even more substantial than social scientists have reported it to be. For one thing, people generally don't like to admit being unhappily married, so their answers to surveys about marital satisfaction are likely to be skewed toward the positive side. Rather than admitting to growing dissatisfaction over time, many individuals simply lower their expectations: "I'm as happy as I can expect to be for someone who's been married *this* long."

Second, we know that very unhappy individuals are generally less likely to participate in surveys and polls, regardless of the topic, so the samples on which social scientists base their conclusions are likely biased toward happier—and more happily married—folks to begin with. Unhappy individuals are wary about opening their doors and sharing the details of their private lives with strangers from a university research office.

Finally, and most important, the most miserable of husbands and wives are not even included in the surveys of married couples, since those who are extremely dissatisfied have gotten divorced. With the U.S. divorce rate hovering at around 50 percent, and with the majority of divorces occurring early in marriage, very few unhappily married couples remain together long enough to stay in a study of marital relations at midlife. Those who do are, by definition, among the happiest of the unhappy. If divorce were not as acceptable as it is, and unhappy couples consequently felt unable to split up, average marital satisfaction scores would surely be a lot lower.

The sad truth is that by about six years into a marriage, wives are only about half as happy as they were during their first year, and husbands are about one-third less satisfied. By the time a couple's firstborn child has entered adolescence, their marriage has, in all likelihood, descended to new depths of dissatisfaction. Ninety percent of wives, and almost that proportion of husbands, report some marital difficulties during the period of their firstborn's adolescence.

STAN AND BARBARA MERRICK

Stan and Barbara Merrick, the architect and publicist you met in the first chapter, were fairly typical in this respect. At the time of our follow-up interview, in their thirteenth year of marriage, Stan seemed to have little interest in Barbara. Barbara was downright hostile toward Stan.

"He acts like a child," she complained. "No—worse—like an oversexed fraternity boy. We can not go out in public without him gawking at young women. It infuriates me. I don't know, I can't tell anymore if he's changed or if I've just become supersensitive to it, but it sure seems like he's always craning his neck to catch an extra-long glimpse of some twenty-year-old." Barbara reached under a stack of *New Yorker* magazines on the coffee table and pulled out a well-worn copy of the previous summer's *Sports Illustrated* swimsuit issue. She held the magazine up so that I could see the cover. "Is it my imagination, or are there more young women walking around out there who look like this? And, honestly, why would Stan save a magazine that is seven months old? He and Brian must have looked at this ten times already." She scowled as she slipped the magazine back under the ones on the table.

"The worst part is that it makes me feel invisible, as if Stan's looking right through me," Barbara continued. The other afternoon, we went out for lunch, just the two of us. It was something we don't get a chance to do very often, but Brian and Jason were both going to be over at friends' houses for the afternoon, and while Stan and I were doing the breakfast dishes, I had suggested going out. Stan said, 'Great,' and suggested a little Italian place we both like. Things had not been going well between us, and I was hoping that this might help."

She paused. "We ended up having a horrible fight."

I asked Barbara if she minded telling me what had happened.

"Not at all. Within three minutes of sitting down, Stan was flirting with the waitress—a lovely little habit he's picked up within the last year. It used to be that he was so stiff and formal when we were in a restaurant that I would get embarrassed. Not anymore. He was joking around with "Melissa" like they were long-lost friends. And that wasn't the worst part. The *worst* part was that he barely seemed to notice that I was there. I seemed like a distraction to him, like my presence was getting in the way of him enjoying the scenery. When I said something to him about his paying too much attention to the waitress, he denied it completely. He joked that I was getting paranoid in my old age.

"Well, you can imagine how that last remark sat with me, even if it was supposed to be a joke. I have not reacted well to aging. Anyway, I lost it completely. I slammed down my wine glass, which spilled red wine all over the tablecloth and my blouse, and I shouted, so everyone could hear it, 'Maybe you'd enjoy lunch more with someone younger and less paranoid, then, like *Melissa*.' Then I stormed out of the restaurant. I knew that people were staring at me, but I didn't care. Stan ended up having to call a taxi to get home. We didn't speak to each other for the rest of the day."

I asked if she and Stan had been arguing more frequently in recent months.

"I suppose so," Barbara replied. "But not a great deal more than in the past. It's not so much that we're fighting more but that we're enjoying each other less. We seem to have less fun. And we certainly have less sex."

I knew what Barbara was referring to. Generally speaking, a drop in marital satisfaction is more often due to a decline in the "positives" (sex, fun, and shared activities) rather than an increase in the "negatives" (arguing, fighting, and disagreements).

Was Stan's inattentiveness a dramatic change in their relationship?

"Oh, it's definitely a change," Barbara replied, "but I don't know that I'd call it dramatic. It's something that has happened gradually, over the past year or two. And, of course, the less attractive I think he finds me, the less I feel like trying. And all *that* does is drive him further away. The problem is, I don't feel as if there's anything I can do. I feel very, very frustrated. Sometimes I get so angry I could spit nails. Most of the time, though, I feel pretty depressed about it."

I had heard similar stories from some of the other wives in our sample, stories which corroborated the picture painted in the more systematic social science surveys: many, many women with adolescent children were quite dissatisfied with their marriage. As it turned out, so were many of the husbands.

"Barbara is always on me about something," Stan Merrick was saying when we met at his office. "I don't pay enough attention to her. I don't give her enough emotionally. We don't spend enough time together. I'm off with Brian and Jason too much of the time." He shook his head. "It kills me. Because when the kids were younger, she complained about just the opposite—that I didn't spend enough time with them. Now that Brian and I have really gotten to be good friends, she gets jealous.

"Frankly, I *would* spend more time with Barbara if she was more fun to be around. Lately, though, she seems so irritable and tense, not only with the boys, which I mentioned to you before, but with me. I hate to say it, but I enjoy myself more when I'm with Brian than when I'm with Barbara."

Has this always been the case?

"No, and that's what's funny about it," Stan said. "It's really been within the last two years, I would say, that things have changed. We had what I thought was a great marriage before then. Certainly better than a lot of our friends. We know couples who've been in and out of marital counseling, some of our friends have done that marriage encounter thing, we've seen a couple of divorces over the years, you name it. Barbara and I always seemed to be able to work things out on our own. But something has really happened to us this time. We can't seem to get things back on track. I keep racking my brains about it but, for the life of me, I can't figure what this is all about."

THE U-SHAPED CURVE OF MARITAL SATISFACTION

In all likelihood, the Merricks' marriage would improve over the next five years, even without their doing anything to alter their situation. Social scientists have discovered something quite curious about the drop in marital satisfaction that seems to afflict most couples during the first fifteen years of matrimony: As soon as the firstborn child begins to move out of early adolescence—past thirteen or fourteen, say—husbands' and wives' marital happiness begins to take a turn for the better. Indeed, by the time most couples have entered the "empty nest"—that is, by the time they have "launched" their youngest child—they are nearly as happy as they were in the early years of marriage.

In other words, marital satisfaction generally follows a U-shaped curve over the course of a marriage. It starts out high, falls steadily until the firstborn child reaches early adolescence, bottoms out, and then starts to rise, continuing to increase into old age. When I interviewed the Merricks, they were just about at rock bottom. For different reasons, Stan and Barbara were each miserable with the way their marriage was going.

Social scientists themselves have had a hard time explaining why couples' happiness tends to follow a U-shaped pattern over the course of married life. Two explanations are commonly given, although neither is completely satisfactory.

THE BOREDOM HYPOTHESIS

The first explanation has to do with the mere passage of time, what we might call the "boredom" hypothesis. The notion is that people enjoy novelty—not only sexual novelty, but novelty in companionship and activity as well—and that husbands and wives simply become bored with each other as the years pass. According to this theory, it makes perfect sense that newlyweds are happier than couples celebrating their tenth anniversary, if only because the newlyweds have not yet gotten tired of each other and the routines of everyday life.

This account makes good sense if we focus just on the first half of the "U," but what about the second half? Why do couples start feeling happier after being married about fifteen years? We might expect that the *rate* of decline in marital satisfaction would slow after a while (that is, that the big drop would occur early on in the marriage), and that couples' dissatisfaction would level off at some point. But we would hardly anticipate that happiness would start to *rise* after fifteen years in the same marriage, if boredom was the culprit responsible for the initial decline. It certainly seems as if something other than the simple passage of time is the crucial factor.

THE MIDLIFE CRISIS HYPOTHESIS

The second explanation for the U-shaped curve in marital happiness centers around what we might call the "midlife crisis" hypothesis. The argument goes something like this: Most individuals are in their mid-twenties when they marry. Fifteen years into a marriage, therefore, coincides with the heart of midlife, which can be a time of profound psychological turmoil. Perhaps the low point in marital satisfaction after around fifteen years of marriage is linked to the intensification of midlife concerns and associated regrets, and the rise in marital satisfaction shortly after is simply due to the midlife crisis becoming less pronounced. In other words, as individuals work through their own personal midlife issues—sometime during their mid-forties—they once again begin to enjoy marriage.

Although this explanation seems reasonable enough at first glance, several pieces of evidence from other studies contradict it. First, when social scientists go back and look specifically at marital happiness among childless couples, they find that changes in marital satisfaction are not nearly as pronounced in this group as they are among couples with children. If changes in marital happiness are due simply to entering and then exiting midlife, we would expect to find similar patterns among parents and nonparents alike. Instead, studies show that the vicissitudes of marital happiness are much more dramatic among couples who are parents than among their childless counterparts. Childless couples do become more dissatisfied over time, but their decline in happiness is far less dramatic than it is for couples with children.

Second, as I discussed earlier, research on the midlife crisis indicates that we probably have overestimated its prevalence. Somewhere between only 10 and 20 percent of adults experience a full-blown midlife crisis. For this small minority of adults, the rise and fall of marital disenchantment may indeed have its roots in the psychological turmoil of the midlife struggle. But for the majority of adults, who do not have a midlife crisis—but whose marital happiness nevertheless hits its nadir after about fifteen years—something else must be happening. I had a hunch that this "something else" is their child's entry into adolescence.

THE ADOLESCENT FACTOR

Several findings from our study fit the "adolescence" hypothesis. First, our results showed that parents' marital satisfaction was more closely related to their firstborn *child's* age than to their own. In other words, a forty-two-year-old father with a teenager was more likely to be unhappily married than a father who was the same age but had younger children. Given two adults at the same point in their own development, the one whose firstborn child was in adolescence was far more at risk for marital discontent. This argued against the "midlife crisis" hypothesis.

Second, parents' marital satisfaction was unrelated to how long they had been married, once their firstborn's age was taken into account. All things being equal, a mother who had been married for sixteen years and who had a fourteen-year-old child was more likely to be unhappy with her marriage than a mother who had also been married for sixteen years but whose oldest child was only ten. This finding argued against the "boredom" hypothesis, since, in theory, the marital unhappiness that comes from being bored should be related to how long a couple had been together and not their child's age.

It certainly looked as if something about having a child enter adolescence was taking its toll on parents' marital relations. But why should this be? Why should having a teenager in the house create problems for a marriage? As we explored this issue further, we identified three reasons.

EMOTIONAL DISTANCING BETWEEN PARENT AND TEENAGER

The first reason has to do with the distancing that goes on between a parent and his or her child as adolescence begins. When this distancing is experienced by the parent as a loss or as a source of regret, the parent often becomes depressed and morose, and this depression, in turn, adversely affects the marriage. I saw this most clearly in the Spencer and Rossi households.

As you may recall, Amanda Spencer reacted poorly to her son, Paul's, attempts at individuation. The more independent Paul became, the more depressed Amanda grew. Her despondency was exacerbated by the fact that, as a full-time homemaker, Amanda had invested a great deal of energy in her parental role. Paul's pulling away shook Amanda's sense of who she was and, more important, who she was going to become. Amanda worried about what was going to become of her once Paul no longer needed so much of her time and energy.

I have noted several times already that the child's movement toward more emotional independence is inevitable—there is little any parent can do to stop this from happening, nor, frankly, should a parent try. The child needs a certain degree of emotional autonomy in order to mature in healthy ways. Although most parents can accept this advice in theory, many have difficulty putting it into practice.

AMANDA AND PAUL SPENCER

Like most parents who experience their child's emotional growth as a personal loss, Amanda Spencer struggled to hold on to Paul as much as possible. But because Paul experienced this holding on as intrusive—even, at times, suffocating—Amanda's attempts were met with resistance. Often, the struggle between them resulted in heated arguments, with Paul accusing his mother of "babying" him, and Amanda accusing Paul of being ungrateful.

One might expect that when a parent feels as if she is losing her child, she will turn to her marriage to compensate for the emotional loss. While this makes sense at first—and, in some regards, this is just what Amanda expected to happen—my experience in working with families of adolescents is that this rarely occurs. In fact, increased distance between parents and children is typically associated with increased *distance* between spouses. Generally speaking, the closer parents are to their children, the closer they are to each other. When things had been better between Amanda and her son, they were also better between Amanda and her husband.

If you think about this a bit, the reason becomes clear. When parents feel distant from their children, they tend to feel angry, anxious, or depressed—especially if the distance is something that has not always been a part of the relationship. Parents who feel this way are not especially pleasant to be around, especially to their spouses. So, even if such a parent attempts to turn to his or her spouse for comfort and emotional compensation, the spouse is typically not forthcoming. In the Spencer household—as was the case for Barbara and Stan Merrick—Amanda's sense of loss ended up driving a wedge into the marriage, alienating Jonathan and driving him toward other activities. Like Stan Merrick, Jonathan Spencer complained that his wife had become less fun-loving and that the time they spent together had become less enjoyable.

"I know that Amanda is unhappy about Paul," Jonathan explained, "but I have no idea what to do. I've suggested different things—getting a job, seeing her friends more often, even going back to school—but she can't seem to motivate herself to follow any of these things up. I know that I should be more sympathetic, but she's got to work this through for herself. In the meantime, we seem to be going our separate ways. I think she just needs a little time, a little space. I'm sure it will pass."

Unfortunately, Jonathan's reaction to Amanda's distress over losing Paul only made their marital problems worse. Jonathan did not experience their son's maturation as a loss—if anything, he felt that Paul's growing into manhood provided them with an opportunity to strengthen their connection. Rather than trying to understand Amanda's difficulty, Jonathan, uncomfortable with and unsure about how to respond to Amanda's despondency, did one of the worst things he could do: He withdrew somewhat from the relationship. The Spencers began spending less and less time together. Unfortunately, this only amplified Amanda's sense of loss—as she put it, she was losing her husband on top of losing her son.

We saw earlier that there are some parents for whom the child's emotional individuation is not experienced as a loss, but, rather, is greeted with pleasure and satisfaction. This frequently was the case among professional mothers who were very invested in their careers, who were happy *not* to have to devote as much time to the day-to-day demands of parenthood as they had previously. For these parents, having a child become more autonomous was a liberating experience, one that affected their mental health positively. Not surprisingly, in many of these cases, it also had a salutary effect on their marriage. Sarah Fein, the science-fiction author, was a good example of someone who fell into this category.

SARAH AND DAN FEIN

"Now that Doug is a teenager," Sarah told me, "Dan and I have more time for each other. I'm happier, because I'm able to spend more time on my writing, which is what I want to be doing with my life right now. And when I'm happier personally, things are better for us as a couple—I suppose that's true for almost everyone. Some afternoons, when Doug is out of the house, Dan will stop by while he's between sales calls. We'll sit and talk, or whatever . . .

"I can remember one time when I had finally finished a chapter that I had really been having problems with. I was delighted, but my neck was killing me from sitting in front of the computer all day. So I decided to treat myself to a nice warm bath. I guess it was about 3:30 or so. I had just gotten in the tub when I heard the front door open. My initial reaction was, 'Oh, darn, Doug is back early from his game.' Not that I don't love him to death, but I was all set just to relax and unwind. Well, it wasn't Doug—it was Dan. He peeked in the door and I said 'Come on in, the water's fine,' which he did. Now, *that* sort of spur-of-the-moment thing did not happen when Doug was younger." Sarah smiled. "Dan and I can't wait for Doug to start dating so that we can have Friday and Saturday nights to ourselves again."

THERESA AND FRANK ROSSI

When a child's entry into adolescence triggers regret in a parent, as it did for Theresa Rossi, the parent's marriage is also adversely affected. Under these circumstances, the regret the parent feels over decisions he or she has made earlier in life spills over into the marital relationship, and the spouse is seen in a new and less flattering light. Theresa could not help but look at her daughter Maria and reevaluate her marriage to Frank.

"I don't know," Theresa replied when I asked specifically about how having an adolescent child had affected her marriage. "As I was saying, I do a lot of daydreaming while I work, a lot of daydreaming about the past. I start thinking about Maria and what she seems to be headed for, and that gets me thinking about my own childhood. I think a lot about how Frank and I ended up together, how things might have been different had I been smarter about my life. I suppose it's not fair to Frank, because I don't tell him what's going on in my head. But after a day of going over everything and feeling sorry for myself, well, I guess I take it out on him when he walks through the door."

I asked Theresa what she meant.

"Oh, I guess I'm not as glad to see him as I should be. I can't help it. I see his face and I just see the Frank I married, and it makes me sad how things turned out."

Frank Rossi could sense that something was wrong in their marriage, but because Theresa had not confided in him, he was more or less in the dark about the source of the problem. "I know that she's not as happy as she was before, but I think it's all the stress we've been dealing with—money, problems with the kids, you name it. She's had a tough life. Hell, we've *both* had tough lives. The problems with Maria, though—those she's brought on herself."

I asked if Frank thought their marriage had been affected by Maria in any way.

"Well," he laughed, "it sure gives us more to fight about. Not that there's ever been any shortage of reasons around here. No question, though: Maria has made things worse between me and the wife."

TEENAGE SEXUALITY AND THE MIDLIFE MARRIAGE

Those of us who study families know that there are some topics people are reluctant to talk about openly. Even under the best of circumstances, with the most adept of interviewers, individuals generally will not confess to having thoughts and feelings that they perceive as socially undesirable. This is one reason that I was always grateful for having questionnaire data to complement our one-on-one interviews, because individuals respond more honestly to sensitive questions when they are posed on anonymous questionnaires than when they are asked in personal encounters.

In the course of analyzing the quantitative data from our study, I came across a finding that I would never have discovered had we relied only on interviews: When adolescents started to date, their fathers' marital satisfaction declined substantially. In fact, the more frequently the teenager dated, the more unhappily married the adolescent's father became. This decline in marital happiness was accompanied by an increase in anxiety and depression if the child was a son. It seemed as if, on some level—perhaps on an unconscious level—men were jealous of their teenager's social life.

Because it is such a sensitive topic, little has been written about how the teenager's budding sexuality may affect his or her parents' feelings about themselves and each other. It is this very sensitivity, however, that makes the issue both especially intriguing and incredibly difficult to talk about with parents. Yet, I suspected that the entrance into the family of an additional sexually mature individual has to alter the dynamics between husbands and wives in profound ways.

Although I felt it was not possible to explore this issue in the course of my interviews with our study participants, I have brought it up with friends and colleagues who have adolescent children, and their answers have been illuminating. Many of the fathers with whom I have spoken have confessed—albeit with a certain degree of embarrassment—to feeling attracted to their son's girlfriends or to their daughter's female friends. One father of a seventeen-year-old with whom I spoke put it this way:

"You wouldn't believe what Tim's girlfriends look like! And how they wait on him hand and foot. One time, he had one of his dates over and they were in the kitchen. I was sitting at the table reading the paper. Now this girl was absolutely beautiful—I mean, a knockout. And there's little Tim—well he's not so little anymore, but I still think of him as a little kid—and he sits down at the table next to me and his girlfriend brings him over a Coke and a sandwich that she's made for him and is standing behind him while he's eating, rubbing his back and playing with his hair. And he looks over at me and flashes this big smile, like, 'Hey, old man, check it out.' And you want to know if I ever get jealous?"

Another father, this one with a sixteen-year-old son, told a story about a recent family vacation to Hawaii. "We were in Maui for a week over Christmas vacation," he said. "My wife, myself, and our two kids, Scott and Alison. We had been there, oh, two days or so, and one night at around nine we're up in the room watching television, and Scott says he is going back down to the lobby to meet this girl he had met on the beach that afternoon. They were going to go for a walk on the beach. I was curious, so I made up a reason to go down to the lobby with him—I said I wanted to buy a magazine to read in bed—and we rode down in the elevator. We get off the elevator and Scott waves to this girl. Now, this girl could have been a model—I kid you not. And Scott introduces her to me and then they head out, his arm around her waist. As I rode the elevator back up to the room, I couldn't help but feel that I wanted to trade places with my sixteen-year-old son."

Even fathers of daughters reported less marital satisfaction the more their child was dating. In this case, the underlying dynamic involved an unconscious competitiveness between the father and the daughter's date and, in some instances, an unconscious attraction toward his own child. Although in our study we heard no stories of sexual abuse or incest (and it is unlikely that we would have been told of such incidents, given the nature of the research), we do know from other research that there is a very real sexual tension that develops between fathers and postpubertal daughters. In one series of studies conducted by John Hill and his colleagues, the researchers observed flirtatious interchanges between fathers and daughters in a large percentage of the families they studied.

In stepfamilies, physical attraction of stepfathers toward their adolescent stepdaughters is especially common, and the feelings this provokes are quite interesting. For example, in response to one of our standard interview prompts—"Tell me about a time when you and your teenager felt especially close"—a stepfather whom I interviewed related the following story about his relationship with his fourteen-year-old stepdaughter, Kelly:

"We were all walking on the State Street mall one Saturday afternoon after lunch. My wife was walking with our nine-year-old son, and I was walking with Kelly, and we were having a really nice conversation. And for a moment, it seemed like Kelly was my date, not my stepdaughter. Sometimes you just . . . I actually thought about it in terms of my own adolescence. And I could remember when it was that way when I was walking down the street with a girl. Yet I never could go back, but it was the closest thing to going back."

As far as I can tell, the sexual reawakening that some fathers feel as their child enters adolescence alters dynamics between husbands and wives in one of two ways. For some couples, like Barbara and Stan Merrick, it dampens sexual desire and diminishes marital happiness, either because the husband is feeling attracted to someone other than his wife (consciously or unconsciously), or because the wife is irritated that the husband simply has been noticing other women. Among other couples, however, the onset of dating by the child actually *en-*

hances the couples' sex life, as it did for John and Linda Forster, who necked in the car after delivering their daughter to her first dance.

JOHN AND LINDA FORSTER

"Seeing Abby getting interested in boys," John told me, "makes me think back to when Linda and I first met, and, I'm not sure why—maybe it's because she looks so much like Linda when Linda was younger—but it is a turn-on. I don't know, have you ever been in a movie theater where there are lots of kids out on dates? It's almost as if you can sense the hormones flowing, or maybe it's just the energy, but whatever it is, when Abby is getting together with her group of friends, boys and girls, Linda and I clearly are affected by it. I don't think it's coincidental that we have had some of our best times together when Abby's been out at some social thing."

Linda had similar sentiments. "I wouldn't say I live *through* Abby," she had told me, "but there is a sort of vicarious thing that happens, I suppose, for all parents. When she comes to me for help with doing her hair or putting on makeup before going out, I really get taken back to my own youth, and it makes me feel younger and, in a funny way, a little charged up. I'm just glad I have a husband who can appreciate it."

Not all parents who were sexually or romantically invigorated by their child's maturation into adolescence had the opportunity to take advantage of this rediscovered energy, however. I still laugh to myself when I recall the complaint of Mary Howe, about her daughter, Christine.

"One of the things my husband and I looked forward to was the day when we could have Saturday night to ourselves again—at home, without going out. You know, just relaxing with each other in front of the VCR or even"—she laughed—"in the bedroom. I figured that as soon as Tina got to be a certain age, we'd have some privacy as a couple.

"Wouldn't you know it?" Mary laughed. "We've got a wallflower for a daughter. A real homebody. Mike and I plead with her to go out, to have some kind of social life, just so we can be alone. Other parents complain about their kids staying out till all hours. We can't get rid of ours.

"There we are, last Saturday, sitting on the couch, watching a movie—I can't remember what it was. Anyway, this sexy scene comes on, and I can tell that Mike is dying to get his hands all over me. Unfortunately, Tina is sitting between us, completely oblivious. I figure I'll give it one more year. Then I'm going to start fixing her up!"

NEW CONFLICTS OVER CHILDREARING

A final way in which the child's entrance into adolescence triggers changes in the parents' marital relationship involves husbands and wives arguing over childrearing. Some couples—many of whom have seen eye to eye during their youngster's childhood years—find that they cannot agree on how to raise an adolescent, and this disagreement leads to fighting and, eventually, to a decline in marital satisfaction. We saw this clearly in the cases of Bob and Laura Peterson and Gray Miller and Ellen Hansen.

In each of these cases, the husband reacted to the child's adolescence by becoming stricter—Bob Peterson, because he was unconsciously jealous of his son's freedom, and Gray Miller, because he felt powerless in the face of his stepdaughter's growing drive toward independence. Bob took his jealousy out on his son, David, by nagging him constantly about his schoolwork, whereas Gray tried to reassert his authority over his stepdaughter Cindy by generating and enforcing a set of rules and regulations that were, by most standards, over issues that were unimportant.

BOB AND LAURA PETERSON

In the Peterson household, Bob's view was challenged—at least in private—by his wife, Laura. "We had some terrible fights about David," Laura told me. "We had always felt that it was important to present a united front, and before David became a teenager, it was pretty easy to do this. If Bob and I disagreed about something, it was usually pretty minor, and we were almost always able to work it out without David knowing that we disagreed.

"But something's changed in Bob during the last few years. He's become more and more strict, instead of the opposite. My feeling is that as a child proves he can be more responsible, you give him a longer and longer leash. Bob worries that if the leash is too long, David will hang himself."

"Laura is too permissive with David," countered Bob during my interview with him. "She is afraid to take a stand with him, I think, primarily, because she is afraid of losing him emotionally. You know, that if you don't give in to each and every whim your child will never forgive you. I keep telling her that kids his age need limits, structure. That parents have to be the bad guys."

I asked Bob how he and Laura handled disagreements about how to raise David.

"Not very well. We're each pretty stubborn about it. I get mad at Laura because I feel that she makes me out to be the villain. She gets mad at me because she feels that I create problems that wouldn't be there otherwise. We'll have an argument and each go to our corners and sulk for a few hours. We're usually fine after a while, but it seems to be happening more and more as David gets older. Frankly, I've spent the night on the living room couch so many times in the last year because of a fight we've had about David that it's starting to feel like it's normal."

For the Petersons, David's entrance into adolescence raised new disciplinary issues and provoked new psychological concerns that had not been apparent earlier. The fact that Bob and Laura disagreed came as a real shock to each of them, since childrearing had in the past never been a source of contention. My sense was that David's maturation was raising difficult psychological issues for Bob concerning his own disappointment in himself and that this was manifesting itself in excessive strictness on Bob's part. Laura, meanwhile, was trying to conduct parenting as usual, and their two styles clashed. Until Bob recognized that he was taking out his own personal frustration on David, their marriage would remain strained.

GRAY MILLER AND ELLEN HANSEN

Gray Miller and Ellen Hansen had similar problems finding common ground in raising their daughter Cindy, but the Millers' disagreement played itself out in different ways from the Petersons'.

This was a second marriage for both Gray and Ellen, and they soon discovered that they had very different ideas about how children should be raised. Gray was from the "spare the rod, spoil the child" school of thought, whereas Ellen was inclined toward a "live and let live" mentality. The collision of approaches was inevitable.

The difference between Gray and Ellen was also exacerbated, I think, by the particular circumstances each brought into this new marriage. Gray, you may recall, had been disengaged from his children's upbringing in his first marriage, and he was determined to correct his mistake the second time around, as a stepfather to Ellen's children. Ellen, in contrast, had grown accustomed to the easygoing style she had adopted as a single mother and had hoped that Gray would permit things to continue along the same disciplinary path. Neither was prepared for what would happen.

I learned during my interviews with both Cindy and her mother that when the Hansen children complained to Ellen about their stepfather's authoritarianism, Ellen often responded angrily. She would remind them that Gray's generosity had allowed them to escape from the near-poverty existence they had suffered after their father had abandoned them. She wanted her children to share her feelings of gratitude for what Gray was providing.

Unfortunately, Ellen knew that in many respects, her children were right. Gray was, as Cindy and her brother liked to label him, "unfair." And, Ellen confessed to me, she knew it was not "fair to the kids to change the rules in the middle of the game."

"But what can I do?" Ellen asked me, in obvious distress. "I can't expect Gray to come in here and bail us out financially and then have no say at all about how the children behave. That's not fair to him, is it? But what do I say to the kids? That I've changed my mind? I can't win. Somebody is always going to be angry at me. Including myself."

Ellen's anger had begun to take its toll on her marriage to Gray. Her sense of being caught in the middle—of having her loyalties divided between her children and her second husband—was making her depressed and anxious, and she began to feel that Gray's presence, regardless of his financial support, was not worth the aggravation it caused in the household. She reminded me that they had sought counseling after Gray and Cindy had fought physically. I asked if the family therapy had helped.

"A little," she replied. "We're much better at resolving conflicts than we were before. But there are just some things you can't really change all that easily. Gray promised to lighten up a little, Cindy promised to respect his opinion more, and I promised to be more open about my feelings, to communicate more honestly with everyone. The therapist said that I was keeping a lot of things in, and that this was not good. But Gray and I just are very, very different people, and I hadn't realized that until now."

Ellen continued, expressing sentiments I had heard from several remarried mothers. "It is lonely being single. And hard, financially. Then you finally meet somebody who seems kind and decent, and you have this vision of how they're going to be with your children, and for a while, at the beginning, they are what you had hoped they would be. It's not like marrying somebody from scratch when you don't have kids. You have to weigh a lot of things. You have these children, and they are already what they are, and so you have to try to think whether this person is going to be able to fit in. And the problem is, you can't tell until it's too late. The day-to-day hassles start to mount up, and you see what they're like up close, under stress. You can't help but feel disappointed. I don't blame Gray. I don't blame anyone. It just is the way it is."

I asked about their marriage.

"To tell you the truth, most of the time it's not very good. My sister is in this relationship now where she sees the fella every week or two. The rest of the time it's just her and the kids. It's wonderful."

In about one fourth of families, the onset of the firstborn's adolescence has little impact on the parents' marital relationship. In some of these households, the couple was quite unhappy before the child reached adolescence, and their relationship was little changed by their child's development. In others, the child's adolescence may have provided a challenge to the marriage, but the couple was able to cope with the demands of the transition and support each other when the going was rough. These couples reported occasional periods of strain but little overall impact on the quality of their relationship. Often, these were families in which husband and wife were both involved in activities outside the home—usually their work—and so were diverted or distracted from many of the day-to-day vicissitudes of childrearing. In some cases, I had the impression that they almost did not notice their child's development.

The majority of couples in our study, however, reported a decline in marital satisfaction over the early adolescent transition. Fathers—especially, fathers of sons—seemed particularly susceptible to this effect, although mothers were by no means immune to it. In general, these were couples in which one or both of the partners reacted negatively to the child's development, for whom the transition was tainted by loss rather than freedom, jealousy rather than joy, regret rather than satisfaction, or powerlessness rather than self-assurance. The negative personal reaction spilled over into the marital relationship and then reverberated back to cause even more personal unhappiness and distress. Although most of the couples who experienced a decline in their marital happiness during this period would rebound from this low point over time, they, of course, could not have foreseen the light at the end of the tunnel. For them, their child's adolescence created or enlarged an abyss in their relationship, and it marked one of the lowest valleys in their marriage.

In a small minority of families, however—about one fifth—marital satisfaction actually increased over the course of the child's adolescence. Generally, these were homes in which both parents experienced the adolescent's maturation as an opportunity to devote more time to their own relationship. Mothers and fathers who found their child's adolescence to be liberating, rejuvenating, or ego gratifying often fell into this category. They were able somehow to plug into the joy and excitement of their child's teenage years and channel some of this energy into their marriage. Some reported a revitalization of their sex life. Others reported an increase in romance. Many simply said they had rediscovered what it was like to spend time together as a couple again, unburdened by some of the daily hassles of raising younger children.

11. THE SPILLOVER INTO WORK

For most of us, midlife is the time during which we abandon our fantasies about potential accomplishments in the world of work and adopt more realistic appraisals of what we actually are more likely to achieve. A corporate vice president accepts the fact that a senior vice presidency, but not the company presidency, is a reasonable aspiration. A clothing manufacturer's sales representative confronts the fact that, although she may be promoted at some future point, she probably will never become a regional manager. A travel agent sees that, despite her lifelong dreams, she will probably never own her own agency. An amateur poet looks over his collected poems and acknowledges that his work, while published locally, is unlikely ever to appear in a national magazine.

THE OCCUPATIONAL PLATEAU

Sometime in their forties, the majority of adults reach a critical turning point in their occupational development—what psychologists call the *occupational plateau*.

The term is somewhat confusing in that the occupational plateau is not a mesa at the top of one mountain. Rather, the plateau psychologists refer to is a sort of landing, where, looking out over one's career vista, it is finally possible to envision how the remainder of one's work life will likely unfold. There may be more distance to climb on the way up the mountain, but once at the occupational plateau, individuals are elevated enough to see what is probably waiting at the highest point they will reach. More often than not, when we arrive at the occupational plateau, we see that we are not going to reach the top.

Hitting some sort of occupational plateau at midlife is virtually inevitable. As a number of other social scientists have pointed out, most occupations are structured like pyramids, not skyscrapers. The higher one climbs, the less room is available. In concrete terms, there are many more would-be law partners than there are law firm partnerships, many more middle managers than opportunities for senior executives, and many more slots on the assembly line than openings for foremen. Feeling squeezed as we move up the career ladder is inescapable.

It is true, to be sure, that some adults enter midlife and emerge as optimistic about the future as they were when they started out on their careers. As they stare out over the expanse of their remaining work years, the future still holds a great deal of promise, perhaps even a certain degree of mystery. They see the top of the pyramid and know that they have a good chance of getting there. Individuals who fall into this category comprise a very small minority, however. Far more common are adults who hit a plateau in middle age and who feel as if they are able to see the "end of the movie."

People have very different responses to this realization. There are those who emerge from the occupational plateau with dashed hopes. They struggle, with considerable pain, to reconcile their actual accomplishments and their realistic expectations for the future against the loftier aspirations and dreams they had entertained when they were younger. They may become depressed or embittered, disappointed in themselves, and sometimes even embarrassed in front of family and friends. Like a major league athlete who "never lived up to his potential," a would-be senior executive who is still stuck in middle management at the age of forty-five may feel that he has let himself and others down.

But there are also many adults whose experience of the occupational plateau is one of relief—a sort of relaxation that comes from accepting who one is and enjoying what one has achieved. Rather than pushing himself harder and harder each year, an accomplished business executive may feel content to leave his firm and become a consultant, so that he can schedule his work at a more relaxed pace.

For some, this inner peace comes from discovering an interest or activity outside of work that is equally, if not more, fulfilling. A reasonably successful attorney may accept—even embrace—the realization that she would rather take on fewer clients and devote more time to her painting.

For others, the contentment comes from acknowledging that additional success has its own costs—typically in the form of additional pressure and responsibility—and that the security of a familiar situation may have very real advantages over the unknown circumstances of a higher position on the career ladder. A number of midlevel executives I know view the day-to-day activities of their superiors not with envy, but with gratitude that they themselves did not end up going that far. Unlike their bosses, they are able to relax with their families on Saturday mornings without the interruptions of urgent faxes and Federal Express deliveries.

And then there are the individuals who decide to make major changes in their occupational careers as a result of insights gained while at the plateau. For these individuals, the plateau provides a sort of psychological rest stop, and while pulled off to the side of the occupational highway, they may decide on a change of itinerary. For many, dissatisfaction experienced and confronted while at the plateau may be transformed into a decision to leave that particular career entirely. This decision may take the form of "I now know that this career wasn't right for me (or isn't right any longer)," or it may take the form of "I now know that I wasn't (or am not any longer) right for this career." In either case, a change in direction feels like the right thing to do.

DIFFERENT RESPONSES TO THE PLATEAU

Given the fact that hitting the occupational plateau itself is more or less unavoidable, it is important to ask why some individuals respond one way while others respond quite differently. What factors explain why some adults at this point in their work life feel angry and bitter, whereas others feel content and satisfied? Why do some individuals react to reaching the plateau with regret over their past mistakes, while others look back on their careers with satisfaction? Why do some midlife adults withdraw from their work emotionally while others invest even more time and energy? Why do some adults continue on in careers in which they are unhappy, while others decide to change occupations entirely?

For many years, psychologists have tried to answer these questions by looking solely at the adult's experiences in the workplace. If a man was successful in middle age (I use "man," because almost all of this research has ignored women), he was expected to be happy and invested in his job. The greater his achievements—the bigger his practice, the more well publicized his accomplishments, the more wealth he had amassed—the more satisfied he was supposed to be.

In theory, we might expect an individual's reaction to hitting the occupational plateau to depend on the distance between his initial *aspirations* (that is, what he had once hoped to accomplish) and his current *expectations* (that is, what he now sees as reasonable). If his expectations exceed his aspirations—e.g., the newspaper editor who, when starting out, had hoped only to someday be able to have his own byline—he should be satisfied, perhaps even overjoyed. If, on the other hand, his initial aspirations far exceed his actual expectations—e.g., the aspiring television producer who sees, at the age of forty-five, that he will never rise above the level of a production assistant—he should be greatly discouraged.

Although intuitively reasonable, this formula falls short when we try to apply it across a range of people. For one thing, it does not explain why some individuals who clearly meet, or even exceed, their aspirations nevertheless feel a sense of disappointment when they reach the plateau. We all know of highly successful individuals who nonetheless feel extremely dissatisfied with their achievements. Often, these individuals find it very difficult to discuss their feelings of inadequacy or discontent, because to outsiders it seems almost inconceivable—and, perhaps, downright irritating—that someone so accomplished would dare to be so disappointed. Yet, many adults at midlife find themselves in exactly this situation—successful, yet disappointed.

CYNTHIA GARRISON

Cynthia Garrison, the single mother who worked as a legislative assistant in the state government, was a good example of someone in this category. As a young girl growing up in rural Wisconsin, Cynthia had been raised to believe that a career was not an especially important facet of a woman's life. Although she had graduated from one of the state university campuses with a respectable record of achievement, she had never given much thought to a career. She expected to devote herself full time to raising a family. When Cynthia first married Michael, she worked as a secretary in the state government to bring in some extra money while Michael finished his residency at the university hospital. Their goal was to begin having children as soon as Michael completed his training.

About one year into their marriage, Cynthia became pregnant with Jessica. She was overjoyed, and the pregnancy went smoothly. However, during the baby's delivery, a number of unusual medical complications arose that necessitated gynecological surgery immediately after Jessica's birth, and when the procedure was completed, Cynthia learned that she would not be able to have any more children. She and Michael were deeply disappointed.

After Jessica entered second grade, Cynthia began to rethink her life plan. Although she had never intended to work outside the home after her children were born, Cynthia began to reconsider this decision. Already she could see that with time Jessica would need her full-time care less and less. And Michael provided little recognition for the special attention Cynthia devoted to being a homemaker—if anything, he disparaged her efforts. Cynthia made an appointment to meet with someone for whom she had worked before Jessica was born, and soon thereafter she was hired as a secretary for a state legislator.

This time, however, Cynthia brought a different attitude to her job. Intent on transforming the job into a career, and sensitive about Michael's complaints that she devoted too much time and energy to their home, Cynthia worked especially hard and took on added responsibilities. Her supervisors recognized her talent and her commitment, and over time, Cynthia was promoted within the legislator's staff. Her divorce from Michael, one year after returning to work, only motivated her to work harder. By the time Jessica had entered fourth grade, Cynthia had become a legislative assistant. Two years later, Cynthia was recruited away by one of the most powerful members of the state senate as his senior staffer. When I met her, Cynthia Garrison was one of the most well-respected legislative assistants in the state capital, with a special interest in education and in programs affecting the state's Native American population.

Without a doubt, Cynthia's career had gone far better than she had ever hoped. But her success did not translate into personal satisfaction or feelings of fulfillment. As you may recall, she was also coping with her feelings of abandonment in her relationship with her daughter.

Although she reported working hard and working long hours, Cynthia reported rather low satisfaction with work but, curiously, scored very high on our measure of *work orientation*, a scale designed to assess how "invested" individuals were in their careers. When I asked Cynthia about her job, her answer corroborated her questionnaire responses: She was working harder than ever, but enjoying it less.

"Work—well, I like it, I suppose. I mean, it's a challenge and I'm always very busy, but some days it feels as if I'm just going through the motions. I guess everything becomes routine if you do it long enough."

I asked Cynthia for an example of something that had triggered this feeling in her.

"I was working on this after-school child-care bill the other day, something that I really care a lot about. While I was sitting at my desk, staring out the window at people walking around the capitol, I began to think that what I was doing really didn't matter all that much. That even if we were successful in getting these programs funded—which we probably won't be, anyway—something else would come up tomorrow that would be just as big an ordeal. And my boss would hand the new project to me, and I would be expected to handle that, too.

"I don't know," Cynthia continued. I spend a lot of time at the office, which is OK, I guess, since Jessie seems to need me less and less. But somehow the job doesn't hold that much interest for me. I feel like I've seen it all already, that there is nothing new to learn. I know I don't have a right to complain—I have a great job by most standards. My friends are really envious. And things like, the other night, I was interviewed on the evening news, and people from back home saw me on television and called to say they had seen it, and that was fun. But I look around sometimes and think, 'Is *this* all there is to it?' And I wonder, how I am going to keep doing the same thing for twenty more years. I think it's easier if you're married. Then, at least you have that to keep you going after the kids leave."

I asked Cynthia how she felt about balancing work and family responsibilities.

"It's different from what I had expected. When Jessie needed me more, I felt stressed out trying to juggle everything, but I think I actually was much happier with work. Now that she wants to be off with her friends all the time, I have more time for my job, but I can't seem to get all that interested in it. It's funny, isn't it?"

One of the classic symptoms of depression is the loss of pleasure in activities that had previously been enjoyable. I sensed that Cynthia's depression over being left behind by Jessica actually was making it difficult for her to enjoy her work.

In addition to the problem of the dissatisfied achiever, social scientists also have had difficulty explaining why some adults whose careers had so obviously turned out to be less than they had expected seemed satisfied and content, despite their apparent "failure." We may even feel a little angry, albeit irrationally, when we discover that someone whom we had pegged as having failed to live up to his potential is nevertheless perfectly happy.

JONATHAN SPENCER

Irritation over his complacent "underachievement" was a reaction often encountered by Jonathan Spencer, the youthful high school teacher whose wife, Amanda, was having trouble coping with their son's emotional maturation.

"I had never expected to go into teaching high school," he told me. "I was in a graduate program in economics at Ohio State, fully intending to get my doctorate and do research. I had finished my master's degree and was just about to start on my dissertation when my mother took ill. When she got out of the hospital, she really needed someone there to take care of her for a while, and with my father gone, there really wasn't anybody else but me to do it. My brother and sister were both married and had their own families. So I left Columbus and moved back to Cleveland.

"I thought I would spend a year back home and then go back to school, but I never got around to finishing my degree. When Amanda and I decided to get married, I figured that teaching was something I could do, because I had been working as a teaching assistant at OSU. So I took some evening courses in education, applied for certification, and got my credential. I taught for a while outside Cleveland, and then we decided to move here. It wasn't what I had planned on doing—and it sure wasn't what people had expected I would do—but I guess becoming an economist just wasn't in the cards."

Looking back, did Jonathan have any regrets about going into teaching?

"Only on payday," he laughed. "Most of the time, I love it. I love the energy the kids generate, and their sense of humor. Actually, I like it more now than when I started out. I'm more relaxed, more sure of myself in the classroom.

"Frankly, it's the parents who make teaching difficult, not the kids. Especially in this town, with all the professors and Ph.D.s running around, teachers aren't exactly held in high regard. Hell, you can't even find a cabdriver in this town who hasn't been to graduate school. Once, at a neighborhood block party, someone—I think he was a doctor at one of the HMOs—actually told me that I seemed too smart to be a high school teacher. He said, 'You must be awfully frustrated.' I told him that I was doing exactly what I wanted to be doing. I said I probably have a lot more fun at work than he ever does.

"No," Jonathan continued, "I'm in teaching for the long haul. I made my peace with that a long time ago. Look, every job has its pros and cons. Teaching high school is no different than anything else. You get out of it what you put into it. I give a lot to my kids, and I get a lot back in return. It's not all that different from being a parent, I suppose."

OCCUPATIONAL DEVELOPMENT AND THE ADOLESCENT FACTOR

How can we account for such apparent anomalies as the dissatisfied success story and the content underachiever? Why is it that some people are unhappy with careers that others would give their eye-teeth for?

Although a variety of influences are potentially important, our study suggested that one factor that has been overlooked in research on occupational development is the influence of having a teenage child. For not only does the occupational plateau coincide with hitting one's forties, it also coincides with having one's child become a teenager. More than 60 percent of the parents in our sample experienced a marked shift in their feelings about their work when their child entered adolescence.

There are a variety of ways that the feelings provoked by having a child come into adolescence reverberate and spill over into the domain of work. As you now understand, the child's transition into adolescence often magnifies the feelings that parents have about themselves. This amplification can make hitting the occupational plateau seem more salient—and feel more painful—than would otherwise be the case. For some parents, the feeling that "something has *got* to change" becomes that much more urgent when they contrast how their life is to the seemingly limitless possibilities open to their child. This happened frequently in families in which a parent identified strongly with the teenager, as was the case for Bob Peterson, the hospital administrator, and his son David.

BOB PETERSON

David's picture sat prominently on his father's desk in his hospital office. When Bob looked at the photo, however, he did not always see his son. Sometimes, if he allowed his mind to drift back twenty-five years, Bob saw himself as a teenager. When he did, he was reminded of his own earlier aspirations to become a physician. In fact, when Bob was David's age, he had spent his afternoons volunteering in his family doctor's office. While he refiled patients' records, thirteen-year-old Bob would fantasize about the day when he would have his own medical practice.

Now, at the age of forty, Bob was not a successful physician, however. Instead, he was an unhappy hospital administrator who was feeling stuck on a treadmill.

Bob thought back bitterly about his struggle to complete the science courses he took as an undergraduate premed student at the university and remembered all too clearly the disappointing grades he had received in biology and chemistry, despite his hard work. He still recalled the day when, as a junior, he met with his premed advisor to discuss his medical school applications. The advisor looked over his transcript and told Bob to stop hitting his head against the wall. It was unlikely that he would be accepted at an American medical school with his science grades. Bob was crushed. Discouraged, Bob changed his career plans and went into health administration.

Initially, Bob was surprised at how much he liked his job, especially given that it was not his first choice of a career. He discovered that he was an able administrator and, for many years, he was quite successful, rising up through the managerial ranks at one of the city's best hospitals. Up until his late thirties, Bob was content with his work.

This changed, however, when Bob's son David entered junior high school and began to express an interest in science and, possibly, medicine. When David first announced this at the Petersons' dinner table one evening, Bob felt a mixture of pride and dread. He was delighted with the possibility that David would pursue a career in medicine and he put David in touch with several of the physicians who worked at the hospital, in the hope that David would be able to secure a summer volunteer position. But at the same time, Bob could not help but be reminded of his failure to reach his own career goal.

Bob's identification with his adolescent son, and the ambivalence it provoked in him, had two interesting effects. At home, Bob became obsessed with David's school performance, riding him constantly about maintaining his grades. David had complained about this when we spoke. I had asked him to tell me about a recent argument with his father.

"We fight a lot about school, I guess. It's ridiculous. He always asks about my homework, wants to check it over and make sure everything is right. He really gets on my nerves. 'Don't make the same mistakes I made,' he always says. He must've said that to me a hundred times. I've heard the story over and over. How he wanted to be a doctor and couldn't get into med school because his grades weren't good enough. How I need to start worrying now if that's what I want to do with my life." Then, David asked me, "How would I know if that's what I want to do with my life? I'm not even in high school yet."

Bob's ambivalence about David's plans was also spilling over into his work at the hospital. Bob told me that he had reached the point where he could see all too clearly how not having an M.D. was going to limit how far he would rise as a hospital administrator. No matter how good a job he did, he said, he would always feel like a second-class citizen within the clubby medical establishment. Although over the years he had become inured to the doctors' air of superiority, David's expression of an interest in medicine reactivated some of Bob's repressed anger and disappointment.

Now, when he stared at the picture of David on his desk, Bob couldn't help feeling disappointed in himself and dissatisfied with his work. More and more frequently, he thought about quitting and getting out of the medical field entirely, but he worried about how he would support his family while he was between jobs. At the office, Bob was often preoccupied; at home, he was cranky and irritable.

THE ADOLESCENT AS CATALYST FOR CHANGE

There were other parents in our sample whose adolescent's developing occupational interests triggered their own reevaluation, but instead of becoming mired in self-pity and regret over their careers, these parents used the occupational plateau as an opportunity to make changes in their lives. Some of these parents were stimulated by their adolescent's newfound freedom to reassess their own life situation and make some changes. Several said that watching their child grow triggered a kind of "now or never" reaction.

One father in my study, a successful business executive, told me that he had always wanted to teach at the college level but had stopped short in his education in order to get a job and make money. One evening after dinner, while helping his son decide on which school subjects to take the following semester, he started telling his son about his own unrealized dreams. Late that night, lying in bed next to his sleeping wife, he began to fantasize about becoming a student himself. He awakened his wife, and they sat up in bed, talking about his hopes and dreams. When they had finished their conversation, he drifted off into a satisfying sleep.

After a number of additional discussions with his wife, the executive decided to go back to school to earn his Ph.D. in history. I asked him if he thought that his decision was motivated by the conversation he had with his son.

"Some of it was, sure. But it wasn't just the conversation with Jimmy that did it. It was more, I guess, that looking at him—seeing him get older—made me realize that time was slipping away for me. I thought to myself, what am I waiting for? I'm forty-three years old. If I wait any longer, it will be too late. And then I started noticing all the people I work with who are unhappy—they feel trapped in a job they don't want to have, trapped by their mortgage payments, college savings plans, the race to keep up."

I said that I thought this feeling was fairly common among men our age.

"You bet," he replied. "There's this group of us that plays cards every Tuesday night—we've been doing it for about eight years now. One night—this is now two years ago—while we were taking a break, I started asking, just out of curiosity, whether anyone ever thought of changing careers. You know what four out of six of them said? 'Every single day.' Can you imagine that? I started to think about this whenever I was on a business trip. I'd look around the airports, at the people in line at the rent-a-cars. All of these forty-year-old guys walking around, one more miserable than the next. And then I would think, 'Who am *I* feeling sorry for? I'm one of them!'

"One morning, a couple of months later, I called my office and told my secretary that I was going to be coming in late. After the kids left for school, I sat at the kitchen table with my wife. We sat down and added up our savings—we'd managed to build up a pretty sizable nest egg—and figured out that we could swing it as long as we cut back on some expenses.

"I still was hesitant, though. I mulled it over for the next month or so—I don't like to do anything impulsive. I wanted to try living with the idea for a while to see how it felt. I kept asking myself what the down side was. I couldn't find a good answer. So I made an appointment with my boss, and over lunch, we talked it through. He knew just how I felt—said he had been there himself more than once. He suggested my taking a leave from work instead of quitting, not burning any bridges. Said I could have a job with the company whenever I wanted to come back. And I took him up on it. And now I'm a student. I've never regretted it—not for one day."

Identification is one mechanism through which the adolescent's maturation affects the parent's occupational identity. A second, equally potent process, involves social comparison. Whereas identification often involves contrast between the adolescent and what the parent *was*, social comparison involves a contrast between the adolescent and what the parent *is*. This was common among parents who reacted to their child's adolescence with jealousy, like Richard Johnson.

RICHARD JOHNSON

As you may recall, Richard, the laboratory technician and baseball-card fanatic, had a good deal of difficulty accepting his son Matt's success. Unlike Richard, who had been lonely and undistinguished as a teenager, Matt excelled academically, athletically, and socially. Although Richard bragged frequently about Matt's achievements to workmates and friends, inside, he was more than a little envious. The brighter Matt shone, the dimmer Richard felt in comparison. One of the ways this manifested itself was in a drop in Richard's work satisfaction. Over the past several years, he told me, he had come to enjoy work less and less.

It was no coincidence that Richard's enthusiasm for work had declined as Matt had begun to come into his own. Before, when Matt was younger, dinner conversations at the Johnson home often revolved around Richard's day at work, and Matt had enjoyed taking trips to the lab with his father on Saturdays and Sundays to check on the progress of various experiments and examine the high-tech equipment. Like many boys, Matt even had gone through a period when he wanted to follow in his father's line of work, and, when asked what he wanted to do when he grew up, would say that he wanted to become a scientist or inventor.

Matt's interest in his father's work began to fade, however, and with it, it seemed, went the interest of the whole Johnson household. Now the Johnsons' dinner conversations seemed focused on Matt's various successes, and when Richard would try to steer the conversation toward his own work, no one seemed to listen. Over time, Richard had even begun to lose interest in his own stories. He began to withdraw from dinner conversation and found himself daydreaming as Matt described his day's activities. Every once in a while, Matt told me, he or his brother Michael would say "Earth to Dad, Earth to Dad" in order to bring Richard back into the conversation.

During our interview, I asked Richard how he felt about his work. He said it was not a particularly important aspect of his life. "Oh, you know, it's usually the same-old, same-old," he said. "By now, most of what I do I can do in my sleep. There was a time when I tried to make it more interesting for myself, but now, when I'm in the lab, my mind is often somewhere else. I know it's a ways off, but I'm already looking forward to retiring. It's hard to keep my mind from wandering. I'm lucky nothing has gone wrong." He knocked on the coffee table for good luck.

FAMILY STRESS INVADES THE WORKPLACE

One of the most common ways in which the child's adolescence affects a parent's work life involves stress. Much has been written about the impact of work stress on the family. But far less has been said about the impact of family stress on work. It became clear to me over the course of our study, though, that when a child's adolescence raised the stress level in the home environment, it often spilled over into the workplace. This was quite prevalent among parents who argued frequently with their adolescent or disagreed markedly with their spouse about childrearing.

Because mothers argue more often with their children than do fathers, the family stress/workplace spillover effect was far more common among women than men. Ironically, while many men complained that they brought work problems home with them more often than they wished, many of the mothers in our sample reported having a hard time leaving family problems at home when they went off to work each morning.

ELLEN HANSEN

Ellen Hansen, who was employed as a medical secretary, was fairly typical. She and her second husband, Gray, were having such a difficult time with her fifteen-year-old, Cindy, that it was hard for her to concentrate at the office.

"I've almost lost my job two different times," Ellen confessed. "I'd be sitting there typing up doctors' notes from a tape, and I just wasn't paying attention. They talk so fast, you know, that you really have to pay attention in order to catch everything they say. And if you let your mind drift at all, you've got to go back over the tape again. I remember one week when Cindy and Gray and I were fighting all the time. I'd listen to a tape and not hear one single word. All I could hear was the fight we had had that morning. Then I'd have to rewind and play the tape all over again.

"I got so far behind that week, they almost fired me. I was lucky, though. One of my supervisors had been through a similar thing with her kid, and so she covered for me when one of the doctors asked where her notes were. Mary said that the tape had jammed and that we had to send it out to be fixed. That saved my neck."

GRAY MILLER

Ellen's husband and Cindy's stepfather, Gray, also had problems on his job, but whereas Ellen's difficulties were due mainly to being distracted by her family's conflict, Gray's were due to something entirely different: Gray's feelings of powerlessness in his relationship with his stepdaughter Cindy were affecting his relationships at the office. The more impotent he felt at home, the more autocratic he became at work. He was well aware of the connection:

"It's like that old cartoon where the boss yells at the guy who takes it out on his wife, who yells at the kid, who kicks the dog. I fight with Cindy and take it out on my secretary. I know it's not right, but I usually walk into the office on Monday all steamed and the last thing I want to hear is someone questioning me—I get *that* all weekend long at home. Let me tell you, since Cindy turned fourteen a year ago, I've gone through three secretaries."

THE MYTH OF THE "EMPTY NEST"

Psychologists have used the term "empty nest" to refer to that time in the family's life when all of the children have moved out of the house. According to popular wisdom, entering the empty nest is supposed to be an extremely difficult transition for parents, especially women. Put most simply, mothers are expected to grow despondent when their children leave home.

Most people are surprised to learn that the empty-nest phenomenon is more or less a myth—a bit of folk wisdom that has never been confirmed in scientific research. In point of fact, it turns out that the idea that women grow depressed when their children leave home is wrong on two counts. First, studies show quite clearly that mothers' mental health *improves* when their children leave home. Second, the little research that has been done on men in this regard suggests that, to the extent that the launching of children is hard on parents, it takes more of a toll on fathers than on mothers—prompting some scientists to label this the "empty den," rather than "empty nest," syndrome.

It seems that mothers, because they have been so involved in the day-to-day work of childrearing, are happy to finally have a break from the parenting role. Fathers, who are typically far less involved in their children's daily lives than mothers, react to their children's departure with regret over what they have missed out on.

Because the oldest children in our sample were still living at home at the time of our study, it was not possible to examine the empty-nest and empty-den phenomena with our data. But in the course of conducting the interviews with mothers and fathers, I discovered something that may explain why scientific research on the empty nest has not corroborated popular belief about the subject. The empty-nest transition is not an abrupt event that occurs when the youngest child leaves home, but a much longer process that actually begins much earlier, when the oldest child first begins to move away emotionally.

One of the reasons that social scientists have had a hard time documenting an empty-nest effect, I believe, is that they have focused too much attention on the final, culminating event—the actual physical departure of the youngest child—and too little on the earlier phases of the process. Instead of focusing on the empty nest and its impact on the adult's mental health, it may be more helpful to think about the "emptying of the nest" and how parents are affected by this.

THE REALITY OF THE "EMPTYING NEST"

When we look at the phenomenon in this light, we find that the early stages of the "emptying" process *do* have an effect on parents' mental health, especially as it pertains to their orientation toward work. In our study, I saw three very different reactions.

For about one third of the parents in our study, the onset of the firstborn child's adolescence diminished their commitment to the workplace. This occurred more often among parents who were already dissatisfied with their work before their child reached adolescence. Not surprisingly, this reaction was more prevalent among blue-collar parents than among white-collar or professional ones. This made sense, since working-class jobs are generally less satisfying and rewarding than either white-collar or professional jobs.

If parents who did not enjoy their jobs were feeling any inner turmoil as a result of what was taking place at home, they would be unlikely to seek comfort in the workplace. Indeed, a stressed-out, work-dissatisfied parent would likely be distracted at work and perhaps even motivated to disengage psychologically from it, a pattern we saw in Theresa Rossi, the data processor who spent her work hours daydreaming about the adolescence she had been deprived of. For her, as for many others in our study, the feelings and thoughts triggered by the imminence of the adolescent's departure made it difficult to concentrate on work. As a result, commitment to and satisfaction with work declined over time.

For a slightly smaller group of parents—about 30 percent—entering the emptying-nest stage of family life had the opposite effect, however. Seeing their children mature provoked increased or renewed commitment to the workplace, motivating an increase in work hours, a return to school for additional training, or an increase in their emotional commitment to their careers. Some parents sought refuge in work as a means of coping with the turmoil caused by the adolescent transition. Others simply took advantage of the opportunity to devote more time to their career now that their child needed less day-to-day attention.

One had the feeling that these parents reacted to entering the emptying nest by anticipating, either consciously or unconsciously, what was going to happen a few years down the road. Because they had been enjoying their work all along, they were able to adjust to the feelings provoked by the thought of the adolescent leaving by throwing themselves into work. Or, for some mothers who had left the labor force after becoming a parent, this was accomplished by throwing themselves *back* into their career. As one might expect, this reaction was more common among parents from white-collar and professional occupations, both because their jobs were more satisfying to begin with and because these occupations provided more flexibility to change. Sarah Fein, who turned to science-fiction writing, and Vicki Dobson, who increased her commitment to her job selling real estate and enrolled in several courses at the community college, were good examples of this.

And finally, there were individuals whose work commitment was more or less unaffected by entering the emptying nest. These parents—who accounted for a little over one third of the sample—kept the worlds of work and parenting separate, not allowing events in one domain to affect those in the other. Although they experienced ups and downs in their satisfaction with work and in their career commitment, these changes had nothing to do with occurrences in their family life. They were driven entirely by events in the workplace.

Which parents were most likely to keep the worlds of work and family separate? For the most part, they were men. In general, the impact of the early adolescent's emotional and physical maturation on parents' commitment to work—whether positive or negative—was far stronger among mothers than fathers. Specifically, we saw increased work commitment in response to the adolescent's maturation in about one third of mothers but in only one fifth of fathers. Similarly, whereas more than one third of mothers decreased their work commitment as their adolescent matured, less than one fourth of fathers fell into this category.

We can look at these numbers a different way. About two thirds of the mothers in our sample, but fewer than half of the fathers, responded to their child's maturation with a discernible change in commitment to the workplace. It would certainly seem that the links between work and family life are stronger among women than they are among men. Men are far more able than women to keep the worlds of home and work separate.

RETHINKING THEORIES OF THE EMPTY NEST

What do our findings say about theories of the empty nest? Mothers are more affected by events that occur in the early stages of the emptying process, such as increases in the child's demand for more privacy or in the child's desire to spend time away from the family. Fathers, in contrast, may be more affected by events that occur during the later stages of the process, such as the child's physical departure from the household. Why should this be the case?

I think the answer is that women, who are generally more attuned to social cues throughout the life cycle than men, are especially sensitive to the subtle changes in the parent-child relationship that occur early in adolescence. This may have short-term costs, such as the bickering and squabbling, the feelings of loss, and so on. But it may also have long-term benefits. By the time the child is ready for actual "launching," many mothers have already made a psychological adjustment in anticipation of the event. Many are even looking forward to it.

Fathers, on the other hand, may fare better in the short run, but worse over the long run. Because men are less interpersonally attuned than women, fathers are more likely than mothers to be oblivious to the changes in the parent-child relationship that occur early in adolescence. They are less likely to get caught up in the day-to-day routines of childrearing. But as a consequence, fathers are easily caught off guard and more psychologically unprepared when their child actually moves out.

Ironically, then, for fathers—whom we have stereotyped as being more or less unaffected by family events—the transition to the empty nest, at least in the traditional sense of the term, may be much more devastating than it is for mothers.

12. THE SPILLOVER INTO PARENTING

"I don't know why," fourteen-year-old David Peterson replied when I asked him whether he thought his father, Bob, was stricter or more lenient now than before, "but he is a lot tougher on me now than when I was younger. It's like . . . like, I've gotten older and everything, but he treats me like I'm still a little kid. He gets so angry, over nothing. I don't know what he's so worried about. I wish he'd just get off my back. Sometimes I want to say, 'Hey Dad—get a life!' "

"Oh, he definitely gives me more freedom now than before," said Matt Johnson when I asked him the same question about his father, Richard. "We used to be a lot closer a few years ago. He'd come to all my games, take me to his office, we'd watch movies on television together. Now it seems like I can come and go as I please and he doesn't really care."

"Stricter?" Jessica Garrison thought for a minute when I posed the question to her. "No, I wouldn't say that my mom's stricter. She's always been pretty good about most things. And I could always talk to her. But now, it's like, she's too involved in my life? I mean, she's nice. She lets me do most of the things I want to do, which is great, but she makes me tell her everything. And it's like she's always there. Even when I just want to be by myself. Or with my friends. It's like she wants to be one of my friends or something. Sometimes I like it. But other times, you know, I wish she'd just be my mother. I wish she'd give me more space."

David Peterson, Matt Johnson, and Jessica Garrison—three "average" teenagers from reasonably similar socioeconomic backgrounds, all growing up in the same town during the same time period, and all approximately the same age. Yet, despite these surface similarities, these three teenagers encountered very different reactions from their parents as they matured from childhood into adolescence.

HOW CAN PARENTS BE SO DIFFERENT?

I was with my wife and son at an outdoor barbecue recently where there were several other families with young children. Even though all of the parents in attendance were from similar backgrounds and lived in the same neighborhood, the variation in how they treated their children was remarkable. One set of parents let their child wander off unsupervised for most of the afternoon—I doubt if the parents exchanged three words with their child within the course of four hours. Another set of parents hovered around their child as if he were a fragile, breakable doll—at times I wondered whether the youngster was getting enough oxygen! A third set seemed to fight with their child constantly, bickering and squabbling about food, activities, manners—you name it.

Consider for a moment the parents you know—the parents who make up your own social network, or the ones you come into contact with through your work or in your community. Have you ever pondered how *different* they are from each other—how some seem incomprehensibly autocratic while others appear insanely lenient? How some parents treat their children with respect and affection, while others are aloof and distant, if not downright hostile?

In our study, I wondered why some parents became more authoritarian during their child's adolescence while others became more permissive. Why did some parents react to their child's adolescence by disengaging emotionally, while others maintained, or even tried to increase, their emotional involvement? How could we account for these differences among parents in their behavior toward their teenagers?

THE FAMILY AS A SYSTEM

I have spent most of my career as a psychologist studying parents and how they behave toward their children. In some of our research programs, we invite parents and their children to come to our offices at the university, where we seat them in our "living room" and give them a problem to discuss. We select the problem from a list of everyday topics that the family has identified as ones that they are currently struggling with, such as getting the teenager to clean up his room or arguing over a youngster's curfew. We know, of course, that families do not interact the same way at home as they do in our artificial situation, but our procedure nevertheless provides an interesting window on the family's style of relating.

While the parents and children are talking the problem over, our staff observes them through a one-way mirror, and their discussion is videotaped. (The families are told that they are being watched and recorded, although we make the observation as unobtrusive as possible.) Later, we watch the videotapes over and over again to try to identify patterns in the family's interaction. Who controls the flow of the conversation? How much disagreement is there in the family? How much affection is expressed? Do individuals listen to each other's opinions?

The differences between the patterns we see in families of nine-year-olds and those we see in families of twelve-year-olds are striking. So are the differences between the families of twelve-year-olds and those of sixteen-year-olds. Compared to families with younger or older children, those with young adolescents—roughly between the ages of eleven and fourteen—argue and interrupt each other far more frequently. At times, their interaction has a strained quality to it, like the sort you'd see among strangers who aren't quite sure how to behave with one another. Relationships within families with young adolescents seem to be in a state of flux. Individuals seem to vacillate between wanting to connect and wanting to be distant. When you watch a tape of a family in this group, the tension between these two desires—connecting and separating—is palpable.

After years of research, psychologists now understand that early adolescence is a time of important shifts in the interpersonal dynamics of the parent-child relationship. During this transitional time period, the family system is being transformed, moving from a state of comfortable routine into a region of uncharted territory. Everyone in the family seems to sense that there is much sorting out and sorting through to be done. But without a clear sense of where the family system is ultimately headed, relationships during these transitional times are renegotiated through trial and error. In early adolescence, teenagers feel on trial, and their parents feel as if everything they do is in error.

It is helpful to think of the family as a system of relationships progressing in and out of various stages of equilibrium over the course of the *family life cycle*. As you know, the family life cycle is the series of stages through which a family develops as its members age and its functions and relationships change. Some stages are relatively brief (for example, the stage surrounding the first child's infancy, which lasts about two years), while other stages are considerably longer (for example, the stage surrounding the child's elementary school years).

When a family has been in a specific stage for several years, it begins to fall into a familiar routine—a sort of steady state. Individuals know their roles and the parts they play in the system, whether these parts have to do with household responsibilities (e.g., Mom does the grocery shopping and Dad takes care of the yard) or emotional relationships (e.g., Mom is the disciplinarian and Dad is the pushover). Sudden, unexpected events—such as a crisis or emergency—can temporarily disrupt the equilibrium, but, in general, most families are able to find their way back again to the earlier script.

When a family enters a new phase in its development, however— when a child is born, when the infant becomes a toddler, when the oldest child enters school, and the like—its members often discover that their old script no longer fits the new characters. Unfortunately, though, it is not clear what the new script should be. Family systems experts refer to this process as one of *disequilibration*—an undoing of the balance that has been established on the way toward the negotiating of a new but different equilibrium. Experts agree that early adolescence is, for most families, a period of tremendous disequilibrium.

There are important differences among families in the way that this disequilibrium manifests itself, however. Although *some* degree of change in the parent-child relationship seems virtually inevitable as children mature into adolescence, the specific form that this change takes varies considerably from one family to another. Some families "go with the flow," gradually adjusting their interaction to the changing needs and capabilities of the developing child. Others change abruptly, experimenting with extremes in strictness or permissiveness, or oscillating between the two. Still others seem stuck in earlier ways of relating, unable to change despite clear evidence that what they are doing is not working.

The lessons I have learned over the years from watching families interact in our laboratory were corroborated in the interviews we conducted with the parents and teenagers in our study. Still now, when I reread the teenagers' interview transcripts, I am struck by the diversity of responses they offered in answer to our questions about how things had changed between them and their parents over the last few years. A few adolescents, of course, reported that things had not changed very much in their home, but these individuals were clearly in the minority and tended to be either relatively younger within our sample (younger than eleven) or relatively older (older than fifteen). As I've explained, these youngsters are likely to be outside the age range when things in the family are changing most dramatically.

Most of the youngsters in our sample, though, could put their finger on at least one dimension of the parent-child relationship that had shifted noticeably. Some, like David Peterson, felt that their parents had really tightened the reins. Often these youngsters felt unfairly treated, complaining that they had done nothing to warrant this increased authoritarianism. Others, like Matt Johnson, wished their parents were *more* involved, noting, sadly, that it seemed as if their parents had taken more of an interest in their life when they were younger. Still others, like Jessica Garrison, complained of feeling suffocated.

THE DETERMINANTS OF PARENTING

Questions about why parents do what they do have received surprisingly little attention from social scientists. Although we certainly know that parents differ in their approaches to childrearing—and that these differences have implications for their children's development—we know far less about the *determinants* of parenting than we do about the *consequences* of parenting. And we know astonishingly little about whether or why parents change their childrearing practices as their youngsters mature.

Most of the research to date on the determinants of parenting has focused on the impact of the child on the parent. These studies show, not surprisingly, that mothers and fathers fine-tune their parenting in response to the behavior and personality of the child. During infancy, for example, parents respond to their child's temperament, raising an active baby differently from a passive one and responding to a perpetually happy child in different ways than they would to a frequently cranky one. During childhood, parents tailor their behavior based on their view of the child's personality. They may see parenting as an opportunity to reaffirm what they view as the child's strong points, for example, by buying watercolors and an easel for an artistically inclined child—or to try and counter what they think are the child's weaknesses, for instance, by enrolling an unassertive child in karate class.

During their child's adolescence, parents also adjust their behavior in response to the changing behaviors of the teenager. An adolescent who demonstrates healthy responsibility and mature self-reliance is likely to elicit more autonomy and independence from her parents. A teenager who is struggling academically may incite more parental involvement in his schoolwork. A parent who discovers that his son is experimenting with alcohol may become more vigilant and restrictive.

Although there is no question that parents' practices are influenced by their children's behavior, the ways that parents treat their children are also profoundly affected by events *outside* the parent-child relationship. Our study pointed to three sets of influences that were especially salient during the adolescent transition: the parents' attitudes and beliefs about effective parenting, or what I called their "childrearing philosophy"; events in the domains of work and marriage; and the parents' psychological response to the child's adolescent transition.

PARENTS AS PHILOSOPHERS

I was surprised to discover how many parents, when asked, could actually articulate what their childrearing "philosophy" was and how they had come by it. All parents have attitudes and beliefs about what a "good" parent does during adolescence—and most have a theory, correct or incorrect, about why certain practices are better for teenagers than others. When I asked Bob Peterson, the hospital administrator, what advice he might give to another parent whose child was about to enter adolescence, here's what he said:

"Love them, but be strict with them. Be a little stricter than you want to be. Show your love by looking out for them. They are at a stage where they think they know it all, but there are things you know as an adult that they just can't see. Sometimes that means that you have to do things that won't win you any popularity contests, but in the end, your child will appreciate you for it."

I asked how Bob had come to this approach.

"I try to balance out my wife," he said. "She's more lenient with David than I am, and I worry that with two lenient parents it would be easy for him to get into trouble, to fall between the cracks. And my parents were pretty strict with me, growing up. And I look back and am grateful for that. They came from the 'spare the rod' school of thought. So I guess I learned some of it from them."

Vicki Dobson, the single mother and real estate broker, came to her daughter's adolescence with a completely different perspective, although it, too, was based on a set of beliefs about what children need. When I asked her what her philosophy was in raising her daughter, Melanie, she responded in the following way:

"Well, I suppose it would be to listen. To try to think what she's feeling. I try to put myself in her place, realizing that I'm not her. I always try to remember to try to empathize with the fact that she is her own person with her own things going on in her head. I make myself go back and remember that nobody really listened to me. So I always try to listen to her."

Where did these beliefs about childrearing come from? Some were based on aphorisms that had been handed down within the family. Others were learned from a spouse—I heard many stories about how the more "knowledgeable" parent shaped a partner's childrearing attitudes and behaviors. Still others were culled from the mountains of parenting advice found in books, in newspapers, and on television.

MY CHILD, MY SELF, MY PARENTS

Perhaps the biggest influence on parents' beliefs and attitudes about childrearing, though, was their own experience growing up. Although this is true throughout all the years of parenting, there seems to be something special that happens during early adolescence. Raising an adolescent typically brings back very vivid memories of one's own experiences as a child being raised by one's parents. This process of recollection seemed to have two different sorts of effects on parents, however.

There were many parents who wanted to replicate the parenting they themselves had received as teenagers. When asked to talk about the influences on their own parenting style, quite a few of the mothers and fathers I spoke with recalled fondly how they had been raised and how fortunate they had been growing up. They hoped that by raising their child in a similar way, they would carry forth the same legacy of happiness.

Watching a child become an adolescent sometimes triggers powerful memories and unleashes strong emotions about one's own parents. Greg, a forty-two-year-old advertising executive, put it this way, "Each new situation that I find myself in with [my son] Peter, well, that makes me think back to my father, and I can't help wondering, 'How would Dad have handled this? What would I do differently? What would I do the same?' Then, all of a sudden, I've taken myself back to my own adolescence and my relationship with my dad. Peter becoming a teenager somehow has brought my own childhood into clearer focus, and I find that lately I've been thinking about my own father a lot. It may be because Dad's getting old, but I think it also has something to do with Peter getting older, which makes me feel older, which makes me think of my own past more. I don't know . . . it's as if I become my son, and myself, and my father all at the same time."

Other parents had similar reactions, although many were less sanguine than Greg. Ellen Hansen, for example, the remarried mother whom you met earlier, described how arguing with her daughter Cindy sometimes dredged up anger she felt toward her own mother. "Lately, when I get into a fight with Cindy, it's like déjà vu, except that I'm the teenager and I'm fighting with my mother. I know it's twenty-five years ago, but I can feel it like it was just the other day.

"My mother and I did not get along, and I wanted to have a different kind of relationship with my daughter. I can't seem to help it, though. Cindy and I have the exact same arguments I had with my mother when I was her age—even though I swore I would never let that happen."

Many parents, like Ellen Hansen, saw their child's adolescence as an opportunity to make up for one or another deficiency in their own parents' behavior. They looked back on their own adolescence with anger or bitterness and resolved that their children would not suffer the same misery that they had been put through. Interestingly, though, the complaints that the mothers and fathers in our sample had about their own parents were not all that different from those that their adolescents had about them. In general, the most common criticisms had to do with having had parents who were too controlling, too constraining, or too aloof.

But an equal number of parents said that raising their own teenager brought back such happy memories that this strengthened their current relationship with their own parents. More than a few said something similar to these words, spoken by a thirty-nine-year-old mother of a thirteen-year-old boy: "It's made me realize how much hard work it is [being the parent of a teenager] and how much my own parents sacrificed for me when I was his age. I feel very, very grateful. And it's made me look at my parents in a more positive light."

REVERBERATIONS FROM WORK AND MARRIAGE

A second set of influences on parents' behavior, in addition to their own experiences growing up, are things that happen in other domains of the parent's life, such as work or marriage. Just as there is spillover from the parent-child relationship into the marriage, and spillover from the parent-child relationship into the parent's job, events in the workplace or marriage reverberate back into the parent-child relationship.

Happily married parents, for instance, tend to have more positive interactions with their children than do spouses who fight a lot—in part, because they have "happy" personalities that transcend these different situations, but in part also because their positive marital relations enhance their well-being, and this spills over into their parenting. When an adult comes home from work after a stressful day at the office, she is far more likely to get into a tussle with her teenager—even if the teenager hasn't done anything to warrant it—than she is if she is returning home relaxed and satisfied with her work.

In essence, marriage, work, and parenting are not separate, independent domains of adult life but interconnected and interdependent realms of activity. Although this idea is a simple one, and perhaps even a bit self-evident, we often overlook it. Our tendency is to think of our lives as compartmentalized into the different settings and roles we occupy, instead of seeing how there are important bridges across settings and links across roles.

One of the most important implications of this view, I think, is that over time the psychologically "rich" get richer, and the psychologically "poor" get poorer. A man who is satisfied and successful at work is likely to be upbeat and happy within his marriage, and this is likely to provoke a positive reaction from his wife, further strengthening his self-esteem and their marital bond. The positive spillover from the happy marriage then enhances the husband's relationship with his daughter, which, in turn, has a salutary effect on her development. Because the daughter is developing in a healthy direction, the father feels happier and more relaxed, which makes him perform better at work, which makes him a better husband, and so on.

In contrast, someone who is experiencing difficulty at work is likely, over time, to carry this strain into his marriage and parenting, which will exacerbate his level of stress, undermine his psychological well-being, and reverberate back into further problems at work. *The general principle is that positive experiences in one of the three domains—work, marriage, and parenting—tend to have positive reverberations in other domains. Conversely, distressing experiences in one domain tend to have negative reverberations in other domains.*

Although it is tempting to ask which domain is most central—that is, which realm of life is likely to "drive" events in the other realms—there is no easy answer to the question. Moreover, it is probably not the right question.

First of all, different domains of activity have different degrees of importance to different individuals; some are more "driven" by what happens in marriage, others are more influenced by events at work, while others are more affected by things that take place in the domain of parenting. As well, different domains take on different degrees of importance at different times in individuals' lives. Most of us have gone through stages where we felt especially work focused and through stages where we were more family oriented, and in each of those stages, the "driving" force in our life may have been very different.

Most important, by the time an intricate process of reverberation among work, marriage, and parenting has been set in motion, it is impossible to tell just where it started.

THE PARENT'S RESPONSE TO ADOLESCENCE

The final set of influences on parenting behavior we examined was the one we were most interested in: the impact of parents' psychological response to the child's maturation.

As we've seen, the child's adolescence provokes very different responses in parents. Some parents, like Amanda Spencer, experience it as loss, whereas others find it liberating. For some parents, like Theresa Rossi, adolescence invites regret, while for others, it engenders satisfaction. Some, like Cynthia Garrison, react to their child's maturation with feelings of abandonment, whereas others feel rejuvenated. Some, like Gray Miller, feel powerless, whereas others feel reassured. Finally, some parents, like Richard Johnson, feel jealous of their child, while others feel joy in their child's accomplishments.

I wanted to know how these different kinds of reactions—loss, regret, abandonment, powerlessness, and jealousy—spill over into parents' actual behavior toward their child. Put another way, do parents' feelings about their child's becoming an adolescent influence the way they interact with the teenager?

In order to examine this question, I needed first to look at the different parenting responses observed in our sample. By *parenting response*, I mean the changes in the overall tenor of the parent-child relationship. A parenting response influences how a mother or father behaves toward the adolescent across a variety of different situations—it isn't simply limited to how the parent deals with specific issues, such as schoolwork, curfew, or socializing. A parenting response touches virtually everything the parent does with the child.

FIVE PARENTING RESPONSES

In our sample, we identified five basic parenting response groups, which collectively accounted for approximately 80 percent of the families we studied (the other 20 percent did not seem to fall neatly into one of these groups). Researchers who have studied parents with children of other ages have found similar categories of parents in their samples, too.

The first response, which we referred to as the *authoritative response*, is characterized by sensitivity to the child's changing needs and capabilities. About 30 percent of the parents in our sample fell into this group. Parents who responded to the adolescent transition this way remained affectionate, involved, and firm in dealing with their child. When asked about their childrearing philosophy, authoritative parents were likely to say that they believe that parents have an obligation to understand their child's needs and feelings, to treat the child's interests and problems as meaningful, and to show genuine concern for the child's well-being. At the same time, however, these parents also said it was important to hold the child to high standards, establish clear rules for behavior, and enforce these strictly and consistently.

Authoritative parents are democratic, in the sense that they solicit the adolescent's opinion on such matters as curfew and family vacation planning. But authoritative parents do not hesitate to assert their authority when the situation demands it. The authoritative household is managed like a well-run, hierarchically structured organization in which the parents are chief executive officers, and the adolescent is a junior partner. For authoritative parents, the primary goal in raising their adolescent is to foster the child's curiosity and self-direction.

A second response is the *autocratic response*. Like the authoritative parents, the autocratic parents in our sample also had high standards for their teenager and set well-defined limits on their child's behavior. But unlike the authoritative parents, the autocratic parents worried that too much warmth or affection would spoil the child and undermine their authority. They were likely to say that they believe that children fare best when their parents are strict, even if it means being a little aloof. Parents who responded autocratically were likely to believe that children should obey their parents at all times and never question their authority.

Another important difference between authoritative and autocratic parents is in the way they run their households. Whereas authoritative parents govern through dialogue and explanation—they insist on talking things out with their children—autocratic parents are more likely to simply "lay down the law" and expect their children to obey them.

For the autocratic parents in our sample, their child's adolescence incited all sorts of fears about the possibility of the child's disobeying, and they saw their role in raising their child as making sure that he or she survived adolescence without getting into too much trouble ("trouble," of course, meant different things in different households). About 10 percent of the parents in our sample were in the autocratic group. Bob Peterson, the hospital administrator whose son, David, wanted to scream, "Get a life, Dad!" demonstrated the classic autocratic response by becoming stricter as his son got older.

A third response we saw fairly often is the *indulgent response*. About 15 percent of the families in our sample were classified in this group. Parents who responded this way became increasingly permissive over time, almost abandoning the rules or limits they had previously set for their child.

Like the authoritative parents, the indulgent parents in our sample remained warm and emotionally invested in their child's welfare, but rather than maintaining their ultimate authority over the child, they tended to leave most day-to-day decisions up to the adolescent. Some maintained that this approach worked because their adolescent was a "good kid" who needed very little hands-on management or guidance. Other indulgent parents, however, seemed to back away from discipline out of fear that they would anger the child or provoke arguments. In either case, the indulgent household tended to be run without a clear sense of who was in charge. For the indulgent parents in our study, the goal of raising an adolescent seemed to be to make it through the adolescent years without rocking the boat.

The *enmeshed response* is the fourth parenting response we identified. The enmeshed parents were warm and loving toward their child, like the authoritative and indulgent parents, but instead of trying to foster their adolescent's curiosity and self-direction, the enmeshed parents became increasingly overprotective and emotionally stifling whenever the adolescent attempted to express independence or individuality. In families headed by an enmeshed parent, it seemed as if the psychological boundaries between individuals were blurred—that the parents were overly involved in "micromanaging" their child's everyday life.

Enmeshed parents tend to govern not through rational discussion (like the authoritative parents) or through the blatant assertion of power (like the autocratic parents), but by using psychological control. They may try to make their child feel guilty for letting the parent down, or they may temporarily withdraw love from the child in order to gain the youngsters' compliance. Enmeshed parents also tend to worry a great deal about the adolescent venturing out in the world and being exposed to danger. For enmeshed parents, the main goal of parenting is to protect the child from dangers that might lurk outside the family.

About 15 percent of the sample reacted to their adolescent in an enmeshed fashion. Amanda Spencer, the mother whose son, Paul, objected to her overinvolvement in his life, is an example of a parent who responded to adolescence with enmeshment. So is Cynthia Garrison, whose daughter, Jessica, wanted more "space."

A final type of response we saw is the *disengaging response*. This was characterized by a pulling back and a lowering of the parent's level of involvement and investment in the adolescent's life. Like the indulgent parents, the disengaging parents became much more permissive as their child aged. But unlike parents in the indulgent group, who maintained their emotional investment in the child, parents in the disengaging group became uninvolved emotionally as well. About 10 percent of the families in our sample fell into this category.

When asked, the disengaging parents in our sample said that they believed that adolescents fare best when their parents leave them alone—that too much involvement on the parent's part would stifle the child's sense of independence. Accordingly, when adolescence arrives, disengaging parents cut back on the rules they have for their child, set fewer limits on the adolescent's behavior, and pull back, if not *out*, of the relationship. When questioned about why they did this, the disengaging parents in our sample often would say things like, "I can't tell her what to do anymore," or, "He needs to learn from his mistakes." For the disengaging parents, the main goal in raising a teenager appeared to be to launch their child into adulthood as soon as it was possible to do so, in order to be able to turn their energy and attention to other matters. In some regards, it was this response that Matt Johnson was complaining about when describing his father, Richard. Theresa Rossi is another example of a disengaging parent. Indeed, her disengagement was so extreme that she actually ran away from her family for a time.

When I began to look at the families that fell into each of these categories, I saw that there was a relation between the feelings adolescence aroused in a parent and the parenting response he or she demonstrated.

PARENTS WHO REACTED POSITIVELY TO ADOLESCENCE

Parents who experienced their child's adolescence as satisfying, rejuvenating, joyful, or self-assuring tended to fall into the authoritative group. They responded to their child's maturation flexibly and were able to shift disciplinary strategies appropriately as their child matured.

Rather than changing abruptly—that is, either letting all discipline go out the window as soon as the child became a teenager or cracking down at the first sign of adolescent independence—these parents were able to let their relationship with their child be transformed gradually. They tended to grant autonomy in steps, taking their cue from the adolescent's behavior. If the adolescent seemed to be able to handle a little more freedom responsibly, the parents might grant a small amount more the next time. They did not see their child's autonomy as either a threat or as a cause for celebration but rather as something that needed patient and steady nurturing. These parents, perhaps because they took pleasure in seeing their child come into maturity, were able to channel their own positive feelings back into the parent-child relationship. John Forster is a good example.

JOHN FORSTER

"Abby and I have a lot of fun together," John Forster said of his daughter. "She's interesting to be around and she, well, she brings a kind of energy to things that is really contagious. Oh, we have our fair share of disagreements—who doesn't?—but she's sensible and willing to listen to reason. And I've tried to be fair with her in return."

I asked for an example.

"OK . . . a few months ago, Abby asked if she could have her curfew extended by an hour. My initial thought was, no way, not yet, she's not old enough. But I kept my mouth shut and gave her a chance to explain. She said that her curfew was much earlier than all of her friends' and that it was embarrassing to always have to be the first to leave people's houses. Now usually, I don't buy the 'everyone else is doing it' argument, and Abby knows that. We've been through that one before. But instead of just complaining, this time she suggested that I call a few of her friends' parents—the ones whose opinion my wife and I respect—and discuss it with them. Which is what I did. And you know what? I think Abby was right—we *were* being too strict. We were holding her to the same curfew she'd had when she was two years younger. And I realized that she had always been responsible. So I told her that, all things considered, she had a point, which I think made her feel good, you know, to see that I wasn't infallible. Not to mention that she got her later curfew."

THE IMPACT OF LOSS OR ABANDONMENT

Parents who experienced their child's maturation as loss or abandon-ment were less likely to respond authoritatively. Instead, these par-ents were likely to respond either with enmeshment or with indulgence. In either case, the parent remained warm and close to-ward the child, but attempted to slow the youngster's emancipation in one of two ways. Those who responded with enmeshment, like Cynthia Garrison, seemed to try to hold on to the child psychologi-cally as a way of stemming their loss. As a single parent, Cynthia had invested a great deal of emotional energy in her friendshiplike rela-tionship with her daughter, Jessica. Now, however, whenever Jessica attempted to move toward spending more time with her friends, Cynthia would try to make her daughter feel guilty for neglecting their relationship. Sometimes, according to Jessica, Cynthia would act hurt and betrayed, and occasionally she would sulk until Jessica suggested that they do something together.

Feelings of loss or abandonment could also be manifested in ex-cessive indulgence, however. In these families, parents seemed to believe that by indulging the adolescent's wishes—typically for more freedom or independence—they could forestall, or at least slow, the child's emotional movement away. Many indulgent parents appeared almost afraid of their child and particularly fearful of get-ting into arguments or disagreements. Some knew full well that what they were doing wasn't particularly sensible but felt as if they had very little alternative.

"What can I do?" one mother of a fifteen-year-old asked me. "If I say, 'Be home by twelve,' and he says, 'I want to stay out until two in the morning,' I have two choices—I can say 'No,' and then we'll fight and he'll storm out and stay out until two anyway, or I can say 'Yes.' Either way, he stays out until two. The only difference is whether we fight about it. I guess I'd rather avoid the fight. I figure the more we fight, the more I will drive him away."

THE IMPACT OF POWERLESSNESS

In contrast, when adolescence provoked feelings of powerlessness in a parent it nearly always incited an autocratic response. Parents who were frustrated in their attempts to assert control over their teen-ager—as Gray Miller was frustrated by his stepdaughter Cindy—fre-quently responded with even stronger attempts at control, typically to no avail. Although the autocratic parent was trying to say, in so many words, "I'll show you who's boss," the teenager was likely to re-spond with "You will, huh?"

In most households, parental autocracy as a response to feelings of impotence usually made matters worse. The Miller-Hansen house-hold survived the transition only with the help of a family counselor. In many other homes, however, the situation spirals out of control, and the adolescent ends up in more serious trouble as a result—in-volved with drugs and alcohol, in trouble with the law, or disengaged from school.

THE IMPACT OF JEALOUSY

Parents who feel jealous of their child typically react in one of two ways. Some, like Bob Peterson, become autocratic, in what is an at-tempt, on some level, to make their child "pay" for his or her good fortune. Bob, for example, sublimated his jealousy of his son's free-dom and opportunity into a near-constant pressure on David to maintain his grades in school—despite the fact that David was a per-fectly good student, irrespective of his father's vigilance.

Other jealous parents, however, became disengaged from their child, almost as if they were protecting themselves from having to face their "competition." We saw this quite clearly in the case of Richard Johnson, who, interestingly, became less and less interested in Matt's achievements the more Matt succeeded. It seemed that as long as their relationship was based on Matt looking up to his father, Richard was able to maintain a high level of involvement and interest in Matt. When Matt began to focus more on himself, and less on his father—and when the Johnson household began to focus more of its attention on Matt and less on Richard—Richard's interest began to wane. Fortunately for Matt, his mother maintained a strong invest-ment in his life, and this offset the adverse effects of his father's emo-tional withdrawal.

Maria Rossi, Theresa Rossi's troubled daughter, was not as fortunate as Matt Johnson, for her mother's disengagement was not compensated for by any increase in involvement by her father. Disengagement was a common response not only among jealous parents, but among parents for whom their child's adolescence triggered strong feelings of regret. In Theresa Rossi's case, for example, watching her daughter mature evoked all sorts of misgivings about the way her own life had turned out, and these ruminations led Theresa deeper and deeper into self-absorption and self-pity.

Maria told me that her mother seemed to have difficulty paying attention to her when she was trying to describe something that happened that day. If her mother *did* pay attention, Maria said, she would always try to relate Maria's experience to something from her own past. "It's like she doesn't really care that this is happening to *me*," Maria said. "She seems so depressed about her own life that mine just isn't that important to her. I tried talking to her about it once, but it didn't really help. So now, I just keep my mouth shut and go my own way. It seems like that's what she wants, anyway."

HOW PARENTING AFFECTS TEENAGERS

One of the reasons that it is so important to understand how parents' feelings about adolescence can spill over and influence their behavior toward their child is that differences in the ways that parents behave affect the adolescent's development. This is something that psychologists know a great deal about, and something that my colleagues and I have been studying for nearly two decades. In several different studies, we have compared youngsters from different sorts of parenting environments on four different indicators of psychological well-being—the teenagers' psychological adjustment (for instance, whether they have high or low self-esteem), their school achievement (for example, the grades they make in school), their involvement in problem behavior (for instance, using drugs and alcohol), and their subjective feelings of distress (for example, feeling anxious or depressed). Over and over, we found that adolescents from authoritative, autocratic, indulgent, enmeshed, and disengaged homes show very different patterns of behavior and adjustment. Moreover, we found that these differences are not transitory—the distinctive patterns associated with each type of childrearing are maintained over time.

In general, adolescents from *authoritative* homes, like Abby Forster, are the most psychologically well adjusted. They are confident, socially self-assured, and have high self-esteem. They perform well in school and have a healthy achievement motive. They are less likely than other youngsters to get into trouble—whether with drugs and alcohol or with other forms of delinquency. And they report the fewest complaints of anxiety, depression, or psychosomatic distress.

Adolescents from *autocratic* homes, like David Peterson, end up being obedient—just as their parents seemed to have wanted—but they pay a great price for this. In general, youngsters raised in these sorts of homes are less well adjusted than other adolescents, scoring lower on measures of self-esteem, self-confidence, intellectual curiosity, and self-reliance. The majority of these youngsters do not get into serious trouble, but some do respond to their parent's autocracy with rebellion, and this can be problematic. Because these adolescents tend to be less self-assured and confident than other children, they are easily swayed by their peers. Those who rebel and fall into a bad peer crowd often have difficulty resisting their friends' pressure to experiment with dangerous activities.

Teenagers from *indulgent* homes, like Peter Rosenstein, are a sort of mirror image of those from autocratic homes. That is, whereas teenagers from autocratic homes tend to be overly compliant and dependent, teenagers from indulgent homes seem to have trouble accepting authority—probably because they have had so little demanded of them by their parents. These youngsters are confident and self-assured, especially around other teenagers. But adolescents from indulgent homes are more likely than other youngsters to get into trouble and to perform poorly in school.

Parental *enmeshment* takes its toll on youngsters' psychological health by raising their level of distress. It is the high level of psychological control in these families, in particular, that does this. When adolescents are made to feel guilty by their parents for asserting their individuality or voicing a difference of opinion, or when they are psychologically manipulated in other ways, the youngsters tend to turn their feelings of anger inward. This is especially true in homes in which the parent is warm and affectionate, because this makes it that much more difficult for the adolescent to disagree out loud. Over time, anger that is not expressed, but is turned inward instead, is transformed into depression, anxiety, nervousness, or psychosomatic problems. Unfortunately, this was the course followed by Jessica Garrison.

There is no question that growing up in an autocratic, indulgent, or enmeshed home takes its toll on the adolescent's mental health. But the adverse consequences of having parents who *disengage* are far worse still. In our studies, we find that young people with disengaged parents, as were Maria Rossi's, score consistently poorly on all our measures of psychological well-being. They have poor self-conceptions, perform poorly in school, are much more likely than other adolescents to get involved in drugs, alcohol, and delinquency. And they report symptoms of distress most frequently. There is little doubt that the absolute worst thing a mother or father can do during his or her child's adolescence is to disengage from the parental role.

Understanding the intricate linkages among work, marriage, and parenting leads to a new way of looking at what is going on with the parent at midlife and why the psychological events of middle age spill over into the domain of parenting. Midlife is a time when multiple forces of change and transformation all collide. An adult who is at the occupational plateau may also be experiencing a low in marital satisfaction and an upheaval in her relationship with her daughter, who herself is moving from childhood into adolescence. Given all of this, it seems inevitable that a parent would change her childrearing practices in one way or another during this phase. Although spillover among work, marriage, and parenting is always a possibility no matter what stage the adult is in, the chances of it happening during the midlife years—that is, during the child's adolescence—are very great indeed.

PART IV

GROWTH AND CRISIS AT MIDLIFE

13. DECLINING AND THRIVING AT THE ADOLESCENT TRANSITION

The psychological turmoil parents feel at their child's adolescence comes in different shapes and sizes.

For some, like Amanda Spencer, the full-time homemaker, or Cynthia Garrison, the successful legislative assistant, the transition of their child into adolescence provokes deep feelings of sadness—mourning, almost—as they face the disappearance of their youngster's childhood and the potential loss of their own self-definition that would accompany it. For Amanda and Cynthia, "losing" their child to adolescence forced them to ask painful questions of themselves: What am I going to do with all this emotional energy now that my child needs—and wants—less of it? Where do I turn for fulfillment and enrichment? Who am *I* now that my child is no longer a child? For them, the child's entry into adolescence incited concerns about the future.

For others, the transition is not so much sad as it is bitter. For parents like Richard Johnson, whose son Matt reminded him of his own adolescent failures, or Theresa Rossi, whose daughter Maria seemed destined to replicate Theresa's own errant youth, their child's adolescence is a time of intense personal disappointment and regret. It is a time dominated by private rumination about their own failures and mistakes, and unspeakable jealousy over the freedom and opportunity that they believe their child is going to enjoy. For parents like

Richard and Theresa, the child's entry into adolescence provokes a different question: Not, "What will I do now?" but "What could I have done differently?" For them, the child's adolescence unearths despair about the past.

And for other parents, like Gray Miller, Cindy Hansen's autocratic stepfather, or Eileen Brown, the overworked travel agent trying to raise two children on her own, their child's adolescence is a time of intense anger—anger over the feelings of impotence and frustration, anger over the feelings of neglect, anger over being exploited and at the same time excluded. For them, the questions their child's adolescence provokes are not questions about the future or the past, but about the *present*: "Why is my child doing this to me? "What did I do to deserve this?" "How am I going to survive these next few years?"

Not all parents experience turmoil as their children enter adolescence, however. As we've seen, there are also the Sarah Feins, the John Forsters, the Vicki Dobsons—parents who not only manage to avoid the turmoil that other, less fortunate, parents suffer, but who seem actually to grow and thrive during their child's teenage years. For Sarah, who turned to writing, her son's adolescence was a time of liberation, of freedom, of relief from the day-to-day demands of raising a younger child. For John, who plugged into his daughter's energy and youthful enthusiasm, Abby's adolescence was a time of rejuvenation, of personal and marital happiness, of fun. And for Vicki, a single parent with a strong network of friends, a satisfying career, and a busy schedule of outside activities, her daughter's adolescence was a time of increased satisfaction and newfound self-assurance.

How can we account for such variability? Why, for example, did Amanda Spencer experience her son's adolescence as a loss, while Sarah Fein experienced her son's adolescence as a gain? Why did Gray Miller turn his relationship with his stepdaughter into a daily power struggle, while Vicki Dobson was able to relax and enjoy her daughter's youth from a position of self-assured, quiet authority? Why did Barbara and Stan Merrick's marriage begin to disintegrate under the strain of their son's entry into adolescence, while Linda and John Forster's bond grew even stronger and more passionate as their daughter matured? It did not appear that there was anything distinctive about any of these teenagers' behavior that would have provoked these particular reactions.

As I began to examine this issue further, I discovered four factors that seem to increase the risk of a parent experiencing psychological turmoil during the child's transition into adolescence:

- *being the same sex as the child making the transition*
- *being divorced or remarried, especially for women*
- *having few sources of satisfaction outside the parental role*
- *having a negative "cognitive set" about adolescence*

THE RISK FACTORS FOR TURMOIL

Risk factors for turmoil during the adolescent transition operate like risk factors for other sorts of problems. The presence of any single factor does not guarantee that the problem will develop—it simply increases the probability that it will.

For example, being a divorced woman is a risk factor for parental turmoil at adolescence in the same sense that eating a high cholesterol diet is a risk factor for the development of heart disease. Not all individuals who eat rich, fatty foods develop heart disease, and not all divorced adults experience psychological turmoil when their children become teenagers. And, just as there are many individuals who follow low-fat diets but who suffer heart disease nevertheless, there are many nondivorced parents who feel a great deal of unrest as their child matures. On average, however, a divorced woman's chances of going through a difficult time when her child becomes a teenager are greater than are those of a nondivorced woman in similar circumstances. In this sense, then, for women, divorce is a risk factor for experiencing psychological turmoil during a child's adolescence.

As with various types of medical and psychological problems, the more risk factors present in an individual's life, the greater the probability of experiencing psychological turmoil when the firstborn child reaches adolescence. For example, a divorced woman whose oldest child is a daughter (that is, who has two of the four risk factors—divorce and a child of the same sex) is more likely to experience turmoil than a nondivorced woman with an oldest daughter (one risk factor) or a divorced woman with a firstborn son (one risk factor). Similarly, a man with a firstborn son who reports low work satisfaction (two risk factors) is significantly more likely to go through a difficult time when his son hits adolescence than is a man with similarly low work satisfaction, but whose oldest child is a girl (one risk factor), or one who reports high work satisfaction, but whose oldest child is a boy (one risk factor).

Individuals with three of the four risk factors are even more likely to experience difficulty than are those with just one or two. And individuals with all four of the risk factors are almost certain to experience a crisis as their child matures.

Why do these particular risk factors—having a child of the same sex, being divorced or remarried, having few satisfactions outside of parenting, and having a negative cognitive set—increase the likelihood of psychological decline for the parent at the child's entrance into adolescence?

Let's look first at the one factor that parents have absolutely no control over: their child's gender.

MOTHERS AND DAUGHTERS, FATHERS AND SONS

Generally speaking, parents whose firstborn child is the same sex— that is, mothers of girls and fathers of boys—are more likely to show a decline in mental health during adolescence than are parents whose child is the same age, but the opposite gender. For instance, a substantial decline in mental health was reported by about half of all mothers of daughters in our sample, but by about 40 percent of mothers of sons. Conversely, about 30 percent of the mothers of boys in our sample were in our group of "thrivers," as opposed to 20 percent of the mothers of daughters.

The same general principle held for fathers. Specifically, whereas about 40 percent of fathers of firstborn sons had psychological difficulty in coping with their child's maturation, the comparable figure for fathers of firstborn daughters was about 30 percent. And while close to 20 percent of the fathers of daughters were thriving, this was true for only about 10 percent of fathers with sons.

There are several reasons for the intensifying effect that having a child of the same sex seems to have on a parent's adjustment to his or her child's adolescence. First, during preadolescence, relationships between parents and opposite-sex children tend to be slightly more distant than they are between parents and same-sex children. That is, mothers and daughters tend to be closer than mothers and sons, and fathers and sons tend to be closer than fathers and daughters. As a consequence, the emotional distancing that goes on between teenagers and parents is felt that much more intensely when the parent and child are the same sex.

Cynthia and Jessica Garrison provide a nice illustration of this. Cynthia, a single mother, experienced Jessica's maturation as a sort of abandonment—she felt left behind as her daughter began to turn her attention more toward her friends and less and less toward her mother. Although Cynthia's "loss" of Jessica was difficult, it was made even more so by the fact that they had enjoyed such closeness and camaraderie previously. Cynthia had come to rely on Jessica almost as a friend, and the emotional distance generated by Jessica's very normal attempts at individuation and emotional autonomy hurt that much more deeply. Although Cynthia was the type of mother who was inclined to have a friendly relationship with her child, their friendship was undoubtedly intensified by their both being female. In families in which the parents and adolescent are less close— whether because of the child's gender or for some other reason—the child's separation is that much easier to handle.

A second reason for the intensifying effect of having a child of the same sex is that similarity between parent and child tends to promote the parent's identification with the child. Parents who can easily see themselves in their child are much more likely to be affected by the child's maturation, whether positively or negatively. Thus, for example, it was Theresa Rossi's ability to see herself in her daughter Maria that triggered Theresa's regretful rumination about her own adolescence and her thwarted plans. I am reasonably certain that had Theresa's oldest child been a son, she would not have had the same sad daydreams while she worked—or at least, she would not have had them so often—as she had as the mother of an adolescent girl in whom she could see herself.

The same can be said for many of the fathers who felt envious of their son's sexual freedom, like Jeff Rosenstein or Jack DeAngelo. These men would look at their son—whether it was Jeff stumbling on his son, Peter, necking with his girlfriend, or Jack, knee-deep in a snowdrift in his driveway, imagining his son Jason with his girlfriend on an unchaperoned ski trip—and find it easy to see themselves in their son's shoes. This identification made it that much easier to feel jealous.

Related to the issue of identification is the third reason for the same-sex intensification effect: social comparison. For many parents, like Richard Johnson, the adverse impact of having a child come into adolescence stemmed from their conscious or unconscious comparison between themselves and their child. Matt Johnson, for example, became a living reminder to Richard of the social clumsiness he had felt when he was a teenager. It was the implicit comparison he drew between himself and his son—Matt, the social success; himself, the former social outcast—that incited much of Richard's envy and, consequently, depression. It is hard to imagine that Richard would have felt this way had he been the father of a socially successful daughter.

THE IMPACT OF DIVORCE AND REMARRIAGE

The adolescent transition takes a different toll on parents' mental health in intact, divorced, and remarried homes, our study found. In particular, divorced, single mothers were more likely than nondivorced mothers to experience a drop in their mental health (55 percent of single mothers versus 43 percent of nondivorced mothers). Interestingly, remarried mothers were even *more* likely to report turmoil during their child's adolescence than single mothers. Over 60 percent of the remarried mothers in our sample saw their well-being decline as their child entered adolescence.

We see the same pattern, except in reverse, when we look at the parents who thrived during this time. Nearly one out of three women in our sample had a change for the better in her mental health as her child matured into adolescence. But the proportion of thrivers in each of the three family structures varied markedly. One third of the nondivorced women in our sample reported improvement in their mental health, as opposed to one fifth of the single women, and only one sixth of the remarried women. It is important to note that all of the remarried women in our sample were living with their biological adolescent and the child's stepfather. I do not know whether we would find the same pattern if we were to study stepmothers and their adolescent stepchildren.

Although we had too few single fathers in our sample to draw any conclusions about this group, we did have a sizable percentage of stepfathers, and we were able to compare these men with their counterparts who were still in their first marriage. Interestingly, the finding that divorced and remarried parents suffered more during their child's adolescence was not true among men. If anything, among men, the reverse was true. More than half of the nondivorced men in our study had declining mental health, compared to only one third of the stepfathers. About equal proportions of each group—one fifth, to be exact—thrived. Being a stepfather, then, was associated with less risk for turmoil, but not necessarily with more potential for positive growth. Again, it is important to keep in mind that we did not study men who were divorced and living with their biological adolescent, either as single fathers or in a marriage to the child's stepmother.

ADOLESCENCE AND THE SINGLE MOTHER

In order to understand why divorce and remarriage exacerbated the turmoil of a child's adolescence among women, but mitigated against it among men, we need to look more closely at the day-to-day lives and the dynamics of parent-adolescent relationships in divorced and remarried households.

The arrival of the adolescent transition disrupted the equilibrium of single-parent households in several ways that were different from the disruption that took place in nondivorced homes. Remember that most single mothers who divorce during their child's elementary school years become more permissive and indulgent following their divorce. Many single mothers in our sample found that the permissive stance they had taken during their youngster's childhood and preadolescent years was difficult to maintain in the face of the very real dangers inherent in raising teenagers. Being lenient about whether a room is kept tidy is one thing; being lenient about whether a child abides by his curfew is another.

In many single-parent households, this situation presented the mother with a difficult dilemma. If she became stricter as the child got older, the adolescent often resisted. Most adolescents understandably enjoyed the permissiveness they had grown accustomed to after their parents' divorce—remember that in most cases, it was friendly indulgence, not hostile neglect. Few were willing to tolerate a return to a stricter, more vigilant atmosphere just at the time when they were beginning to get a taste of what their independence might buy them. Even if the parent's intent was to shift simply to a more authoritative style—not autocratic, but authoritative—to the child it seemed like taking several steps backward.

At the same time, however, the alternative—maintaining the same level of permissiveness even as the child moved into adolescence—was a frightening prospect. The youngsters in our study were coming of age at a time when drugs were available, teenage sex was prevalent, and crime was on the rise, even in our moderate-sized midwestern town. The risks of excessive permissiveness were very great and very real.

Few single mothers in our sample with a prior record of permissiveness found a simple solution to the problem of control that surfaced at the onset of their child's adolescence. Some, like Eileen Brown, the travel agent, reacted erratically, vacillating unpredictably between autocratic control and disengaged neglect. This was more often seen among parents who did not have a close emotional relationship with their adolescent—as was the case between Eileen and her daughter, Becky.

Others, like Cynthia Garrison, came away feeling frustrated and helpless and, not surprisingly, depressed. This was more characteristic of mothers who had maintained close emotional ties with their children all along, as Cynthia had with her daughter, Jessica. In either case, the struggle over control (whether an actual struggle between the parent and adolescent, as in the Brown family, or a psychological struggle that took place within the parent's mind, as in the Garrison home) took a grave toll on the single mother's mental health.

Cynthia Garrison's situation in particular also provides a window on the second aspect of life in a single-parent household that makes their child's adolescence difficult for mothers: the special intensity of the parent-adolescent relationship, especially between single mothers and daughters. As I noted in an earlier chapter, single mothers in general did *not* complain about having problems managing their children. In general, they had emotionally close relationships with their children, and many had established what looked on the surface to be a close friendship with their oldest child. This was certainly true in the Garrison household.

But this closeness proved problematic when the emotional changes of adolescence set in. Just as the adolescent's individuation was more difficult for parents to handle if their child was the same sex, so too was individuation a problem when it was pursued within the context of the intimate friendship that many single parents and their child had enjoyed. Not only was Jessica Garrison attempting to individuate from her mother—she was attempting to individuate from one of her best friends. Any of the parental feelings of loss or abandonment that this process triggered, even under the best of circumstances, were amplified in single-parent households where relationships had been emotionally close.

ADOLESCENCE IN STEPFAMILIES

A different set of dynamics exacerbated the turmoil of the adolescent transition in stepfamilies. In most of the single-parent households we studied, the challenge the family faced was to restore equilibrium to a stable family system that was disrupted by the normal changes of adolescence. In the stepfamilies we studied, however, the family's problem frequently was to deal with *two* difficult adaptations simultaneously: the adjustment to remarriage and the adjustment to a child's adolescence. Adapting to either of these challenges alone is difficult enough. Adapting to both at the same time was more than many families could handle.

As a rule, the longer a stepfamily had lived together as a unit prior to the oldest child's entry into adolescence, the more smoothly its adjustment went. Indeed, among stepfamilies in our sample in which the remarriage had taken place six or more years prior to the oldest child's entry into adolescence, the transition into adolescence was as smooth as it was in families that had never experienced divorce.

Few stepfamilies with adolescents fall into this category, however.

More than two thirds of our stepfamilies had been formed five years or fewer when they joined our study, and nearly half had lived together only one or two years. In our sample, the typical scenario was more like that in the Miller-Hansen household, with the remarriage occurring sometime during the oldest child's late elementary school years. We found, as have other researchers, that, in these homes, adolescence was an extremely difficult transition for children and parents alike. Teenagers living in stepfamilies were more likely than other teens—including those in divorced, single-parent homes—to have academic difficulties and behavior problems. And the parents in these homes—especially the biological mothers—reported the highest level of turmoil in our sample.

The reasons for the extreme level of distress reported by remarried mothers with adolescent children have to do, I think, primarily with the problem of divided loyalties. The entrance of the stepfather into the family has to be viewed in light of the very close relationship likely to have been formed between the oldest child and her single mother.

In many families, the oldest child previously had enjoyed special status as the mother's confidante, parental assistant, and social companion. Following the remarriage, however, the child was expected to relinquish these roles to the stepfather. For a younger child, the potential benefits of having an additional adult in the home might have outweighed this sacrifice. But to an older child, they simply did not. If anything, the entrance of a stepfather into the family was anything but a benefit. It typically meant more rules, more limits, and more hassles—as it certainly did for the Hansen children. Above all, the stepfather's arrival meant less time with Mom.

I noted in an earlier chapter that marital happiness is usually positively associated with close parent-child relationships; that is, women who have close relationships with their husband also, on average, have close relationships with their children. We saw a fascinating exception to this general rule in stepfamilies, however. Here, instead, the closer the stepfather and mother's marriage, the more *distant* the mother and child are likely to be. Understanding why this is helps shed light on why adolescence is so hard on the mental health of the remarried mother.

The remarried mother finds herself in a no-win situation. The closer she moves emotionally toward her new husband, the more she risks alienating her adolescent child, and, as we've seen, distance in the mother-child relationship is a major contributor to psychological turmoil for women. On the other hand, the closer the newly married mother remains to her child, the less happy her husband is likely to be, and this marital tension will take its toll on her well-being, too. This was precisely the situation we found Ellen Hansen in, caught between the demands of her husband, Gray, and her daughter Cindy. Although the struggle over divided loyalties involves the stepfather as well as the mother and adolescent, it does not appear to take a toll on the stepfather's mental health. I noted above that stepfathers were, in fact, *less* likely to report feeling turmoil than were fathers living with their biological child. Why should this have been so?

The answer is that stepfathers, without a biological link to the adolescent, are much less likely to identify with, or compare themselves to, the adolescent, especially if they have been living with the child for only a few years. In addition, stepfathers' lack of closeness with the adolescent—in our study, as in most others, relationships between stepfathers and adolescents were cordial but quite distant—protected them from the potentially adverse effects of having the adolescent pull away emotionally. Ironically, then, the very factor that makes day-to-day parenting so difficult for stepfathers—the lack of a strong emotional bond with their stepchild—may, in the end, protect their personal mental health from the turmoil that comes with the child's entry into adolescence.

PROTECTIVE BUFFERS

The third risk factor we identified concerned the extent to which the parent found satisfaction in activities outside the parental role. Those who did—whether in their work, their marriage, or their outside interests—were less likely to experience turmoil as their child matured into adolescence. In contrast, those who did not have satisfying nonparental lives were far more vulnerable.

Interestingly, the critical protective variable was not, as some might expect, whether or not an individual invested a great deal in parenting. Although one might have anticipated that mothers and fathers who had invested a great deal in parenting would be most at risk for turmoil as their child matured, this was not the case. High investment in parenting was neither a risk factor nor a protective factor. It was the *absence* of nonparental investment, not the presence of parental investment, that was crucial.

In concrete terms, a career-oriented mother who was also very involved in parenting was no more likely to experience turmoil than one who was equally career-oriented, but less invested in being a parent. However, a woman who was dissatisfied with work and marriage was at risk for experiencing turmoil *whether she was heavily invested in parenting or not*. Put another way, the protection against parental turmoil at the adolescent transition came from having other interests in addition to being an involved parent, not from disengaging from parenting.

THE PROTECTIVE BUFFER OF SATISFYING WORK

For many of the parents in our sample, the absence of a satisfying work life made them far more vulnerable to experiencing turmoil as their child matured. Some of the parents in this group were women who had put their careers on hold when their children were younger and who had been full-time homemakers for some time, like Amanda Spencer. Others were employed full- or part-time, but either had lost interest in their work, like Bob Peterson, whose job as a hospital administrator had grown stale and frustrating, or had never seen it as anything other than a source of income, like Eileen Brown, whose work as a travel agent was little more than a means of paying her family's household bills. Thus, it was not the amount of time a parent worked that made a difference, or how much money the parent earned, but rather, how much pleasure the parent derived from work. John Spencer, the teacher; Paula Johnson, the nursing professor; and Vicki Dobson, the real estate broker, all profited from the protective buffer of satisfying employment.

Some of the parents in our sample thrived during the adolescent transition not because of investment in a paid career, but because of investment in a worklike hobby. Sarah Fein decided to write her first novel. Another mother became very involved in community activities, donating considerable amounts of time and energy to her school's parent-teacher organization. Another parent, who had grown increasingly bored and unhappy with his work as a surgeon, decided at the age of forty-two to learn how to play jazz piano and would practice several hours each evening after dinner. None of these parents let their outside interests diminish their commitment to parenthood. Yet all of these parents experienced less turmoil as a result of their additional investment outside the parental role.

We saw in an earlier chapter that one of the possible spillovers of parental turmoil at the adolescent transition is the negative impact the situation makes on the parent's work life. Many parents became more dissatisfied with their work as a result of confronting the psychological issues triggered by their child's maturation. And, although it is certainly true that one's feelings about work can be *affected* by one's experiences as a parent, it is also true that one's feelings about work can serve a protective function against crises in the family before such crises even arise. Investment in a career or in some other productive activity outside the home buffers the parent against the potential adverse effects of having a child mature.

For some parents, then, like Bob Peterson, the turmoil incited by the adolescent transition exacerbated an already difficult situation at work. Bob's initial dissatisfaction at the hospital, due largely to his inability to rise within its administrative ranks, left him more vulnerable to the negative effects of seeing his son, David, mature. But David's maturation, in turn, only made Bob more disenchanted with his work, for watching David grow up reminded Bob of his own failure to achieve his dream of going to medical school.

THE PROTECTIVE BUFFER OF A HAPPY MARRIAGE

There were other parents in the sample whose vulnerability to the turmoil of adolescence came not from an unsatisfying career, but from an unhappy marriage. They were not as fortunate as John and Linda Forster or Sarah and Dan Fein, whose happy marriages protected them against the psychological unrest triggered by their children's adolescence.

Theresa Rossi's turmoil over her daughter Maria's becoming a teenager was exacerbated by her unhappy marriage. Theresa, as you may remember, had never been happy in her marriage to Frank—a marriage that had been forced by an unplanned and unwanted pregnancy when Theresa was still a teenager. Although she and Frank had stayed together over the years, there was little love between them.

The gap in Theresa's emotional life caused by her unhappy marriage left her open to being hit hard by her daughter's maturation. With Frank unavailable much of the time (he would spend most weekday evenings out with his friends) and psychologically inaccessible even when he and Theresa were together (when he was home, he would usually drink beer and watch television), Theresa had a great deal of free time to review her life and ruminate about the mistakes she had made as a teenager. Her daughter's imminent difficulties, reminiscent of the problems Theresa herself had gotten into as an adolescent, only intensified her regret and sharpened her feelings of self-pity.

Richard Johnson suffered from a similar lack of marital buffering. His wife, Paula, had grown tired of Richard's withdrawn, antisocial behavior. Early on in their marriage, she had been able to coax Richard out of his shell and persuade him to accompany her to dinner parties, community affairs, and neighborhood bridge games. Occasionally, Richard even enjoyed himself—although he was reluctant to admit it to Paula. But as the years went by, Richard became less and less willing to go along with Paula's requests. The more Paula nagged at Richard to be more social, the more insistently introverted he became. By the time their son Matt reached adolescence, the Johnsons had decided, by default, to lead separate social lives.

As Paula pulled away from Richard in her social activities, however, she also pulled back emotionally. I imagine that at some level she felt that this was only fair; since Richard was no longer willing to give her what she wanted, she was no longer willing to give him what *he* desired. Unfortunately, Paula's emotional withdrawal left Richard feeling isolated and alone. Although he wasn't interested in socializing with other people, he missed his wife's companionship and support. And when his son Matt's entrance into adolescence triggered feelings of jealousy and envy, Richard did not feel he could turn to his wife to express them. As a consequence, the turmoil Richard felt grew that much stronger.

HOW THE BUFFERS WORK

Marriage, work, and outside interests buffer parents against the potential ill effects of seeing a child mature in two different ways. First, these outside interests provide a distraction, which tends to diffuse the focus of the parent's life. Adults without satisfying interests outside of parenthood understandably tend to focus a tremendous amount of energy and attention on their children. They are therefore more likely to react to each and every event in their children's lives, no matter how minor or inconsequential. And when major events take place—such as a child's transition into adolescence—they take on gargantuan importance.

The second reason for the buffering impact of outside interests has to do with the adult's sense of competence and self-worth. Although parenthood may make a mother or father feel happy, it generally does not increase the individual's sense of competence or self-esteem. Accomplishments in work and marriage tend to do this, however. Thus, the parent who has satisfactions outside the parental role stands a better chance of being a more confident, more self-assured individual, and this confidence and self-assurance provides an added layer of psychological protection against the unrest caused by the child's adolescence.

THE COGNITIVE SET

The final risk factor I identified was the hardest to quantify but, in some senses, was potentially the most important. This was the "cognitive set" the parent came to adolescence with. By *cognitive set*, psychologists mean the expectations individuals have for a given situation, the way in which a set of events is perceived, and the sorts of explanations or attributions individuals make after something has happened.

In clearly defined situations, cognitive sets do not matter very much, because it is difficult for an individual to define the situation in a way that differs from what it really is.

For example, I recently had a severe pain in my tooth that necessitated my going to the dentist for a root-canal procedure. If you've had one of these, you know that, while it isn't excruciatingly painful, it is uncomfortable. Given what I knew about the procedure, I couldn't realistically tell myself as I was driving to the dentist's office that the root canal was going to be fun, and given the actual procedure itself, I had little opportunity while in the dentist's chair to define the situation as pleasant, since it isn't—not by any stretch of the imagination. This was a situation in which my cognitive set mattered very little.

Cognitive sets *are* important in vague situations, though, where individuals' definitions and perceptions are very much subjective. In vague situations, the way in which we perceive, define, and interpret the situation may be more important than the situation itself.

In the university psychology department where I teach, for example, each of our doctoral students must successfully complete an oral defense of his or her dissertation. At the defense, the student sits at the head of a long conference table and must answer any questions about his or her research that are raised by the faculty members on the student's dissertation committee.

The other afternoon, one of my students who had just set a date for his dissertation defense made an appointment to see me in advance of the meeting. Aaron wanted to know what to expect at the defense so he would be able to prepare for it. I said, "Well, you'll begin the defense with a brief statement about your research and what you think you've accomplished in it, and then we'll go around the table and people will ask you questions."

"What are they likely to ask?" Aaron wanted to know. "Will the questions be difficult?"

"I have no idea," I replied. "Every defense I've been to is different. Don't worry about it, though. You know more about your own dissertation than anyone on the faculty does, so I'm sure you'll do just fine. If you're feeling anxious, why don't you call the other members of your committee and ask them if there's anything special you should be worried about."

"No," he said, "I don't think I want to do that. That would take all the fun out it. It will be a more interesting meeting if I just let it happen. Actually, I'm kind of looking forward to it. I've heard it can be pretty stimulating."

I thought this was quite a remarkable attitude. Other students in the same situation usually respond very differently. Rather than defining their defense examination as a potentially interesting and enjoyable intellectual challenge, they see it as a difficult and unpleasant ordeal to be survived. When they speak to their fellow students—just as Aaron did—they hear nothing but horror stories. I have even had some students walk into their defense and whisper to me as the exam was beginning, as if they were about to have a root canal done, "Well, in two hours it will all be over." It is hard to imagine that these students got very much out of the experience, except perhaps, the beginning of an ulcer.

One of the reasons that cognitive sets are so important is that they often become self-fulfilling prophecies. My experience as a doctoral advisor is that the students who enter their dissertation-defense examination expecting to find an interesting intellectual challenge typically do find it to be so, whereas those who expect it to be nerve-racking have their worst nightmare confirmed. One reason is that the individual's expectation influences what he or she attends to in the situation. Thus, an optimistic student at a defense will tend to notice the affirmative head shaking that the faculty members engage in when they agree with a point that has been made, whereas the pessimistic student will notice each and every grimace and frown. Moreover, the students will differ in how they interpret the same events: The optimistic student will interpret faculty interruptions as indicative of how interested they must be in the research, whereas the pessimistic student will interpret the same interruptions as signs of frustration or irritation.

The child's transition into adolescence is one of those situations that is vague. Most of what happens as the child matures is not clear cut. And most of what happens is subject to multiple interpretations. Rather than being black *or* white—easy *or* difficult, good *or* bad—the family's transition in the child's adolescence is complicated and multifaceted. And how it is experienced is very much influenced by the parent's cognitive set.

As an example, consider how different parents respond to their child's demands for more privacy. Most families face the following situation sooner or later. When their adolescent is home, her bedroom door is closed. When the phone rings for her, she asks to take the call in another room. When she is asked what she and her friends did at the mall on a Saturday afternoon, she says, "Oh, you know, nothing." I have heard this same story from parents dozens of times. But I have seen parents respond to the situation in very different ways.

Some parents react by worrying: "What is my daughter hiding from us?" they ask. "Why won't she tell me more about her life? Does this mean that something is wrong?" Part of the reason they worry is that their cognitive set about adolescence is that the period is going to be difficult, that teenagers are drawn toward trouble, and that any effort at establishing privacy must mean that the adolescent has something to hide. This was certainly the view held by Gray Miller, Eileen Brown, and Bob Peterson.

Other parents respond to the identical situation entirely differently, however: "I remember how much fun it was to share secrets over the phone with my friends," or "I'm glad she can take the bus to the mall with her friends and spend the whole afternoon there—that's one less activity I have to organize for her." Part of their cognitive set about adolescence is that it is fun and natural for teenagers to spend more time with their friends and less with their parents, and that expressing a desire for privacy is a healthy sign that their child is maturing, not heading for trouble. Think, for example, of Vicki Dobson, John Forster, or Ed O'Hara, the police officer.

In our study, the cognitive set that parents had about adolescence was an important influence on the degree of turmoil they experienced during this transition. Parents who expected the worst to happen during adolescence often had their expectations fulfilled. These parents came to the adolescent transition expecting that they would not get along with their child. They anticipated that their child was going to change in dramatic ways, and they defined adolescence as a time of loss—of losing the child, of losing control and authority, of losing status in the child's eyes, or losing one's role as a parent. They also tended to see any temporary shifts in family relationships as permanent alterations, always for the worse.

In many regards, this was the crux of the problem faced by Amanda Spencer, Theresa Rossi, Cynthia Garrison, Gray Miller, and Richard Johnson. Because of who they were and their own developmental histories, each came to his or her child's adolescence with negative preconceptions and expectations. And this led them to have a negative interpretative framework within which they viewed their teenagers and their relationships with them.

Some parents came to their child's adolescence with a negative cognitive set specifically because of their own problems as a teenager. They had been "difficult" teenagers, and expected the same from their children. Some had had strained relationships with their own parents and expected that this was the normal course of events in all families. Some, like Theresa Rossi, Richard Johnson, or Bob Peterson, had not really worked through their own adolescent conflicts, and these conflicts came back to haunt them in their relations with their children.

Other parents had negative preconceptions about adolescence because of what they had read or been told by friends. They had seen the bookstores filled with "survival" guides to adolescence or had heard from friends or distant relatives about the difficult times they had experienced during their child's teenage years. I was often surprised by these parents, since many could not point to any specific instances in their own child's life that would have led them to such pessimistic expectations.

And still others, like Amanda Spencer and Gray Miller, had negative outlooks in general, and this global negativity colored their view of their child's development at all stages. These were the sorts of parents for whom the glass was always "half empty," whether the "glass" in question was their work, their marriage, or their child.

THE EFFECT OF A NEGATIVE COGNITIVE SET

Regardless of their origin, though, these negative expectations, once confirmed as self-fulfilling prophecies, became psychological filters through which the adolescent's behavior was interpreted and explained. What began as an emotional reaction to the onset of adolescence became an interpretive framework for subsequent events. Amanda Spencer filtered her son's behavior through a lens of loss.

Gray Miller looked at his stepdaughter's behavior through a lens of powerlessness. Cynthia Garrison viewed her daughter's behavior within a framework dominated by her own fears of abandonment. Given the negative cognitive set these parents brought to adolescence, their turmoil and unrest were virtually inescapable.

Not all parents come to the adolescent transition with such negative expectations, however. Many, like Linda Forster, Ed O'Hara, or Jon Spencer are positive and upbeat, realistic without being afraid. They see adolescence as a time to strengthen their relationship with their child and as an opportunity to explore new dimensions of parenthood. These parents greet their child's adolescence with open arms, and they tend to be the parents who thrive during this time.

14. OPPORTUNITIES FOR GROWTH AND CRISIS

For Richard Johnson, the central emotion in his struggle with his son's adolescence was jealousy. Despite his genuine wish to be as good a father as possible, he could not seem to make himself feel proud of Matt's accomplishments. Fortunately for Matt, Richard's wife, Paula, was able to give Matt the attention that he wasn't receiving from his father.

I was confident that, because of Paula's attention and affection, Matt would continue to grow and blossom. But for Richard, I had no such positive prognosis. As long as Matt continued to achieve and Richard continued to envy him, Richard would remain depressed, and his marriage and work would suffer.

Cynthia Garrison's concern was abandonment. As a single mother with a strong investment in her relationship with her daughter, Jessica, Cynthia could not help feeling left behind as her daughter's social and emotional world began to widen. Unfortunately, the harder Cynthia tried to hold on to her unusually intense friendship with Jessica, the more her daughter felt the need for breathing room. The gap between them grew.

Cynthia's feeling of abandonment intensified. She began to have trouble sleeping. I thought it probably was just a matter of time before her enmeshment would drive Jessica away even further, to escape the psychological suffocation she was feeling. Jessica herself was beginning to show signs of internalized distress, complaining of a loss of appetite and frequent headaches. I felt particularly sorry about what was happening to Cynthia and Jessica, because they had enjoyed such a close relationship previously.

The turmoil that Amanda Spencer, the full-time homemaker, experienced when her son, Paul, hit adolescence revolved around loss. Once Amanda began feeling as if she were losing something by Paul's growing up, she could not help seeing each stride her son took toward becoming independent as confirmation of her worst fears.

For Amanda, Paul's maturation triggered a loss of self-definition. As her sense of loss intensified, Amanda grew more and more despondent. She was having difficulty concentrating, and she suffered increasingly frequent bouts of nervousness. Her depression was taking its toll on her relationships at home. She was bickering with Paul frequently and distancing herself from her husband, Jon.

In the Miller-Hansen household, the central issue was powerlessness. Each time his stepdaughter Cindy asserted her individuality, Gray Miller took it as a threat to his authority as the man of the house. The more threatened Gray felt, the more angry he became. The more Cindy resisted Gray's attempts at control, the more impotent Gray felt.

Ellen Hansen, Cindy's mother, was caught in the middle of this feud between her daughter and her new husband. When I met Ellen, she was feeling completely stressed out. Family counseling had helped stop things from spiraling out of control, but the distance between Gray and Cindy, and, as a result, between Gray and Ellen, was widening nevertheless. In the end, Ellen's loyalties would probably rest with her children. I thought it was likely that she and Gray would eventually divorce.

For Theresa Rossi, one of the working-class mothers in our study, the defining issue was not loss, but regret. As her daughter Maria moved into adolescence, Theresa was overwhelmed with regret about her own life—so much so, that she could barely pay attention to what was going on in Maria's. As Theresa began to disengage from parenting, her daughter's problems increased.

Adolescents in similar circumstances often end up on a downward trajectory of detachment from school and problems with delinquency, sex, and drugs. Maria was already among the most troubled youngsters in our sample, with a poor record in school and an extreme susceptibility to peer pressure. Unless her parents' level of involvement rose, Maria was headed toward serious behavior problems.

PARENTS AT MIDLIFE

The little information we have on how parents' psychological well-being is affected by changes in the family system comes from research at the two ends of the parental career: the birth of the first child, the so-called transition to parenthood, and the launching of the last, the so-called transition to the empty nest. This research has been illuminating. But to focus on these extremes and ignore everything in the middle is to assume a constancy in adult development and family life that is mythical. Such a viewpoint surely misses out on the very important changes that take place *in the parent* as the child grows and matures.

Our study is a starting point in assessing the impact that changes in the family at the adolescent transition have on parents' mental health and well-being. But it is just a beginning, and there is much to be learned. We are still in the process of mapping out what is largely uncharted territory. For example, we focused on parents during the early part of their firstborn's adolescent years. We do not yet know whether developments during the rest of the child's adolescence have comparable effects.

Our understanding of psychological development during middle adulthood is growing at a rapid pace. As recently as twenty-five years ago, most social scientists did not even acknowledge that there *was* development in adulthood. Now, it seems that a new book on middle age enters the bookstores weekly.

But even the recent flurry of books and articles on menopause—inspired, no doubt, by the movement of the baby-boom generation into this stage of the life span—give only passing mention to the fact that the adults undergoing the change of life are parents as well as spouses, mothers and fathers as well as employees. None pays any attention to the way in which the development of the child affects the psyche of the parent.

THE TEENAGER AS TRIGGER

What is it about the child's entrance into adolescence that has the potential to incite psychological unrest in his or her parents? Our findings point to six specific "triggers":

• *Puberty* Few aspects of the adolescent passage are as noticeable or as striking to parents as the changes in the child's physical appearance that come with puberty. Changes in the child's emotions, personality, or behavior can be dismissed as temporary, but the transformation of a parent's little boy into a man, or little girl into a woman, provides incontrovertible evidence that the child is really growing up. For many parents, the unshakable facts of growth spurts and facial hair, breast buds and menstrual periods, do not just signal that a new phase in their children's lives is beginning. They also say that an old phase in their own lives is ending.

• *Sexuality* Seeing one's child mature sexually is one of the most difficult aspects of the adolescent passage for parents, especially in households with adolescent girls. For many parents, their adolescent's sexual maturation unleashes a torrent of emotions and conflicts about their *own* physical attractiveness, their *own* sexuality, their *own* sexual experiences as teenagers, and their marriage. More often than not, the effects are negative ones, making parents feel unattractive, envious of their child's potential, longing for their own "lost" youth, and, if married, dissatisfied with their spouse.

• *Dating* Watching an adolescent begin to date also triggers turmoil for many parents, because they both identify with and compare themselves to their child. Having a son or daughter date increases mothers' feelings of self-doubt, their regret over past decisions, and their desires to change things about their life. Fathers of sons (but not of daughters) who are dating report a combination of more anxiety and depression but higher self-esteem, especially if their son begins dating early. Regardless of whether the child is a son or a daughter, though, when the adolescent begins dating, fathers frequently report a drop in their own marital satisfaction.

• *Independence* There are families in which each movement the adolescent makes toward independence leaves the parents feeling as if they are giving up some piece of authority. In these homes, parents may feel powerless, nervous, or out of control. For parents whose own midlife anxieties are already intense at the time of their child's adolescence, coping with the adolescent's strivings for independence only amplifies the parents' sense of internal chaos. Many parents who feel this way attempt to dominate their adolescent as a means of imposing some structure on a life they feel is either in, or heading toward, disarray.

• *Emotional Detachment* Many, many parents have difficulty coping with the adolescent's emotional detachment. Adverse reactions to this are especially common among mothers with daughters, probably because the mother-daughter bond is the closest of any parent-adolescent relationship. Nevertheless, numerous fathers experience this loss too, especially if their oldest child is a son.

• *Deidealization* One of the best predictors of parents' mental health during the adolescent transition is the extent to which their children have deidealized them—have come to see them as fallible, imperfect, at fault. Parents whose children see them through these critical lenses frequently feel depressed and dissatisfied as a result. They often suffer from low self-esteem and are wrapped up in rumination about their past. For some parents, their child's criticism produces intense feelings of self-doubt.

DECLINERS, THRIVERS, AND SURVIVORS

Roughly speaking, about 40 percent of parents in our sample experienced psychological difficulty of one sort or another during their child's transition into adolescence. This decline was manifested by a drop in two or more of our indicators of well-being, that is, a decline in self-image or life satisfaction, or an increase in midlife rumination or in symptoms of psychological distress, such as depression, anxiety, or psychosomatic ailments. In other words, four in ten adults see their mental health deteriorate as their child becomes a teenager.

At the other end of the spectrum are parents whose mental health takes a turn for the better during this same transition. Over time, these men and women show significant improvement in their psychological well-being, reporting increased self-esteem and life satisfaction, and less rumination and psychological distress. About one fifth of the parents we studied—two in ten—fell into this group.

The remaining individuals—about 40 percent—fall between these two extremes. They neither decline nor improve in any dramatic way as their children enter adolescence. Some of these parents are simply not affected by the transition. Others may be affected, but not in ways that translate into visible changes in their own mental health. That is, they may feel proud or disappointed in their child, or happy or sad that this phase in their child's life is beginning, but these feelings do not influence their *own* well-being in one direction or another.

How do these findings jibe with other research on adults at midlife? In general, I think they are consistent with more recent and more systematic research on middle-aged adults. Not everyone with an adolescent child experiences psychological unrest, and even among those who do, there are important differences in the form and intensity that the turmoil takes. Consistent with more recent studies of midlife, our study uncovered considerable diversity in individual experience in middle age.

MOTHERS AND FATHERS AT MIDLIFE

Although both men and women were well represented in all three groups of parents—the "decliners," the "thrivers," and the "survivors"—more women than men reported a change in well-being, either positive or negative, as their child became a teenager.

Nearly half of the mothers in our sample saw their mental health take a turn for the worse; among fathers, though, it was only about one in three. At the same time, approximately twice as many women as men enjoyed a change in their mental health for the *better*: nearly one in three women, but fewer than one in six men, fell into this category. Another way of putting this is that men were disproportionately overrepresented in the "survivor" category: about half of the men we studied, but only one fourth of the women, were in this group.

There are a number of different lessons about similarities and differences between mothers and fathers at midlife to be gleaned from these figures:

• About six in ten parents experience a noticeable change in their mental health as their children become teenagers. Of the proportion who *do* change, twice as many decline as improve. It is important to keep in mind that these individuals were studied over a relatively short time period—just two and a half years. Over a longer time frame, the proportion of individuals who would report a change in their well-being—either positive or negative—would likely be greater. I imagine, though, that the relative ratio of "decliners" to "thrivers" would remain fairly constant at about two to one. In other words, the effect of the adolescent transition on parents' mental health is twice as likely to be negative as positive.

• Women seem especially likely to be affected by the passage of the child into adolescence. Indeed, given the fact that nearly half of all the women in our sample experienced a drop in well-being during this period, it seems safe to say that *the child's entrance into adolescence represents a significant threat to mothers' mental health*. It is not just that raising an adolescent child is difficult—it is that the experience of watching one's child mature can incite difficult and painful psychological turmoil in women.

• At the same time, however, the fact that nearly one in three women reports substantial improvement in well-being during the identical time period indicates that there is a great potential for personal growth.

• In some regards, the observation that women are more affected by the child's transition into adolescence than are men is consistent with longstanding notions about sex differences in influences on psychological well-being. In general, we tend to think of women's mental health as being more closely linked to events in the family than is the mental health of men. And to large measure, our study corroborates this view. Nevertheless, our findings clash with the widely held view that midlife is a more difficult time for men than women. This portion of midlife—or at least, this *aspect* of midlife—appears equally critical for women and men, if not more critical for women.

• *Women's personal crises at midlife do not come from launching their adolescents but from living with them.* It is time we abandoned once and for all the notion of the "empty nest" as a crisis in women's lives. It is the transition *into* the child's adolescent decade, not the transition out of it, that causes unrest for mothers. Entering the *emptying* nest is more stressful than entering the empty nest.

• Although men are more likely to simply "survive" this transition unchanged than are women, it would certainly be incorrect to come away from this study with the idea that men's mental health is *untouched* by their child's development, which is also part of the prevailing stereotype about the differences between men and women. Half of the fathers we studied reported a change in well-being during their child's transition into adolescence.

• A far higher proportion of men whose mental health changed during this time reported a change for the worse than for the better. Very few men thrived during this period, and men who declined outnumbered those who improved by more than two to one. Thus, although the chances of passing through this stage psychologically unaffected—that is, as a "survivor"—appear greater among men than women, the proportion of men who actually *thrive* during this transition is considerably lower.

• Although the "empty nest" is probably less stressful for women than the popular stereotype holds, the imminence of the "empty den" is a significant source of concern for many fathers. *The child's adolescence may trigger intense regret among fathers over the time they did not devote to their children when they were younger.*

DIVERSITY IN DISTRESS

It is tempting to lump together the Amanda Spencers, the Cynthia Garrisons, and the Theresa Rossis, or the Richard Johnsons and the Gray Millers, into general, overarching categories of mothers or fathers who had a "difficult time" during their youngsters' adolescence. Doing so, however, ignores the fact that despite their shared distress, these parents' particular experiences and emotions were quite different from each other. To borrow from Tolstoy's *Anna Karenina*, "Every unhappy parent of a teenager is unhappy in his or her own way."

The diversity we uncovered in the types of turmoil parents experience is important to understand, because different reactions to the child's entrance into adolescence have quite different consequences for the adult's work, marriage, and parenting.

• Parents whose primary experience is *loss* tend to react in ways similar to those seen in depressed individuals. Those who are married may have difficulty finding pleasure in their relationship, and those who are employed may feel empty and bored at work. As parents, these individuals tend to try to hold on to their child through various forms of psychological control, such as inducing guilt or withdrawing love. Some may form an enmeshed relationship with their adolescent in an attempt to stop the child from moving away emotionally. Others may become more indulgent in an effort to win the adolescent's favor through permissiveness and leniency.

• Parents whose primary experience is *regret* tend to spend a good deal of time ruminating about and reviewing their own life story. They may think a great deal about their own adolescence and their young adult years. If married, this frequently leads to a reevaluation of the relationship and, in some instances, to severe marital disenchantment. At work, these adults may have difficulty concentrating, spending time daydreaming about what they might be doing instead of their present job. As parents, adults who react this way often disengage from parenting. Because they focus so much energy on themselves, they often have little left for their child.

• Parents whose primary experience is *abandonment* are tempted to turn outside the parental role for emotional and psychic compensation. For instance, as marital partners, these parents may seek more intimacy and involvement from their spouse; if employed, they often increase their work hours or take on added responsibilities. Not surprisingly, the mental health of these parents is linked to what they find in these other domains. Some are able to shift their focus to work or marriage and are fortunate enough to find new satisfaction in one or both of these spheres. However, those who try to find solace in other activities but fail may fare especially poorly. As parents, these mothers and fathers tend to shift between extremes: clinging to their adolescent in an enmeshing response or disengaging from the relationship as a protective device.

• Parents whose primary experience is *powerlessness* often have difficulties in their marriage and work life as a result. In most cases, these parents have responded to the child's maturation with an increase in autocratic parenting, which has likely prompted resistance and rebellion on the part of the teenager. They and their adolescent may fall into a coercive cycle of arguing and bickering, with each escalating the other's frustration and irritation. The anger that this experience arouses in the parent is easily carried over outside of the parent-child relationship. Such parents often report high conflict in their marriage and frequent interpersonal problems at work.

• Parents whose primary experience is *jealousy* may respond by trying to make some drastic change in their life, typically in an effort to recapture their own youth. Some become quite concerned about their own physical state, worrying about their appearance, health, or stamina. They may feel dissatisfied with their marriage and look elsewhere for sexual excitement. They may daydream on the job about starting over in a new line of work. As parents, these adults frequently let their envy interfere with their better parental instincts. Their jealousy may lead them to turn autocratic, in an attempt to "even the score" with their child; or indulgent, in an effort to demonstrate that they are still fun loving and "with it."

The other half of Tolstoy's observation about happy and unhappy families—that "happy families are all alike"—applies to our findings as well. In general, the parents who thrive during their child's adolescence are alike in many important ways. Their marriages tend to be revitalized and energized, and many report renewed interest in sex and romance. In their work lives, these parents manage to find satisfaction and gratification, whether in continuing to strive to move ahead within their career, or in contenting themselves to remain in the same position. The few who change careers during this period tend to do so with an optimistic, youthful excitement, and without bitterness, fear, or a sense of desperation. As parents, these adults tend to react authoritatively, remaining engaged, flexible, and appropriately in control.

LESSONS FOR LIVING

The findings to emerge from this study show that the child's entrance into adolescence is often a difficult personal period in parents' lives—perhaps even more difficult for parents than it is for their children. This is not simply because raising teenagers is an arduous task. It is because watching our children mature unearths complicated and intense emotions deep inside us. That these emotions typically rise to the surface during midlife, a time with its own trying psychological agenda, makes matters that much more difficult.

Yet one of the most important lessons I think this study teaches us is that the turmoil parents feel at the adolescent transition, while common, is not inevitable.

I am frequently asked by parents—parents whose children *are* teenagers and those whose children are about to *become* teenagers—how they can better handle this period in their family's development. At these moments, I find myself thinking not about the parents in our study who were thrown into a period of unrest, but about those whose mental health actually improved. What lessons can we learn from listening to *these* parents—the John and Linda Forsters, the Ed O'Haras, the Sarah Feins, the Jon Spencers, and the Vicki Dobsons? What can parents do to make adolescence a wonderful time—a time of growth—not only for their child, but for themselves?

• *Make sure you have genuine and satisfying interests outside of being a parent.* The thrivers in our sample all had in common a real zest for something in addition to their child. For some it was marriage, for others, work, and for others still, an outside hobby or interest. If you are fortunate enough to have a happy marriage, a satisfying career, or a stimulating hobby, do what you can to strengthen your commitment to it even further. If you are not so fortunate, it is important that you take steps to establish a satisfying foothold outside the parental role.

Don't fall for the fallacy that one has to choose between work and family. The happiest, most well-adjusted adults tend to have strong commitments to both.

• *Don't disengage from your child emotionally*. Another characteristic of the thrivers in our study was that they all had warm, involved, and emotionally close relationships with their children. Remember, it is the absence of investment in nonparental activities, rather than being invested in parenting, that places adults at risk for difficulty during this transition.

Disengaging from your child will not protect you from the psychological effects of seeing your child mature. It will, however, jeopardize your child's well-being, and this, in turn, will adversely affect your own. The healthiest children, and the healthiest parents, have a relationship that is authoritative—warm, firm, and communicative.

• *Try to adopt a positive outlook about what adolescence is and how your child is changing*. Start by disabusing yourself of the stereotypes you may hold of adolescence as a family nightmare. It isn't. But if you approach your child's adolescence as if it is, you may well turn it into one, not only for your child but for yourself as well.

Instead of viewing your child as challenging your authority, remind yourself that raising a curious, assertive child is wonderful, not problematic.

Instead of seeing your child's emotional growth as the end of your relationship, try to imagine how the relationship you have with your son or daughter can be strengthened by your child's new maturity.

Instead of viewing your child's independence with fear and trepidation, try to reframe it as something that is not just inevitable but desirable. Don't view your child's striving for autonomy as a sign that he or she does not want to be emotionally close to you. Adolescents learn *healthy* independence best in the context of a close parent-child relationship.

• *Don't be afraid to discuss what you are feeling with your mate, your friends, or, if need be, with a professional counselor*. All parents have ambivalent feelings about their children growing up. We simply haven't been socialized to express them—not to others, and not to ourselves. This is a special problem for fathers, who have been led to believe that they are psychologically impervious to events and changes in the family. Whether you are a mother or a father, you may find comfort in venting some of what you are feeling, and solace in learning that you are not alone.

GROWTH, CRISIS, AND THE ADOLESCENT FACTOR

Psychologists are fond of pointing out that the Chinese symbol for "crisis" is formed by combining the characters for danger and opportunity. In this sense, the child's transition into adolescence would appear to be a crisis for most parents—a time of danger, but also a time of opportunity.

Most of what has been written to date about the changing dynamics of family relationships over the life course has concentrated on how parents affect their children. As any of the parents in our study will attest, though, this is only half the story.

Processes of influence in families flow in both directions—parents affect their children, to be sure, but children also affect their parents. Not only is the parent-child relationship a two-way street, it is also an extremely important influence on adults' well-being. Mothers and fathers are as affected by events within the family as are their sons and daughters.

The stories of the families who participated in this study indicate that those writing about menopause and the midlife crisis have given us only a partial picture of psychological functioning in middle age. I don't wish to suggest that the biological and occupational changes of middle adulthood—the foci of those writings—are not important events in the adult life cycle. But the lessons to emerge from our study point to the family as an equally if not more significant arena for change and crisis in the lives of middle-aged men and women.

The child's entry into adolescence is a crucial time for mothers and fathers, for it is a period in which a critical developmental transition in the child's life, puberty, coincides with a critical developmental transition in the adult's, midlife. For the midlife parent, the crossing paths of adolescence and middle adulthood provide remarkable opportunities for growth. If these opportunities are not seized, though, the juxtaposition of the transitions of adolescence and midlife also may create a tremendous potential for psychological turmoil.

NOTES

1. CROSSING PATHS (PAGES 15–19)

Adolescence as a tumultuous period for the family: W. A. Collins, "Parent-Child Relationships in the Transition to Adolescence: Continuity and Change in Interaction, Affect, and Cognition," in *Advances in Adolescent Development: Vol. 2. The Transition from Childhood to Adolescence*, R. Montemayor, G. Adams, and T. Gullotta, eds. (Beverly Hills, CA: Sage, 1990); Laurence Steinberg, "Autonomy, Conflict, and Harmony in the Family Relationship," in *At the Threshold: The Developing Adolescent*, S. Feldman and G. Elliot, eds. (Cambridge: Harvard University Press, 1990).

Previous studies of family relationships: Laurence Steinberg, "Transformations in Family Relations at Puberty," *Developmental Psychology* 17 (1981): 833–40; Laurence Steinberg, "The Impact of Puberty on Family Relations: Effects of Pubertal Status and Pubertal Timing," *Developmental Psychology* 23 (1987): 451–60; Laurence Steinberg and Susan Silverberg, "Influences on Marital Satisfaction During the Middle Stages of the Family Life Cycle," *Journal of Marriage and the Family* 49 (1987): 751–60; Susan Silverberg and Laurence Steinberg, "Psychological Well-being of Parents at Midlife: The Impact of Early Adolescent Children," *Developmental Psychology* 26 (1990): 658–66; Susan Silverberg and Laurence Steinberg, "Adolescent Autonomy, Parent-Adolescent Conflict, and Parental Well-being," *Journal of Youth and Adolescence* 16 (1987): 293–312.

Studies of the "transition to parenthood": Jay Belsky and John Kelly, *The Transition to Parenthood* (New York: Delacorte, 1994); Carolyn Cowan and Philip Cowan, *When Parents Become Partners* (New York: Basic Books, 1992).

Studies of the transition to the "empty nest": K. Cooper and David Guttman, "Gender Identity and Ego Mastery Style in Middle-aged, Pre- and Post-empty Nest Women," *Gerontologist* 27 (1987): 347–52; Marjorie Lowenthal and David Chiriboga, "Transition to the Empty Nest: Crisis, Challenge, or Relief?" *Archives of General Psychiatry* 26 (1972): 8–14.

Overview of the research study: This research project has been described in articles published between 1987 and 1991 in the following journals: *Child*

Development, Journal of Marriage and the Family, Journal of Youth and Adolescence, Developmental Psychology, and the *Journal of Early Adolescence.*

Struggles to redefine the parent-child relationship: Collins, "Parent-Child Relationships"; Judith Smetana, "Concepts of Self and Social Convention: Adolescents' and Parents' Reasoning about Hypothetical and Actual Family Conflicts," in *21st Minnesota Symposium on Child Psychology,* M. Gunnar, ed. (Hillsdale, NJ: Erlbaum, 1988); Steinberg, "Autonomy, Conflict, and Harmony."

2. THE MERRICKS (PAGES 20–30)

Coasting through their teenage years smoothly: In retrospect, I should not have been surprised. Other studies have found similar things. See, for example, Elizabeth Douvan and Joseph Adelson, *The Adolescent Experience* (New York: Wiley, 1966); Daniel Offer, *The Psychological World of the Teenager* (New York: Basic Books, 1969); Daniel Offer, Eric Ostrov, and Kenneth Howard, *The Adolescent: A Psychological Self-portrait* (New York: Basic Books, 1981).

3. PARENTS IN CRISIS (PAGES 31–51)

Erik Erikson's theory of the life cycle: Erik Erikson, *Identity and the Life Cycle* (New York: W. W. Norton, 1959).

Sheehy's best-selling book on midlife: Gail Sheehy, *Passages* (New York: Dutton, 1976).

Marking time in terms of years left to live: Berenice Neugarten, "The Awareness of Middle Age," in *Middle Age,* R. Owen, ed. (London: BBC, 1967).

Levinson's study of men at midlife: Daniel Levinson et al., *The Seasons of a Man's Life* (New York: Ballantine, 1978).

Women and the "empty nest": Neugarten, "The Awareness of Middle Age."

Family life and the well-being of men: A similar conclusion was reached by Michael Farrell and Stanley Rosenberg, in *Men at Midlife* (Boston: Auburn Press, 1981).

The empty nest as a source of relief for women: Also not a surprise, given more recent empirical studies of the empty-nest syndrome. See, for example, Norval Glenn, "Psychological Well-being in the Postparental Stage: Some Evidence from National Surveys," *Journal of Marriage and the Family* 37 (1975): 105–9; Florence Livson, "Patterns of Personality Development in Middle-aged Women," in *Becoming and Being Old,* J. Hendricks, ed. (Farmingdale, NY: Baywood, 1981); Sara McLanahan and Aage Sorensen, "Life Course Events and Psychological Well-being Over the Life Course," in *Life Course Dynamics,* G. Elder, Jr., ed. (Ithaca, NY: Cornell University Press, 1985).

Middle adulthood as a turning point, not a crisis: See, for example,

Winifred Gallagher, "Midlife Myths," *The Atlantic* 271 (1993): 51–68.

Pervasive dissatisfaction at midlife: Farrell and Rosenberg, *Men at Midlife*; Roger Gould, *Transformations* (New York: Simon and Schuster, 1978); George Vaillant, *Adaptation to life* (Boston: Little, Brown, 1977).

Midlife unhappiness about work: Levinson, *Seasons*.

Marital satisfaction follows a U-shaped curve: S. Anderson, C. Russell, and W. Schumm, "Perceived Marital Quality and Family Life-cycle Categories: A Further Analysis," *Journal of Marriage and the Family* 46 (1983): 105–14; R. Collins, *Sociology of Marriage and the Family* (Chicago: Nelson-Hall, 1985); Lois Tamir, *Men in Their Forties* (New York: Springer, 1982).

Disenchantment with parenthood: L. Hoffman and J. Manis, "Influences of Children on Marital and Parental Satisfactions and Dissatisfactions," in *Child Influences on Marital and Family Interaction: A Life-span Perspective*, R. M. Lerner and G. B. Spanier, eds. (New York: Academic Press, 1978).

Excruciating self-assessment: Gould, *Transformations*; Levinson, *Seasons*.

Change in time perspective: Neugarten, "Awareness."

Depression and suicide at midlife: Good reviews of the literature on mental health at midlife may be found in Farrell and Rosenberg, *Men at Midlife*; and Judith Stevens-Long, *Adult Life*, 3d ed. (Mountain View, CA: Mayfield, 1988).

Symptoms of midlife crisis among blue-collar adults: Farrell and Rosenberg, *Men at Midlife*.

Alcohol and drug use in midlife: Farrell and Rosenberg, *Men at Midlife*.

Measures of the midlife crisis: We employed or adapted many measures that had been used in previous studies of mental health in the general population, including Farrell and Rosenberg, *Men at Midlife*; Gould, *Transformations*; A. Campbell, P. Converse, and W. Rodgers, *The Quality of American Life: Perceptions, Evaluations, and Satisfactions* (New York: Russell Sage Foundation, 1976); Morris Rosenberg, *Society and the Adolescent Self-image* (Princeton, NJ: Princeton University Press, 1965); Lenore Radloff, "The CES-D Scale: A Self-Report Depression Scale for Research in the General Population," *Applied Psychological Measurement* 1 (1977): 385–401; and Kenneth Keniston, "Scales for the Measurement of Identity" (Unpublished manuscript, Yale University School of Medicine, 1963).

4. THE TEENAGER AS TRIGGER (PAGES 52–76)

Age at which people get married: U.S. Bureau of the Census, *Marital Status and Living Arrangements*, various years.

On-time versus off-time events: Berenice Neugarten and Gunhilde Hagestad, "Age and the Life Course," in *Handbook of Aging and the Social Sciences*, H. Binstock and E. Shanas, eds. (New York: Van Nostrand Reinhold, 1976).

Family life cycle: Roy Rodgers, *Family Interaction and Transaction: A De-*

velopmental Approach (New York: Prentice-Hall, 1973).

Biological changes of adolescence not a source of stress for teenagers: Jeanne Brooks-Gunn and Edward Reiter, "The Role of Pubertal Processes," in *At the Threshold: The Developing Adolescent*, S. Feldman and G. Elliott, eds. (Cambridge: Harvard University Press, 1990).

Puberty more salient in girls than boys: Brooks-Gunn and Reiter, "Pubertal Processes."

Earlier maturation of girls: Brooks-Gunn and Reiter, "Pubertal Processes."

Men's self-esteem tied to accomplishments: Levinson, *Seasons*.

Establishing a sense of autonomy: Steinberg, "Autonomy, Conflict, and Harmony."

Parental anxiety about adolescent independence: Stephen Small, Gay Eastman, and Steven Cornelius, "Adolescent Autonomy and Parental Stress," *Journal of Youth and Adolescence* 17 (1988): 377–92.

Demands for privacy at adolescence: Laurence Steinberg and Ann Levine, *You and Your Adolescent: A Parent's Guide for Ages 10 to 20* (New York: Harper & Row, 1990).

Detachment: Anna Freud, "Adolescence," *Psychoanalytic Study of the Child* 13 (1958): 255–78.

Mother-daughter bond: See Terri Apter, *Altered Loves* (New York: St. Martin's Press, 1990); Laurence Steinberg, "Recent Research on the Family at Adolescence: The Extent and Nature of Sex Differences," *Journal of Youth and Adolescence* 16 (1987): 191–98; and James Youniss and Jacqueline Smollar, *Adolescents' Relations with Mothers, Fathers, and Friends* (Chicago: University of Chicago Press, 1985).

Individuation: Peter Blos, "The Second Individuation Process of Adolescence," *The Psychoanalytic Study of the Child* 1 (1967): 183–98.

Parental identification with children: Theresa Benedek, "Parenthood as a Developmental Phase: a Contribution to the Libido Theory," *Journal of the American Psychoanalytic Association* 7 (1959): 389–417.

5. JEALOUSY (PAGES 79–97)

Parental self-esteem is lower: I am grateful to Professor Carol Ryff, Department of Psychology, University of Wisconsin—Madison, for sharing these preliminary findings with me.

"I find myself wishing that I had raised my children in a different way": Item from Silverberg and Steinberg, "Psychological Well-being."

"I will probably feel a little empty when my children all leave home": Item from Silverberg and Steinberg, "Psychological Well-being."

6. ABANDONMENT (PAGES 98–114)

Fewer than one fourth of parents and teenagers have strained or unhappy relations: Michael Rutter et al., "Adolescent Turmoil: Fact or Fiction? *Journal of Child Psychology and Psychiatry* 17 (1976): 35–56.

Most common complaint among single parents concerns finances: Other major studies of divorce reach similar conclusions. See, for example, the collection of papers in E. Mavis Hetherington and Josephine Arasteh, eds., *Impact of Divorce, Single Parenting, and Stepparenting on Children* (Hillsdale, NJ: Erlbaum, 1988).

Emotional distance in the parent-child relationship: Blos, "Individuation."

Closeness in the family is a good thing: Steinberg, "Autonomy, Conflict, and Harmony."

Beneficial effects on the parent: Silverberg and Steinberg, "Adolescent Autonomy."

Separation-individuation: Margaret Mahler, F. Pine, and A. Bergman, *The Psychological Birth of the Human Infant* (New York: Basic Books, 1975).

Similarities between adolescent and toddler: Blos, "Individuation."

7. LOSS (PAGES 115–130)

"I find myself wondering if I've put too much emphasis on certain things in life while neglecting other important things": Item from Silverberg and Steinberg, "Psychological Well-being."

Puberty as a trigger of changes in family relations: Steinberg, "Autonomy, Conflict, and Harmony."

Depression and loss: Charles Wenar, *Developmental Psychopathology*, 2d ed. (New York: McGraw-Hill, 1990).

Psychological control: Diana Baumrind, "Parenting Styles and Adolescent Development," in *The Encyclopedia of Adolescence*, J. Brooks-Gunn, R. Lerner, and A. C. Petersen, eds. (New York: Garland, 1991); Earl Schaefer, "Children's Reports of Parental Behavior: An Inventory," *Child Development* 36 (1965): 413–24; Steinberg, "Autonomy, Conflict, and Harmony."

8. POWERLESSNESS (PAGES 131–147)

Arrival of a stepfather: Frank Furstenberg, Jr., "Child Care After Divorce and Remarriage," in *Impact of Divorce, Single Parenting, and Stepparenting on Children*, E. M. Hetherington and J. D. Arasteh, eds. (Hillsdale, NJ: Erlbaum, 1988); E. Mavis Hetherington and Edward Anderson, "The Effects of Divorce and Remarriage on Early Adolescents and Their Families," in *Early Adolescent Transitions*, M. D. Levine and E. R. McAnarney, eds. (Lexington, MA: Lexington Books, 1987).

Brief honeymoon after remarriage: E. Mavis Hetherington, *Studying Family Transitions: Families, Lives, and Videotapes*. Presidential address presented at the biennial meeting of the Society for Research on Adolescence. Atlanta, Georgia, 1990.

Occupational plateau: Levinson, *Seasons*.

Uncontrollable situations and health: Martin E. P. Seligman, *Helplessness:*

On Depression, Development, and Death (San Francisco: Freeman, 1975).

Ranking different aspects of parenting: Susan Silverberg, "Psychological Well-being of Parents with Early Adolescent Children" (Ph.D. diss., Department of Child and Family Studies, University of Wisconsin—Madison, 1986).

Parental abdication of responsibilities: Susie Lamborn et al., "Patterns of Competence and Adjustment Among Adolescents from Authoritative, Authoritarian, Indulgent, and Neglectful Homes," *Child Development* 62 (1991): 1049–65.

9. REGRET (PAGES 148–164)

Middle class emphasis in research on midlife: See Stevens-Long, *Adult Life*, for a review.

Working-class adults use different words in describing the crisis: Farrell and Rosenberg, *Men at Midlife*.

"I find myself wishing that I had the opportunity to start afresh and do things over, knowing what I do now.": Item adapted from Farrell and Rosenberg, *Men at Midlife*.

Life review: Robert Butler, "The Life Review: An Interpretation of Reminiscence in the Aged," *Psychiatry* 26 (1968): 65–76.

Early marriage and divorce: Douglas Teti, Michael Lamb, and Arthur Elster, "Long-range Socioeconomic and Marital Consequences of Adolescent Marriage in Three Cohorts of Adult Males," *Journal of Marriage and the Family* 49 (1987): 499–506.

Effects of parental disengagement: Laurence Steinberg et al., "Over-time Changes in Adjustment and Competence Among Adolescents from Authoritative, Authoritarian, Indulgent, and Neglectful Families," *Child Development*, 1994, in press.

10. THE SPILLOVER INTO MARRIAGE (PAGES 167–186)

Sampling biases in survey research: Charles Judd, Eliot Smith, and Louise Kidder, *Research Methods in Social Relations*, 6th ed. (New York: Holt, 1991).

New depths of dissatisfaction in marriage: Boyd Rollins and Harold Feldman, "Marital Satisfaction Over the Family Life Cycle," *Journal of Marriage and the Family* 32 (1970): 20–28.

Upturn in marital satisfaction after adolescence: Anderson et al., "Perceived Marital Quality"; Rollins and Feldman, "Marital Satisfaction."

Boredom and marital happiness: Elaine Walster and William Walster, *A New Look at Love* (Cambridge: Addison-Wesley, 1978).

Midlife crisis and marital happiness: Levinson, *Seasons*; Rosenberg and Farrell, *Men at Midlife*; Sheehy, *Passages*.

Impact of children on marital happiness: McLanahan and Sorensen, "Life Course Events."

Proportion of adults with full-blown crisis: Farrell and Rosenberg, *Men at Midlife*.

Closeness of marriage correlated with closeness of parent-child relationship: Brian Barber, "Marital Quality, Parental Behavior, and Adolescent Self-esteem," *Family Perspective* 21 (1987): 244–368.

Adolescent autonomy as a liberating experience: Lowenthal and Chiriboga, "Empty Nest."

Flirtatious interchanges between fathers and daughters: John Hill, "Adapting to Menarche: Familial Control and Conflict," in *21st Minnesota Symposium on Child Psychology*, M. Gunnar, ed. (Hillsdale, NJ: Erlbaum, 1988).

11. THE SPILLOVER INTO WORK (PAGES 187–205)

Occupational plateau: Levinson, *Seasons*.

Men's happiness tied to work success: Daniel Offer and Melvin Sabshin, *Normality and the Life Cycle* (New York: Basic Books, 1984).

Measure of orientation to work: Item taken from Silverberg and Steinberg, "Psychological Well-being."

Social comparison between parent and adolescent: H. Meyers, "The Impact of Teenaged Children on Parents," in *The Middle Years*, J. Oldham and R. Liebert, eds. (New Haven: Yale University Press, 1989).

Mothers argue with children more than fathers do. Steinberg, "Transformations in Family Relations."

Mothers' mental health improves when children leave home: Lowenthal and Chiriboga, "Empty Nest"; McLanahan and Sorensen, "Life Course Events."

Empty den: Farrell and Rosenberg, *Men at Midlife*.

Looking forward to launching: Cooper and Guttman, "Gender Identity."

12. THE SPILLOVER INTO PARENTING (PAGES 206–226)

Family relationships in a state of flux in early adolescence: Steinberg, "Transformations in Family Relations."

Family life cycle: Rodgers, *Family Interaction*.

Familial reactions to disequilibrium. Salvador Minuchin, *Families and Family Therapy* (Cambridge: Harvard University Press, 1974).

Determinants of parenting: Jay Belsky, "The Determinants of Parenting: A Process Model," *Child Development* 55 (1984): 83–96.

Categories of parenting: Diana Baumrind, "Parenting Styles."

Patterns of adjustment maintained over time: Lamborn et al., "Patterns of Competence"; Steinberg et al., "Changes in Adjustment."

13. DECLINING AND THRIVING AT THE ADOLESCENT TRANSITION (PAGES 229–248)

Relations between parents and same-sex children are closer: Youniss and Smollar, *Adolescents' Relations*.

Parents identify with same-sex child: Silverberg and Steinberg, "Psychological Well-being."

Parent-child intimacy in single-parent homes: Frances Sessa and Laurence Steinberg, "Family Structure and the Development of Autonomy in Adolescence," *Journal of Early Adolescence* 11 (1991): 38–55.

Arrival of stepfather: Hetherington and Arasteh, *Effects of Divorce and Remarriage.*

Absence of nonparental investment is crucial: Grace Baruch, Rosalind Barnett, and Caryl Rivers, *Lifeprints* (New York: McGraw-Hill, 1983).

Absence of satisfying work life increases vulnerability: Silverberg and Steinberg, "Psychological Well-being."

Unhappy marriage increases vulnerability: Kelly Koski and Laurence Steinberg, "Parenting Satisfaction of Mothers During Midlife," *Journal of Youth and Adolescence* 19 (1990): 465–74.

Accomplishments in work and marriage bolster self-esteem: Baruch et al., *Lifeprints*

14. OPPORTUNITIES FOR GROWTH AND CRISIS (PAGES 249–261)
Recent books and articles on menopause: For example, Gail Sheehy, *The Silent Passage* (New York: Random House, 1992); Gallagher, "Midlife Myths."

BIBLIOGRAPHY

Anderson, S., C. Russell, and W. Schumm. 1983. Perceived marital quality and family life-cycle categories: A further analysis. *Journal of Marriage and the Family* 46: 105–14.

Apter, T. 1990. *Altered loves.* New York: St. Martin's Press.

Barber, B. 1987. Marital quality, parental behavior, and adolescent self-esteem. *Family Perspective* 21: 244–368.

Baruch, G., R. Barnett, and C. Rivers. 1983. *Lifeprints.* New York: McGraw-Hill.

Baumrind, D. 1991. Parenting styles and adolescent development. In *The encyclopedia of adolescence,* ed. J. Brooks-Gunn, R. Lerner, and A. C. Petersen, 746–58. New York: Garland.

Belsky, J. 1984. The determinants of parenting: A process model. *Child Development* 55: 83–96.

Belsky, J., and J. Kelly. 1994. *The transition to parenthood.* New York: Delacorte.

Benedek, T. 1959. Parenthood as a developmental phase: A contribution to the libido theory. *Journal of the American Psychoanalytic Association* 7: 389–417.

Blos, P. 1967. The second individuation process of adolescence. *The Psychoanalytic Study of the Child* 1: 183–98.

Brooks-Gunn, J., and E. Reiter. 1990. The role of pubertal processes. In *At the threshold: The developing adolescent,* ed. S. Feldman and G. Elliott, 16–23. Cambridge: Harvard University Press.

Butler, R. 1968. The life review: An interpretation of reminiscence in the aged. *Psychiatry* 26: 65–76.

Campbell, A., P. Converse, and W. L. Rodgers. 1976. *The quality of American life: Perceptions, evaluations, and satisfactions.* New York: Russell Sage Foundation.

Collins, R. 1985. *Sociology of Marriage and the Family.* Chicago: Nelson-Hall.

Collins, W. A. 1990. Parent-child relationships in the transition to adolescence: Continuity and change in interaction, affect, and cognition. In *Advances in adolescent development: Vol. 2. The transition from childhood to adolescence,* ed. R. Montemayor, G. Adams, and T. Gullotta. Beverly Hills, CA: Sage.

Cooper, K., and D. Guttman. 1987. Gender identity and ego mastery style in middle-aged, pre- and post-empty nest women. *Gerontologist* 27: 347–52.

Cowan, C., and P. Cowan. 1992. *When parents become partners*. New York: Basic Books.

Douvan, E., and J. Adelson. 1966. *The adolescent experience*. New York: Wiley.

Erikson, E. H. 1959/1980. *Identity and the life cycle*. New York: W. W. Norton.

Farrell, M., and S. Rosenberg. 1981. *Men at midlife*. Boston: Auburn Press.

Freud, A. 1958. Adolescence. *Psychoanalytic Study of the Child* 13: 255–78.

Furstenberg, F. F., Jr. 1988. Child care after divorce and remarriage. In *Impact of divorce, single parenting, and stepparenting on children*, ed. E. M. Hetherington and J. D. Arasteh, 245–61. Hillsdale, NJ: Erlbaum.

Gallagher, W. 1993. Midlife myths. *The Atlantic* 271: 51–68.

Glenn, N. 1975. Psychological well-being in the postparental stage: Some evidence from national surveys. *Journal of Marriage and the Family* 37: 105–9.

Gould, R. 1978. *Transformations*. New York: Simon and Schuster.

Hetherington, E. M., and E. R. Anderson. 1987. The effects of divorce and remarriage on early adolescents and their families. In *Early adolescent transitions*, ed. M. D. Levine and E. R. McAnarney, 49–68. Lexington, MA: Lexington Books.

Hetherington, E. M., and J. Arasteh, eds. 1988. *Impact of divorce, single parenting, and stepparenting on children*. Hillsdale, NJ: Erlbaum.

Hetherington, E. M. March 1990. *Studying family transitions: families, lives, and videotapes*. Presidential address presented at the biennial meeting of the Society for Research on Adolescence. Atlanta, Georgia.

Hill, J. 1988. Adapting to menarche: Familial control and conflict. In *21st Minnesota symposium on child psychology*, ed. M. Gunnar, 43–77. Hillsdale, NJ: Erlbaum.

Hoffman, L. W., and J. D. Manis. 1978. Influences of children on marital and parental satisfactions and dissatisfactions. In *Child influences on marital and family interaction: A life-span perspective*, ed. R. M. Lerner and G. B. Spanier, 165–213. New York: Academic Press.

Judd, C., E. Smith, and L. Kidder. 1991. *Research methods in social relations*. 6th ed. New York: Holt.

Keniston, K. 1963. Scales for the measurement of identity. Yale University School of Medicine.

Koski, K., and L. Steinberg. 1990. Parenting satisfaction of mothers during midlife. *Journal of Youth and Adolescence* 19: 465–74.

Lamborn, S., N. Mounts, L. Steinberg, and S. Dornbusch. 1991. Patterns of competence and adjustment among adolescents from authoritative, authoritarian, indulgent, and neglectful homes. *Child Development* 62: 1049–65.

Levinson, D., et al. 1978. *The seasons of a man's life*. New York: Ballantine.

Livson, F. 1981. Patterns of personality development in middle-aged women. In *Becoming and being old*, ed. J. Hendricks. Farmingdale, NY: Baywood.

Lowenthal, M., and D. Chiriboga. 1972. Transition to the empty nest: Crisis, challenge, or relief? *Archives of General Psychiatry* 26: 8–14.

McLanahan, S., and A. Sorensen. 1985. Life course events and psychological well-being over the life course. In *Life course dynamics*, ed. G. Elder, Jr. Ithaca, NY: Cornell University Press.

Mahler, M., F. Pine, and A. Bergman. 1975. *The psychological birth of the human infant.* New York: Basic Books.

Meyers, H. 1989. The impact of teenaged children on parents. In *The middle years*, ed. J. Oldham and R. Liebert. New Haven: Yale University Press.

Minuchin, S. 1974. *Families and family therapy.* Cambridge: Harvard University Press.

Neugarten, B. 1967. The awareness of middle age. In *Middle Age*, ed. R. Owen. London: BBC.

Neugarten, B., and G. Hagestad. 1976. Age and the life course. In *Handbook of aging and the social sciences*, ed. H. Binstock and E. Shanas. New York: Van Nostrand Reinhold.

Offer, D. 1969. *The psychological world of the teenager.* New York: Basic Books.

Offer, D., E. Ostrov, and K. Howard. 1981. *The adolescent: A psychological self-portrait.* New York: Basic Books.

Offer, D., and M. Sabshin. 1984. *Normality and the life cycle.* New York: Basic Books.

Radloff, L. 1977. The CES-D scale: A self-report depression scale for research in the general population. *Applied Psychological Measurement* 1: 385–401.

Rodgers, R. 1973. *Family interaction and transaction: A developmental approach.* New York: Prentice-Hall.

Rollins, B., and H. Feldman. 1970. Marital satisfaction over the family life cycle. *Journal of Marriage and the Family* 32: 20–28.

Rosenberg, M. 1965. *Society and the adolescent self-image.* Princeton, NJ: Princeton University Press.

Rutter, M., P. Graham, F. Chadwick, and W. Yule. 1976. Adolescent turmoil: Fact or fiction? *Journal of Child Psychology and Psychiatry* 17: 35–56.

Schaefer, E. 1965. Children's reports of parental behavior: An Inventory. *Child Development* 36: 413–24.

Seligman, M. 1975. *Helplessness: On depression, development, and death.* San Francisco: Freeman.

Sessa, F., and L. Steinberg. 1991. Family structure and the development of autonomy in adolescence. *Journal of Early Adolescence* 11: 38–55.

Sheehy, G. 1976. *Passages.* New York: Dutton.

———. 1992. *The silent passage.* New York: Random House.

Silverberg, S. 1986. Psychological well-being of parents with early adolescent children. Ph.D. diss. Department of Child and Family Studies, University of Wisconsin—Madison.

Silverberg, S., and L. Steinberg. 1987. Adolescent autonomy, parent-adolescent conflict, and parental well-being. *Journal of Youth and Adolescence* 16: 293–312.

———. 1990. Psychological well-being of parents at midlife: The impact of early adolescent children. *Developmental Psychology*, 26: 658–66.

Small, S. A., G. Eastman, and S. Cornelius. 1988. Adolescent autonomy and parental stress. *Journal of Youth and Adolescence*, 17(5): 377–92.

Smetana, J. 1988. Concepts of self and social convention: Adolescents' and parents' reasoning about hypothetical and actual family conflicts. In *21st Minnesota symposium on child psychology*, ed. M. Gunnar, 79–122. Hillsdale, NJ: Erlbaum.

Steinberg, L. 1981. Transformations in family relations at puberty. *Developmental Psychology* 17: 833–40.

———. 1987. The impact of puberty on family relations: Effects of pubertal status and pubertal timing. *Developmental Psychology* 23: 451–60.

———. 1987. Recent research on the family at adolescence: The extent and nature of sex differences. *Journal of Youth and Adolescence* 16: 191–98.

———. 1990. Autonomy, conflict, and harmony in the family relationship. In *At the threshold: The developing adolescent*, ed. S. Feldman and G. Elliot, 255–76. Cambridge: Harvard University Press.

Steinberg, L., and A. Levine. 1990. *You and your adolescent: A parent's guide for ages 10 to 20*. New York: Harper & Row.

Steinberg, L., and S. Silverberg. 1987. Influences on marital satisfaction during the middle stages of the family life cycle. *Journal of Marriage and the Family* 49: 751–60.

Steinberg, L., S. Lamborn, N. Darling, N. Mounts, and S. Dornbusch. n.d. Over-time changes in adjustment and competence among adolescents from authoritative, authoritarian, indulgent, and neglectful families. *Child Development*. In press.

Stevens-Long, J. 1988. *Adult life*. 3d ed. Mountain View, CA: Mayfield.

Tamir, L. 1982. *Men in their forties*. New York: Springer.

Teti, D., M. Lamb, and A. Elster. 1987. Long-range socioeconomic and marital consequences of adolescent marriage in three cohorts of adult males. *Journal of Marriage and the Family* 49: 499–506.

U.S. Bureau of the Census, *Marital Status and Living Arrangements*. Various years.

Vaillant, G. 1977. *Adaptation to life*. Boston: Little, Brown.

Walster, E., and W. Walster. 1978. *A new look at love*. Cambridge: Addison-Wesley.

Wenar, C. 1990. *Developmental psychopathology*. New York: McGraw-Hill.

Youniss, J., and J. Smollar. 1985. *Adolescents' relations with mothers, fathers, and friends*. Chicago: University of Chicago Press.

INDEX

ABOUT THE AUTHORS

Laurence Steinberg, Ph.D., is Professor of Psychology at Temple University, where he directs the university's program in Developmental Psychology. Dr. Steinberg has taught previously at Cornell University, the University of California at Irvine, and the University of Wisconsin at Madison. He was educated at Johns Hopkins University and Vassar College, where he was elected to Phi Beta Kappa and graduated with honors and distinction in psychology; and at Cornell University, where he received his Ph.D. in human development and family studies. He is a fellow of the American Psychological Association.

A nationally recognized expert on psychological development and family relations during adolescence, Dr. Steinberg is the author of numerous scholarly articles on growth and development during the teenage years, as well as the books *Adolescence, When Teenagers Work: The Psychological and Social Costs of Adolescent Employment* (with Ellen Greenberger), and *You and Your Adolescent: A Parent's Guide for Ages 10 to 20* (with Ann Levine).

Wendy Steinberg is a free-lance writer who has written both fiction and nonfiction. She was educated at Mills College, where she received her B.A. in English, and at Temple University, where she received her M.A. in English in the university's Creative Writing program.